BYLINE, RICHARD WRIGHT

BYLINE
Richard Wright

ARTICLES FROM THE *DAILY WORKER* AND *NEW MASSES*

Edited by Earle V. Bryant

University of Missouri Press
Columbia

University of Missouri Press, Columbia, Missouri 65211
Printed and bound in the United States of America

First paperback printing, 2016

Cataloging-in-Publication data available from the Library of Congress.
ISBN 978-0-8262-2092-9

This paper meets the requirements of the
American National Standard for Permanence of Paper
for Printed Library Materials, Z39.48, 1984.

Cover design: Susan Ferber
Design and composition: Bruce Leckie
Typeface: Utopia

For Larry Godfrey, magister et amicus,
and Oscar Boise, who planted the seed for this work

CONTENTS

PREFACE

Richard Wright, whom Margaret Walker once characterized as "the father of black literature in the twentieth century," is best known for his fiction and his critically acclaimed autobiography *Black Boy*.[1] Wright's novels—especially *Native Son,* which took the literary world by storm in 1940 and went on to secure the position of an American classic—are invariably ranked alongside some of the finest works of modern fiction, and *Black Boy* remains one of the most widely read and critically praised autobiographies in twentieth-century literature. Wright's position in American literature, then, is firmly established on the basis of his fiction and autobiographical masterpiece. However, what many readers are not aware of is that before there was Richard Wright the celebrated novelist, short story master, and internationally recognized voice of black protest, there was Richard Wright the journalist, the cub reporter who conducted interviews, researched stories, edited copy, wrote articles, and even served as his newspaper's bureau chief. The newspaper was the *Daily Worker,* the organ of the American Communist Party. For seven months in 1937, Wright diligently labored at the *Daily Worker*'s Harlem bureau, turning out over two hundred articles. In those articles, Wright focused on most of the major and minor events, personalities, and issues percolating on the local, national, and global scene at the time. Whether detailing Harlem's rampant poverty and despair or celebrating heavyweight champion Joe Louis's victories in the ring, and whether tracking developments in the Scottsboro case or clarifying the Communist Party's beliefs and objectives, Wright's newspaper articles provided in-depth coverage with an unmistakably human touch.

Wright's time at the *Daily Worker,* however, has too often been consigned to a footnote in his literary career, and for over seventy-five years the articles he wrote for the newspaper, when not altogether ignored, have been given short shrift or dismissed as meritless. Such negative critical response to Wright's early journalism is unfortunate and unwarranted. In truth, Wright's *Daily Worker* articles and his essays in the leftist literary journal *New Masses* were written with close attention to detail and in disciplined, sculptured prose; they are for the most part models of diligent research and fluent writing, relentless in their probing and wide-ranging in their scope. In all probability, the reason for the critical neglect of Wright's early journalism is that no effort has been made to examine these pieces and assess their importance collectively. That is precisely what this collection of over one hundred of Wright's early articles and essays seeks to do. Its objective is to introduce readers to the journalistic nuggets that for so long have lain unappreciated on microfilm and in archival file cabinets while Wright's posthumously published fiction—works such as *Rite of Passage* and *A Father's Law*—have meanwhile received much-deserved critical attention.

The range of Wright's news assignments at the *Daily Worker* ran the gamut from the plight of Harlem's quarter-million black residents to the treatment of black war veterans, from the Spanish Civil War to the state of the African American theater scene in New York, from icons like Joe Louis and Leadbelly to lesser-known figures like war hero Walter Garland and activist Ralph Bates. All of these subjects and more are treated in this collection. Readers familiar with Wright's fiction or with his widely acclaimed autobiography or even with his nonfiction works like *Twelve Million Black Voices* or *White Man, Listen!* will discover in these articles another, earlier Richard Wright, and they will discover that this Wright is as compelling a journalist as he is a novelist and short story master. For readers unacquainted with Wright, these articles will provide a suitable introduction, one that will motivate them to read the works Wright is best known for.

A sterling testimony to the enduring quality of those articles is that their value remains undiminished after three-quarters of a century. But of what value are they? Why were they worth reading in the thirties, and why are they worth revisiting today? For modern readers, much of their value is that they are reminders. Like a well-made historical documentary, they return us to a period when an entire nation rallied behind a young black athlete named Joe Louis and anointed him the champion of democracy and justice. They return us to a time when artistic talent in New York found outlets for expression in the new Harlem Community Arts Center and on the stage of the fabled Lafayette Theater, an era when freedom-loving people united to crush the fascist monsters ravaging Spain, and a period when untold millions were themselves crushed by what historian Meyer Weinberg has termed "the most destructive economic catastrophe [in] American history"—the Great Depression.[2] Wright's articles are valuable because they are prose portraits of a time and a place that will forever exert a grip on the national consciousness. Many of these articles, a virtual kaleidoscope of issues and events, are played out against the backdrop of one of the nation's most famous and fabled communities. Captured forever in prose is Harlem, suffering from not only the ravages of the Depression but also from the greed of slumlords and merchants, from deplorable housing and white apathy. Captured is Harlem's response to fascist aggression abroad and racial injustice at home, and Harlem's pride and elation at the victories of "Young Black Joe," as Langston Hughes once dubbed Louis. In fine, Wright's articles preserve the past. But unlike many historical accounts, his articles illuminate and vivify that past, introducing and interpreting its events and figures from the perspective of a consummate literary artist. They are without a doubt worth revisiting.

It would be disingenuous, however, to omit pointing out that a few of Wright's friends from his Chicago days saw little redeeming merit in his *Daily Worker* articles. One of those friends was the almost always hypercritical Abe Aaron, the man who in 1933 had introduced Wright to the John Reed Club (and hence to the Communist Party). Aaron saw next to no value in Wright's articles and did not hesitate to tell him so. In a letter to Wright dated August 25, 1937, Aaron chided Wright about his *Daily Worker* pieces. "Your stuff in the DW, Dick, [is] pretty bad," he wrote, continuing,

"You're a serious, hard-plugging workman, and I do not believe your heart is in this stuff you're doing. Some of the stuff actually can't be read, doesn't make sense, [and] violates every rule in the book. . . . As a reporter, Dick, you're a flop, just as I would be."[3]

Later in the same letter, Aaron toned down his criticism and offered what he saw as a possible explanation for Wright's "pretty bad stuff": "I imagine you're . . . asked to produce when you're not in the mood for production, when you're hungry, worried, down at the heel and down in the mouth. Uncertain of the future, you can't treat the present adequately, and therefore the failure."[4]

Another one of Wright's close friends from Chicago, Herbert Caro, also failed to see much in Wright's "newspaper stuff." "You should be spoken to severely," he told Wright in a letter dated August 16, 1937. "I've seen 3 by-lined stories of yours in the *Daily Worker*. You're so obviously less than interested that the stories are unilluminating. Indeed, you don't even bother to write sentences or take any concern with construction."[5] And then, like Aaron, he went on to attribute Wright's "unilluminating" articles to hunger and stress: "I quite seriously ask whether this is due to a weariness consequent on worry and lack of food. If it is I think we'd better give you a hand from here for a while."[6]

In their evaluation of the quality of Wright's articles and the level of his interest in the stories, Aaron and Caro are wrong, terribly wrong. It is true, as Aaron and Caro say, that Wright was "hungry" and thus needed the money (he never claimed otherwise), and also true is Aaron's claim that Wright was "hellishly pushed for time" (most journalists as a rule usually write under the gun). It is decidedly untrue, however, that Wright's "stuff in the DW," as Aaron refers to it, was slipshod hackwork, so poor that some of it "can't be read, doesn't make sense, [and] violates every rule in the book." It is just as untrue, as Caro charges, that Wright's articles are "unilluminating," weakly structured, and mechanically unsound. On the contrary, far from being, as Aaron maintains, a flop as a newspaperman, Wright was a remarkably skilled journalist, easily on a par with Ernest Hemingway and Jack London when they worked for newspapers early in their careers. Wright's *Daily Worker* articles, moreover, far from being "pretty bad," as Aaron puts it, are well researched and smoothly written and have certainly stood the test of time.

What is also remarkable about Wright's *Daily Worker* articles is that many of the issues they covered were ones often ignored by both black and white newspapers of the day. For instance, the *New York Age* and the *New York Amsterdam News,* the two New York African American newspapers prominent at the time, did not devote a great deal of attention to Harlem's deplorable housing conditions or to the rent strikes staged by tenants in reaction to those conditions. Nor did they cover the stories of African American soldiers who fought courageously in the Spanish Civil War or report much on white-on-black assaults. Likewise the white press largely failed to cover these stories and ones like them. The reluctance of the press to cover this kind of stories is not an indictment of them. Black and white mainstream newspapers of the day did what they were established to do—cover stories the editors deemed newsworthy and at the same time keep from offending sensibilities, and not too many of their editors deemed poverty newsworthy. The *Daily Worker,* on the other hand, did not have to worry about offending sensibilities. Consequently, the stories Wright covered—the stories *he* considered newsworthy—filled a very real void in the thirties and provided a valuable service to a reading public wanting to be kept informed.

The articles in this collection are arranged thematically rather than chronologically. The reason for this is that Wright's assignments varied from week to week (indeed, from day to day). For example, on one day he would interview and write about musical legend Leadbelly and then a few days later he would find himself covering the inner workings of a meeting of the Harlem branch of the Communist Party. A article dated November 29 reveals how Thanksgiving Day in Harlem is anything but joyous ("Few Harlem Tables Weighted by Turkey"), while one a little over a week later shifts to the heroism of a man who lost his life while rescuing two black children from a burning tenement. In short, the subject matter of Wright's articles hops, skips, and jumps all over the map. As such, chronological arrangement of his newspaper stories would fail to reveal the journalistic tapestry that Wright wove during his time at the *Daily Worker.* Accordingly, the articles collected here are arranged thematically, in five sections, after an introductory chapter that details Wright's arrival in New York in 1937 and his settling down to what he once termed the "hard, hard grind" of newspaper work. This introduction also presents a graphic look at the Harlem that Wright lived and worked in, and it further provides important background on the *Daily Worker,* his home base. In addition, it addresses Wright's attitude toward his duties at the *Daily Worker* and whether or not his time at the paper contributed to his expertise and success as a fiction writer.

Many of Wright's articles for the *Daily Worker* foreground Depression-racked Harlem, and section 1, "The Shame Spot of New York," features forty-seven pieces that focus on Harlem's battered and bruised souls suffering during the Depression. As historians have long noted, of all the sections of New York City, Harlem was the one most severely damaged by the Depression, and Wright's articles fully attest to that. His Harlem articles are vivid, often unsettling stories of hunger, evictions, unemployment, callous neglect of the sick and dying, deprivation of human dignity—in short, all the ills attendant on poverty. Additionally, a number of Wright's articles on Harlem spotlight the abuse, physical and emotional, leveled at Harlem's black populace by police, storekeepers, medical professionals, representatives of big corporations, and even teachers. Many of these stories also chronicle the black response to such abuse, a reaction that often took the form of protest: boycotts, pickets, strikes, and rallies.

Quite a few of Wright's Harlem articles expose the deplorable living conditions that African Americans there were forced to endure: rat- and roach-infested firetraps, exorbitant rents, heartless landlords who profited from this misery. But also in this cluster of articles are "victory pieces," stories of tenants united to combat this injustice. Particularly noteworthy among them is Wright's wonderful article on the opening of the Harlem River Houses, a valiant undertaking by the New York Housing Authority and the federal government to provide decent, affordable housing for Harlemites.

Another salient issue that Wright addressed in a number of his *Daily Worker* articles was war, specifically wars raging in Spain and China during the late 1930s. Articles about these conflicts appear in section 2, "The Winds of War." Both the Spanish Civil War and Japan's invasion of China garnered intense international attention and concern, and Wright did his share—and commendably so—to report on these conflicts, profiling (and even interviewing) some of those involved in the war effort. Each article in this section homes in on some aspect of each of the two wars, be it recognition of the African American heroes of the Spanish Civil War or Harlem's cooperation in the boycott of Japanese-made products.

The subject matter of Section 3, "Heroes Sung and Silent," is heroism. Two-thirds of the articles in this section are devoted to two figures Wright regarded as truly heroic. One was known almost globally—heavyweight boxing champion Joe Louis, the Brown Bomber. The other was hardly known at all. His name was William Campbell, and he was a white truck driver who dashed into a burning building in Harlem to rescue two young black children, only to die. Wright's articles on Louis and Campbell not only celebrate their achievements but also foreground Harlem's response to those achievements. Wright's essays on Joe Louis, published in *New Masses,* rank among his best short fiction.

"A Burst of Fists on a New Horizon," section 4, includes those articles whose subject matter was among the most personal to Wright, at least at the time he wrote them. These are the pieces that center on the Communist Party, its beliefs and objectives. Wright's purpose in these articles was to set the record straight, to dispel the cloud of mystery and myth that hung over the party. He was fully aware of the popular misconceptions about the Communist Party, of how the general public viewed the party with distrust, suspicion, and certainly ignorance. In his articles on the party he clarifies, largely by humanizing its members, why the party does what it does and why it believes what it believes. Although some Wright scholars have dismissed these articles as inconsequential propaganda pieces, they are anything but that.

Included in section 4 are over two dozen articles that focus on what is still regarded as one of the most flagrant miscarriages of justice in the annals of the US criminal justice system: the case of the "Scottsboro Boys." The defendants' ordeal stretched out over years and years, and even though the tragedy had begun six years prior to Wright's arrival in New York, the ongoing case was still a major news story during his time at the *Daily Worker.* The articles devoted to the Scottsboro case are some of the briefest pieces Wright wrote for the newspaper, but in them he succeeded in keeping his readers informed as various stages of the case developed. Wright made sure he stayed abreast of not only the constantly incoming details of the case but also of the rallies and fund-raisers in support of the defendants, and he made equally sure that he relayed those updates to a reading public following the multiple trials and appeals.

Section 5, "Art for Life's Sake," consists of articles unquestionably close to Wright's heart. Here issues of hunger and homelessness, war and sports, boycotts and strikes, and even political ideology are temporarily left behind. In their stead, Wright's readers are treated to a compelling portrait of musical icon Leadbelly; an account of the grand opening of the Harlem Community Arts Center, which would go on to produce such artists as Jacob Lawrence; Wright's astute analysis of the state of Depression-era theater in Harlem, and a rare look at the birth of *New Challenge,* a literary magazine that would unfortunately become the literary Left's one-hit wonder of 1937. In sum, all the articles in this section are concerned with art in one form or another.

The book's conclusion assesses Wright's time at the *Daily Worker* and his contribution there. In doing so it addresses such issues as why Wright left his job at the paper, how he regarded the worth of his newspaper work, and why, in the final analysis, that work remains worth reading. All in all, the hundred-plus *Daily Worker* articles and the two *New Masses* essays collected here represent an attempt to bring Wright's early newspaper work out of obscurity and into the light where it can be read and appreciated.

ACKNOWLEDGMENTS

I owe a special debt of gratitude to Clair Willcox, editor-in-chief at the University of Missouri Press, for his belief in the merits of this book and for expertly steering it to its final form. I am equally indebted to the phenomenal staff at the University of Missouri Press, especially Sara Davis and Lyn Smith, and to freelance copy editor Chris Dodge. This book would not have gotten off the ground were it not for the various travel grants I received from my home institution, the University of New Orleans, most notably from Robert "Bob" Cashner in the Office of Research, Richard "Dick" Engstrom in the Africana Studies Program, and the late John Cooke, my department chair, who believed in and funded my project in its infancy. I am also profoundly grateful to the remarkable archivists at Yale University's Beinecke Rare Book and Manuscript Library, the Schomburg Center for Research in Black Culture (most notably Schomburg archivist Sharon K. Howard), and the Amistad Research Center at Tulane University, all of whom went out of their way to assist me in locating the materials I needed. Truly indispensable in moving this book forward was Teresa "Terri" Albano, editor of the *People's World*, who graciously gave permission to publish these articles and essays. Thank you, Terri, and *gracias* to the *People's World*. My deepest appreciation also goes out to Raymond Brookter for his unwavering aid and support. I cannot overlook the invaluable assistance given me by my son Dante, whose computer expertise was indispensible in the preparation of the final manuscript. And by no means least, I thank my wife, Loretta, for her patience and understanding during my many and long research trips to New York and New Haven.

BYLINE, RICHARD WRIGHT

INTRODUCTION

ARRIVAL

At the outset of Rudolph Fisher's short story "City of Refuge" (1925), King Solomon Gillis, a naive but likable black man fleeing a murder charge in the South, arrives in Harlem and is awestruck by what he sees when he emerges from the subway at 135th Street and Lenox Avenue: "'Done died an' woke up in Heaven,' thought King Solomon, watching, fascinated."[1] Fisher's short story is set at the height of the Harlem Renaissance, a time of "a dramatic upsurge of creativity in literature, music, and art within black America," a period most scholars generally agree runs from about 1919 to 1935 (the year of the Harlem riot incited by the arrest of a teenager for shoplifting a penknife).[2] King Solomon Gillis's characterization of 1920s Harlem as heaven was echoed by a host of real-life figures, both during and after the Renaissance. For James Weldon Johnson, Harlem was a place teeming with "movement, color, gayety, singing, dancing, boisterous laughter and loud talk."[3] For Claude McKay, one of the leading lights of the Renaissance, Harlem was "the queen of black belts."[4] Arna Bontemps described it as a place "too wonderful for words"; living there, he rhapsodized, was "a foretaste of paradise."[5] The legendary Cab Calloway, upon his arrival in Harlem in the late twenties, recalled being "awestruck by the whole scene." "It was beautiful. Just beautiful," he reminisced.[6] In like manner, another musical icon, Duke Ellington, who arrived in Harlem in 1923, exclaimed, "Why, it [was] just like the Arabian Nights."[7]

Indeed, for untold thousands, black and white alike, Harlem during the twenties was exactly that—a magical place, an enchanted isle. African Americans migrated there in droves from all points of the compass. To many of them it represented the Promised Land, a northern Canaan whose siren song beckoned, promising a chance for a better life. "Harlem for blacks," Nathan Huggins has observed, "like New York for whites, was synonymous with opportunity."[8] Black artists from all parts of the country yielded to Harlem's lure. From the Midwest came poet Langston Hughes and painter Aaron Douglas, and from the West arrived writers Wallace Thurman and Arna Bontemps. From the South traveled sculptor Augusta Savage and the inimitable Zora Neale Hurston, while from New England journeyed nineteen-year-old writer Dorothy West and her equally young cousin, poet Helene Johnson. For black artists, then, Harlem was, as Huggins says, "[the] platform from which the new black voice would be heard around the world, and [the] intellectual center [for] the New Negro."[9]

White New Yorkers too felt Harlem's magnetic pull, though for a different reason: for them it was a garden of delights, an after-hours, hedonistic playground unparalleled in its sensuous offerings and its ability to gratify any taste. Manhattan whites followed Duke Ellington's advice and took the A train, or directed their chauffeurs to heed the directive in the popular song "Drop Me Off in Harlem." There, despite Prohibition, liquor flowed freely in the area's many nightclubs, cabarets, and speakeasies. Live entertainment abounded, and whites swarmed to popular clubs like Smalls' Paradise, Connie's Inn, Barron's, and the fabled Cotton Club to get their fill. Famed performer Jimmy Durante went a long way in summing up white Manhattan's fixation with Harlem when he remarked, "You go sort of primitive up there."[10] This, in fine, was 1920s Harlem—the "world's greatest Negro metropolis," the Negro Mecca, the queen of black belts, the black cultural capital of America. Little wonder, then, that Rudolph

Fisher's character King Solomon Gillis believed that he had "died an' woke up in Heaven."

A decade after King Solomon Gillis's fictional hegira from the South to the Negro Mecca, another southerner—a real one—arrived in Harlem, suitcase in hand. His name was Richard Wright, and he was ultimately to become what one literary critic has termed "the father of the contemporary black writer."[11] Twenty-eight years old, talented, and ambitious, Wright arrived in New York in late May 1937 and before long rented a furnished flat in a rooming house at 809 Saint Nicholas Avenue, deep in the heart of Harlem. The Harlem that Wright found, however, was a far cry from the earthly paradise extolled by so many ten years earlier. A feverish misery had replaced the once touted good times. Instead of seeing comfort and hearing laughter, Wright witnessed poverty and pain. Where previously there had been a spirit of boundless optimism in the air, there was now a pervasive malaise akin to despair. Sky-high unemployment. Rampant poverty. Deplorable living conditions. Homelessness and hunger. Crime and disease. This was the Harlem that Richard Wright found when he arrived in 1937. In the years following the end of the Renaissance, Harlem had devolved, as many historians and social scientists have noted, from a ghetto to a slum. The queen of the black belts had become, as Wright has termed it, the shame spot of New York.

Harlem had suffered such a downward spiral for the same reason that the entire country was in such agonizing straits—the Great Depression, an unparalleled catastrophe that "smashed into the nation with such fury that men groped for superlatives to express its impact and meaning."[12] As urban planning professor Peter Marcuse has remarked, "Shanties erected in Central Park, marches on Washington, breadlines and soup kitchens, unemployment, overcrowding, mortgage foreclosures, political agitation, and radical organizations characterized the times."[13] In short, America during the 1930s was, in historian Edward Ellis's apt phrase, a nation in torment. One of the hardest hit communities was Harlem. "For virtually everyone in Harlem," history professor Mark Naison points out, "the Great Depression was a traumatic experience. The economic crisis had the same general impact as in the rest of America—massive unemployment, evictions, bank failures, loss of family savings, loss of business—but in every instance it was far more serious [in Harlem]."[14] With its rampant poverty, high unemployment (the jobless rate for black Harlemites reached 40 percent by 1937), widespread hunger, and staggering number of evictions, Harlem had indeed "suffered the worst ravages of a collapsing economy."[15] Indeed, it was "more badly hit by the Depression than any other section of New York City."[16]

Arriving during the depths of the Depression, Wright brought with him very little in the way of worldly possessions—a suitcase, a small portable typewriter, and a sheaf of manuscripts, which he guarded with his life. The material in those manuscripts—rough drafts of short stories and even a novel—Wright would polish and burnish until one day, he was firmly convinced, they would be published. To be a published writer—this had been his lifelong ambition. It was in part to bring this dream to fruition that he had left the South at nineteen, "full of a hazy notion that life could be lived with dignity."[17] Dignity, after all, like opportunity, equality, and safety, was certainly not something that African Americans enjoyed in the Jim Crow South of Wright's youth. Born in rural Natchez, Mississippi, in 1908, he grew up in a fatherless household (his father, a sharecropper, deserted the family when Wright was only four years old). Surrounded by poverty and hemmed in by racial bigotry, all of which he was to chronicle so cogently in *Black Boy,* Wright waged an unrelenting battle for the preservation of his dignity and selfhood—and at times for the preservation of his very life. In 1927 he left the South, "that . . . swamp of despair and violence," traveling first to Chicago, where he spent ten years, then to New York—to Harlem.[18] He would ultimately go on to achieve fame as a novelist and short story writer, earning international recognition and acclaim as both a writer and a powerful voice of black protest. His magnum opus, *Native Son,* would take the literary world by storm in 1940 and go on to secure the position of an American classic. It would be followed in future years by the autobiographical *Black Boy,* the critically acclaimed tale "The Man Who Lived Underground," and compelling novels such as *The Outsider*

(1953) and *The Long Dream* (1957). Long before his untimely death in 1960, he had firmly established himself as "a prototype of black literary achievement in the United States."[19]

But before he enjoyed seasons in the sun as a literary heavyweight, Wright plugged away at the *Daily Worker,* which paid his bills and kept him fed. The pride of the Communist Party, the paper was launched in Chicago in 1924 and opened a New York branch in 1927, moving into a building at 50 East Thirteenth Street in Union Square. Truly in a class by itself, the *Daily Worker* was enormously influential, never more so than during the 1930s, when its popularity peaked. "There was no other daily like it in America," historians Kelly Rusinack and Charles Lamb have observed.[20] There wasn't. Probing and informative, provocative and unafraid to tackle controversial issues head on, no other newspaper of its kind matched its degree of investigative reporting. Sacco and Vanzetti, the Scottsboro Boys, unjust labor practices, corporate greed, lynching, slum conditions in Harlem—the *Daily Worker* covered (and opined on) all these and more.

Aware that Harlem, with its 250,000-plus African Americans, was an ideal community to be served, the *Daily Worker* decided to open an office in Harlem. On September 12, 1936, the newspaper announced in a prominently placed sidebar on page 6 that it would soon "establish a Harlem bureau" that would cover Harlemites' "struggles against police terror, slum housing, denial of jobs—all [their] insufferable conditions of oppression."[21] The Daily Worker kept its promise. On the front page of its September 23 edition, the newspaper proudly announced the bureau's opening. In bold caps, the headline read, "DAILY WORKER GETS HARLEM NEWS BUREAU." The article, in time-honored journalistic format, provided the who, what, where, and when, if not the why:

> Washington . . . Chicago . . . Detroit . . . Cleveland . . . Pittsburgh . . . and now a Harlem News Bureau of the Daily Worker, headed by Ben Davis, Jr., former Editor of the Negro Liberator. Two hundred and fifty thousand Negro people inhabit Harlem. The Harlem News Bureau will depict their struggles, problems, experiences as

> never before in the press. Hear the opening gun this Wednesday night 8 P.M. at Finnish Hall, 15 West 126th St., New York! Hear Ben Davis, Jr., himself discuss the new *Daily Worker* and the Harlem News Bureau in relation to Harlem's vital needs.[22]

According to the newspaper's own accounts, it did not take long for the bureau to prove a success. A week after the bureau's opening, the paper ran a 350-word piece by Ben Davis, Jr., on the editorial page, touting the infant branch.[23] As the *Daily Worker* took every opportunity to remind its readers, the newly opened Harlem branch was managed by Davis, one of the party's most dynamic members. A graduate of Amherst College and Harvard Law School, Davis had been raised in a moneyed and prominent southern African American family. Not only an eloquent speaker and fluent writer but also a skillful organizer, Davis was vaulted into the national spotlight as lead defense attorney for Angelo Herndon, the African American Communist jailed for leading a nonviolent protest march in Atlanta, Georgia, in 1932. Davis's hunger for justice and racial equality and his hatred of racism and discrimination radicalized him, as he reveals in his autobiography, and steered him into the Communist Party, where he was welcomed with open arms.[24] By the time the party tapped him for management of the *Daily Worker*'s newly opened Harlem bureau, Davis was near the height of his popularity with both the party and the Harlem community. It was under his leadership that the Harlem news bureau took root, and it was under his direction that Wright worked.

Davis and Wright got along well. Wright liked Davis's combination of intelligence and wit, and he found Davis downright pleasant, not dour like so many of the party members he had worked with over the years (he had joined in Chicago in 1933). For his part, Davis was impressed with this earnest, intense young man, a fellow southerner from a neighboring state. The two soon became close friends (a friendship that lasted until Wright's break with the party in 1942 and the publication, a year later, of his apologia, "I Tried to Be a Communist"). Davis, in fact, was best man at Wright's wedding in 1941. So impressed was Davis with Wright's talent and energy that he appointed Wright branch editor of the *Daily Worker*'s Harlem bureau in the spring of 1937. With his demanding schedule and load of responsibilities, Davis was no doubt greatly relieved to have Wright take over the newspaper work that he had been directing for over a half year, work that had certainly taken him away from the many other party matters he was involved with. Wright thus found himself not only with a job that paid a modest salary but also with the responsibility of running the newspaper's satellite branch.

It should come as no surprise that Wright found a job at the *Daily Worker* almost immediately after his arrival in New York. Despite a serious falling out with the Chicago branch of the Communist Party in the spring of 1937, he was still in the party's good graces when he arrived in New York on Memorial Day weekend. Since he was a writer with a proven track record (he had by then been published in *Partisan Review,* the *New Masses,* and other left periodicals), as well as a card-carrying party member, a position at the *Daily Worker* was a natural fit for both him and the newspaper. Nobody in the New York branch of the party was troubled (at least at first) by Wright's falling out with the Chicago branch, which Wright later detailed in *American Hunger* and which was partly responsible for his departure from Chicago. In leaving Carl Sandburg's hog-butchering City of the Big Shoulders, Wright was not so much running away from anything as he was running *toward* something. That something was literary success. The primary reason that Wright moved to New York was to better establish himself as a writer, a point that Margaret Walker reaffirms in an interview for Madison D. Lacy's video biography of Wright. "He had learned in [his] ten years [in Chicago] just about everything he could learn . . . about writing," Walker reveals. "And he was ready to publish [books], and he knew he wasn't going to get published in Chicago the way he could get published in New York."[25] To get published was what Wright wanted above all else. Until such time as he could realize his dream of literary success, his position at the *Daily Worker* would pay the bills.

Newspaper work, however, was not what he wanted to do for the rest of his life. By his own admission, he was not entirely pleased with his new job as a journalist. His writing, he was convinced, was destined for loftier purposes. He was determined to write short stories and novels that would address the country's racial and social problems and articulate the plight of its black populace—works that would stir the heart and rouse the conscience of America. Like other black literary artists before him—Charles Chesnutt, for example, and Frances Watkins Harper—Wright saw the moral education of white America as his mission. He was eager to reach a considerably wider audience than the *Daily Worker*'s and to give full vent to his literary creativity, something that he found all but impossible to do as a journalist. As he lamented to poet and teacher Sterling Brown in a letter in early October 1937, "This newspaper work leaves me absolutely no time at all for anything else and it's ephemeral."[26] He sounded a similar note a month later when he told his close friend and ardent admirer Ralph Ellison that he had not come to New York to spend what seemed like every waking minute slaving at a newspaper. "I'm working from 9 A.M. to 10 P.M.," he complained to Ellison, "and it's a hard, hard grind. Can't do any work [on fiction], haven't the time. . . . I seem to be turning my life into newspaper copy from day to day."[27] But Wright needed the money that the *Daily Worker* was paying (however little it was) and thus he gave himself over to that "hard, hard grind" that was an inescapable part of his position at the paper.

The grind that Wright complained of to Ellison would in all probability have been less onerous if it had been a learning experience for Wright, which is to say if it had sharpened his writing skills or in some way contributed to his development as a writer. That was not the case, however. Though Wright unquestionably learned a great deal about Harlem while working for the *Daily Worker* and staffing its Harlem branch, his time at the newspaper cannot rightly be called a literary apprenticeship: he was already a skilled artisan when he started working at the paper. Recall Margaret Walker's testimony that when Wright left Chicago he had already learned "just about everything he could learn . . . about writing. And he was ready to publish."[28] Truth by told, Wright's time as a reporter for the *Daily Worker* furthered his career more than it did his writing craft. By the time Native Son was published in 1940, his name had become a familiar one to a multitude of readers nationwide, due in no small part to his byline in the paper. The *Daily Worker* was a national newspaper with a wide readership, one not confined exclusively to the Left. Recall too Rusinack and Lamb's observation: "There was no other daily like it in America."[29] Not only was that true but also, on the *Daily Worker*'s staff, there was no other journalist quite like Wright. His byline appeared continually, and that, combined with his compelling prose, could not help but provide him with a name recognition that would later help his career as a writer. Wright's newspaper work, however, was not the crucible for his fiction.

When Wright arrived in New York and started his job at the *Daily Worker,* he had already finished writing "Big Boy Leaves Home" as well as his essay "Joe Louis Uncovers Dynamite." "Big Boy Leaves Home," one of the five tales in *Uncle Tom's Children* (1938), is by all accounts Wright's best short story, a mini-masterpiece. In a similar vein, "Joe Louis Uncovers Dynamite" is far and away Wright's best early essay, a riveting work of undeniable artistry. Both works were written in 1935, two years prior to Wright's arrival in New York. Wright biographer and anthology editor Michel Fabre is thus on target when he too asserts that Wright "had little to learn from the newspaper world in terms of craft."[30]

While Wright's time as a newspaperman did not teach him anything about the nuts and bolts of fiction writing, it certainly gave him grist for the mill. That is to say, long after he left the *Daily Worker* and the "grind" of newspaper work behind him, the conditions he observed in Harlem, the people he encountered there, and the incidents he wrote about all remained with him, indelible deposits in his memory bank. He would later draw on these to create realistic depictions of black life in some of his major works. In *Native Son,* for example, his magnum opus, the world that Bigger Thomas inhabits—with its dingy pool halls where crimes are planned, its abandoned buildings where rape and murder find a safe haven, its street corners where trouble hangs out—is the same world that Wright lived in and wrote about every day in Harlem, the same world that comes alive in his newspaper articles. Moreover, the hovel that Bigger and his family live in is a facsimile of the rat-infested firetraps that Wright saw and reported on in his *Daily Worker* articles, especially his lengthy piece on the Harlem River Houses. It is highly probable that the fictional Mr. Dalton, from whom Bigger and his family rent their squalid one-room apartment, is a composite of various slumlords Wright encountered while researching and writing his articles on Harlem's execrable housing conditions. In characters such as the private investigator Britten and the prosecuting attorney Buckley he also drew on the raft of Harlem's racist law enforcement officers and government officials that his *Daily Worker* articles so sharply profiled. All in all, the spirit of despair and violence and injustice pervading Bigger Thomas's world is the same spirit that Wright witnessed hovering over Harlem. *Native Son,* of course, is not set in Harlem but in Chicago, the city where Wright spent ten years before moving to New York. But its template was assuredly Harlem, whose mean streets Wright became all too familiar with during his time at the *Daily Worker.*

Native Son was not Wright's only major work that benefited from his time spent as a journalist in Harlem. The year after *Native Son* took the literary world by storm, Wright published *12 Million Black Voices,* his pictorial folk history of African Americans. There is little question that Wright's familiarity with all facets of Harlem more than adequately prepared him for writing *12 Million Black Voices,* a book that a reviewer for the *New York Times* termed "striking" and "eloquent" and that another reviewer characterized as "magnificent in its . . . directness and force."[31] In chapter 3 of the book, "Death on the City Pavement," Wright homes in on the Great Migration, that mass exodus of African Americans from the rural, agricultural South to the urban, industrial North that began around the turn of the twentieth century. "We went [North] innocently," Wright states, "longing and hoping for a life that the Lords of the Land [in the South] would not let us live. Our hearts were high as we moved northward to the cities."[32] One of those northern cities that the migrants fled to and one that figures prominently in the chapter is Harlem. "So many of us crowded into New York City that Harlem's black population doubled between 1900 and 1920," Wright points out.[33] The heart of the chapter is Wright's graphic exposition of the conditions the black migrants encountered upon their arrival in the big city. To be sure, Wright does not dwell exclusively on Harlem. He draws attention, for instance, to conditions in Chicago and Philadelphia and Detroit. But in the chapter, Harlem emerges as the prototypical Canaan, the Promised Land that turns out to be nightmarishly harsh and brutal. That harshness and brutality, detailed so graphically in the chapter, were what Wright had written about time and again in his *Daily Worker* articles. Harlem had been his home and his beat while he was a journalist, and just as he had done with *Native Son,* so too did he do with *12 Million Black Voices*—that is, he drew on that bank of memories and experiences deposited during his *Daily Worker* days to fashion one of the twentieth century's most compelling "docuhistories."

Later in life (a year before his untimely death in 1960), Wright's time as a journalist in Harlem would again inform one of his finest works. Although written over twenty years after Wright left the *Daily Worker,* his posthumously published novella *Rite of Passage* also bears the imprint of his newspaper days. Unlike *Native Son, Rite of Passage* is set squarely in Harlem. One of the novella's concerns is juvenile crime and its root causes. The book's protagonist, fifteen-year-old Johnny Gibbs, becomes engulfed in crime and gang violence as a result of the ineptitude and callousness of the city's social welfare system. In his depiction of the heartlessness of that system, which is also responsible for the plight of other youthful characters in the book, Wright certainly drew on what he had observed and written about as a journalist covering what used to be known as the relief system. For example, in his *Daily Worker* article "300 at Harlem ERB Sit In," he reported on the inhumane treatment that aid recipients received at the hands of the relief agency in Harlem, citing the chilling example of a woman forced into homelessness because of a case worker's crass indifference and neglect of duty. And again in his piece "Mother, Three Children Are Evicted in Harlem," he shined a light on a relief system so mired in bureaucratic red tape and indifference that it turns a blind eye to the human suffering that it is supposed to help alleviate. The same blindness to misery emerged in "Bar Negro Relief," where again he highlighted an unfeeling, uncaring social welfare machine. In fine, Wright's knowledge of the workings of the relief system in Harlem proved invaluable in his composition of *Rite of Passage.*

In the final analysis, although Wright's time as a journalist did not teach him anything about writing that he had not already mastered, it did provide him with a wealth of material that he would later put to good use when he emerged as the author he had dreamed of becoming before and after his days at the *Daily Worker.* It would be wrong to believe, however, that since Wright's deeply rooted and abiding interest lay in fiction writing, he was therefore a mere time-server at the *Daily Worker,* a hack who cranked out pulp. Nothing could be further from the truth. Wright's articles for the newspaper (despite what his friends Abe Aaron and Herbert Caro argued) were all written with a fluency and punch that were on a par with that of leftist journalistic luminaries like Mike Gold and Edwin Seaver. With the notable exception of Gold's columns, Wright's *Daily Worker* articles stand out from those written by his colleagues at the paper. One can scour the pages of the paper during Wright's tenure there and not find the kind of quality coverage that Wright brought to his pieces. For example, in his treatment of how the Great Depression had a death grip on Harlem, he takes great pains to individualize and humanize poverty's victims. This he does by painting vivid, compelling portraits of women and men: a homeless mother of five begging for food on the streets, an elderly woman who collapses and dies while waiting for assistance at a welfare office, an out-of-work father and husband struggling to provide for his family. Wright makes readers know these people and care about them. Likewise, in his article giving a behind-the-scenes look at what happens at a typical branch meeting of the Communist Party in Harlem, he breathes life into the party members gathered there and into the meeting itself. Aside from Gold, no one on the staff of the *Daily Worker* ever reached those heights.

What has been insisted upon above bears repeating. Even though Wright knew that he wrote better than all the others on the staff at the *Daily Worker,* he was not a bumptious know-it-all who considered newspaper work so beneath him that he dished out fodder, with no regard for style or accuracy. Not so. Wright's articles on the rampant poverty in Harlem, the Spanish Civil War, the opening of the Harlem River Houses and the Harlem Community Art Center, the importance of the Federal Theatre Project productions, Harlem's boycott of Japanese-made goods, and many other significant issues were all carefully researched, double-checked for accuracy, and fluently written. To read them attentively is to realize this. From articles as lengthy as "What Happens at a Communist Party Branch Meeting in the Harlem Section?" to the two- or three-paragraph pieces on sundry topical subjects, Wright always approached his writing for the *Daily Worker* with the utmost professionalism, contrary to what some of his Chicago friends thought and said. Wright, in fine, was no hireling. Even though his ruling passion was fiction writing, he took his work at the paper seriously.

SECTION ONE

THE SHAME SPOT OF NEW YORK

Harlem is New York's shame spot when it comes to housing.

RICHARD WRIGHT

One of the impressive features of Wright's articles for the *Daily Worker* is their sheer variety. In the two hundred or so pieces he wrote for the newspaper, Wright covered crucial national and world events as well as major issues on the local scene in Harlem and elsewhere in New York City. With skill and feeling, Wright's articles captured an America and a world rife with turmoil and angst yet occasionally enlivened by the joy and hope that are testimony to the resilience and pluck of the human spirit. Some of the best of those articles vividly chronicle the plight of Harlem's quarter-million black residents suffering, to a greater or lesser degree, from the effects of the Great Depression. One such article ("Negro, with 3-Week-Old Baby, Begs Food on Streets") relates the dolorous tale of Esther Bostwick, the mother of five young children, a woman deserted by husband and evicted from her apartment, forced to wander the streets of Harlem with her children in search of food and shelter. Touching without being mawkish, Wright's feature story on this woman graphically captures the human misery brought about by the Depression. While Wright depicts Mrs. Bostwick as a flesh-and-blood individual, he also portrays her as representative of the multitudes of suffering souls racked by the country's dire economic circumstances.

One noteworthy point that Wright touches on in the article is the reason that Mrs. Bostwick's husband deserted his family: he lost his job and was thus unable to provide for them. Such behavior was hardly unique. Sociologists and historians have often maintained that one of the Depression's myriad disastrous effects was the shattering of the family structure. Baldly put, men ran away from their homes, leaving their wives and children behind to fend for themselves. While such was the case nationwide, the incidents of husbands deserting their families were especially high in Harlem. "The Depression inevitably disrupted family life [in Harlem]," historian and professor Cheryl Greenberg notes, ushering in "an increase in . . . desertion cases."[1] These desertions were directly attributable to unemployment. Edward Ellis accurately captures a reason underlying the record-high number of desertions when he argues, "The Depression castrated some men by dethroning them from their position as the breadwinner and the head of the family."[2]

But not all Depression-era men in Harlem abandoned their families. Many dug in and remained, struggling alongside their wives and children, providing for them as best they could. In his article on Mrs. Bostwick, Wright incorporates the portrait of another Harlem family that has fallen on hard times, the Theus couple and their young child. Their story forms a poignant complement to that of the Bostwick family. The Theus family too has been evicted and is wandering the streets of Harlem, but there is an important difference between the two families: the husbands. Husband and father Theodore Theus has, like Mrs. Bostwick's husband, been "pink slipped," but Theus does not bolt—he toughs it out beside his wife and child. So do a few other family men Wright homes in on in some of his other articles (Mr. Branum, for instance, in Wright's story on the Harlem River Houses, and Adolphus Green in Wright's article on the intolerable burden placed on consumers by the increase in milk prices).

Even though Theodore Theus and other husbands and fathers like him resist the kind of "castration" that Ellis writes of, their resistance does not lessen their misery—and Wright excels at chronicling such misery. Especially gripping is his coverage of the added stressful burden that the holidays place on Harlem families. One of those holidays, Thanksgiving, receives close attention as Wright interviews a number of typical Harlemites who have little or no reason to be thankful. The article comes close to being a virtual tour of a Harlem teeming with hungry people whose pantries are empty. An even bigger holiday is Christmas. In "Santa Claus Has a Hard Time Finding Way to Harlem Slums," Wright interviews a fairly representative Harlem family (one in which again the husband, having been laid off, has deserted). A particularly poignant piece, the article juxtaposes the gaiety of the Christmas season with the grinding poverty that forces parents to go so far as to cut back on buying milk so that their children will have a toy or two.

Far more compelling is Wright's story of Florence Christopher, a sixty-five-year-old black woman who suffers a heart attack, collapses, and dies on the floor of the Emergency Relief Bureau in central Harlem. One reason the story is so gripping is Wright's revelation that the woman's body lay on the floor of the crowded relief station for half an hour before a doctor arrived. Another hour had then passed waiting for an ambulance. The ambulance, Wright points out, never arrived, and at length the woman's body was draped with "a dirty burlap bag," unceremoniously "shoved . . . into a police wagon," and carted off to the morgue. While exposing such blatant inhumanity, the article also indicts the system responsible for it—a system, the article charges, that provides no emergency health aid at Harlem relief stations (despite regular fainting in those stations), that funnels money away from the poor and gives it to Wall Street bankers, and that allows the body of an elderly woman to be treated with something akin to desecration.

While Wright's account of Harlem's battered and bruised souls is heart-rending, his intent is not to evoke tears. "If you are the type to weep," he writes at the conclusion of "Negro . . . Begs Food," then "you can have a good cry over this and then feel good, 'purged,' you know. But tears can't stop starvation."[3] Wright's primary purpose is to effect action, reform. It is significant, then, that he opens the same article with a direct reference to that Victorian apostle of social reform, Charles Dickens. Wright, we know from both his autobiography and his biographers, was a voracious reader, and one of his favorite authors was Dickens. An attentive reader, Wright well knew that while Dickens's novels tugged at the heartstrings, they did so in order to hammer home the need for social change. In his articles on Harlem's "disinherited" (to use Wright's own word), he does the same.

Other *Daily Worker* articles that Wright penned also laid bare the indignities heaped on Harlem's poor people and the rampant social injustice they suffered. One piece, for example, exposes the unconscionable disregard for the care of black patients at Harlem Hospital, where Wright reports insect-ridden medicine being dispensed to patients. Another article tells of the eviction of a single mother and her three children from their Harlem apartment, the eviction being overseen by a contingent of police officers there to ensure no interference. Still another article recounts the life-threatening predicament faced by a black man, John Jones, who had settled in Harlem after fleeing for his life from the South ("Negro, Who Escaped Lynch Mob in South, Ordered to Return by Harlem Relief Officials"). The article, one of the last Wright wrote for the *Daily Worker,* is among his most jarring. The article discloses that Jones fled the South and his hometown in Florida after a fistfight with a white man led to the formation of a lynch mob. Jones escaped to the supposedly sheltering bosom of Harlem, where bureaucratic ineptitude and indifference within the Harlem Emergency Relief Bureau threatened to force Jones back to the South, straight into the arms of the mob he had eluded. An important, engrossing story, it was one not covered by any other reporter for any other paper.

Other stories by Wright expose instances of job discrimination against black workers, even against black doctors at Harlem Hospital, while several others reveal brutality against blacks by storekeepers, teachers, and the police. This issue was one with which Wright was all too familiar. Having grown up in the Jim Crow South, where blacks routinely suffered brutality, humiliation, and emotional torment at the hands of whites, he had not only heard firsthand accounts of blacks being beaten, raped, and lynched, he had also witnessed (and in some cases even experienced) his share of these atrocities, as he reveals in Black Boy and "The Ethics of Living Jim Crow." Wright was thus uniquely qualified to report on stories of white violence against blacks.

One of his first *Daily Worker* articles, along with its follow-up piece, highlights a then-important story of white-on-black brutality: the beating of a fourteen-year-old African-American boy, John Wilson, by a white store clerk. The boy, the article relates, had been sent to the store (Phillips Market on Fulton Street in Brooklyn) by his family to buy some hot dogs but had forgotten to get his change. When the youth went back for the money, the store clerk assaulted him. (The photo accompanying Wright's story showed the boy's swollen, bandaged face.) For twenty-first-century readers, a store clerk's assault of a customer may seem nothing more than a blip on the radar screen of neighborhood news. At the time, however, the incident caused a volatile situation. After word spread about what had happened, hundreds of angry people gathered outside the store. (The *Amsterdam News* placed the number of people in the crowd at over eight hundred, while the *New York Age* gauged it at two thousand.) The situation grew so tense that police were called to the scene. When they arrived, they arrested the store clerk, Leo Toscana, and charged him with assault. New York authorities, it seemed, were not about to run the risk of having a riot break out. The 1935 Harlem riot was still fresh in the minds of everyone in the city. Black Harlemites recalled how two years earlier Harlem had exploded after rumors spread that a white store clerk at a five-and-dime had savagely beaten a youth, sixteen-year-old Lino Rivera. The assault on John Wilson was thus an acutely troubling matter to 1937 Harlem, and Wright was well aware of this even though he had been in Chicago in 1935. He also knew that conditions in Harlem, which were the underlying cause of the riot, had not improved greatly, and hence the beating of Wilson had the potential to spark another outbreak of mass violence. It mattered little that the incident happened in Brooklyn. The victim was black and young; his attacker was white and adult. In his follow-up article on the assault, Wright detailed steps that were being taken to ensure justice in the case. He reported how Toscana, the clerk, had been jailed, and then had been fired by the store owner, one A. Philips. Wright went on to relate that in a community meeting attended by over five hundred people, Philips had apologized for the incident and agreed to hire a black clerk to replace Toscana, as well as a black butcher. Wright did not mention that Philips even took out an ad in the *New York Age* decrying what he called "the ill-advised and brutal action of his former clerk" and announcing at the bottom of the ad, "COLORED HELP EMPLOYED.") Unfortunately, not all Wright's articles end on such a positive note—but then, life in Harlem during the 1930s was not conducive to happy endings.

In a related article written about a month later ("Harlem Crowd Shows Feelings on Chiseling"), Wright again reported on a near-riot stemming from "a small incident based on a misunderstanding." The incident in question occurred when a white clerk in a shoe store in Harlem refused to pay a black youth the full amount of money agreed upon for electrical work the youth had done in the store. A minor scuffle broke out between the youth and the clerk, but it was soon quelled, and the youth left the store unharmed. Somehow, though, a rumor circulated that the youth had been beaten by the store owners (again, a rumor similar to the one that sparked the 1935 riot). Before long a crowd formed in front of the store and began smashing its windows. It was only when the youth returned to the store and showed everyone that he was unhurt that the angry crowd dispersed. Though brief, the article is noteworthy because, like Wright's piece on the assault of John Wilson, it reveals that racial tension in Harlem was still high and that a rumor of white-on-black aggression had the potential to set off a riot comparable to the one two years earlier. Just as important, the article homes in on some of the root causes of this "high . . . pitch of resentment in Harlem": "exploitation by landlords, storekeepers, and businessmen." Wright would go on to devote many of his *Daily Worker* articles to exposing this and other forms of racial injustice.

One particularly painful form of injustice that African Americans in Harlem faced was price gouging, especially by landlords. It was no secret, though white realtors adamantly denied it, that the rent black Harlemites paid was exorbitant, way out of proportion to that paid by white renters in Manhattan or Brooklyn, or even by members of other minority groups living in East Harlem. Scores of committees and commissions were set up throughout the 1930s to study and rectify the housing problem in Harlem. The City Affairs Committee, the Slum Clearance Committee, the Housing Commission, the Citywide Citizens' Committee on Harlem, the Mayor's Commission—all these bodies arrived at essentially the same conclusion, one voiced as early as 1929 by Richard Moore, an outspoken African American Communist: "Rents in Negro Harlem are . . . often double and sometimes triple those in other sections of the city."[4] In the words of the City Affairs Committee's 1937 report, "Negro tenants [in Harlem] pay one percent to twenty percent more of their income for rent than any other group."[5] In Central Harlem, Cheryl Greenberg goes on to reveal, "rents never fell below $31 a month, and often ran as high as $70. The average resident of Central Harlem paid $52."[6] This was despite the Depression, when rents were much lower elsewhere. Additionally, the apartments (or tenement flats) for which black Harlemites paid such exorbitant rent were nothing more than hovels, dank and squalid, decaying and rat-ridden. Testifying in December 1937 at a court hearing that grew out of a state-commissioned inquiry into housing conditions in Harlem, New York City Housing Authority Commissioner Langdon Post painted a harrowing picture of tenement life in Harlem. (Wright covered Post's testimony for the *Daily Worker* in an article that appeared in the paper's December 15, 1937, edition.) At the hearing, Post detailed the disease, infant mortality, and crime that resulted from such squalid housing and went on to deliver a scathing indictment of the landlords responsible. "There is no doubt," he concluded, "that we are faced with an emergency in Harlem."

Post was neither exaggerating nor being melodramatic; if anything, he understated the problem. Little wonder, then, that not infrequently Harlem tenants would launch rent strikes against their slumlords. "More than any other time," Mark Naison contends, "the 1930s was the period when the tenant movement 'came of age'"[7]—a period, he adds, "of extraordinary ferment among tenants."[8] One of the spots where that movement and that ferment were most pronounced was Harlem, where rent strikes were repeatedly staged. Wright covered some of these rent strikes, reporting on their course and outcome (many of them successful).

One bright spot in the otherwise grim housing situation in Harlem was the construction of the Harlem River Houses, a valiant joint effort by the New York City Housing Authority and the federal government (the Public Works Administration) to provide decent housing for Harlemites. Construction plans were drawn up in mid-1935, and the project was completed and ready for occupancy in late August 1937. Built by WPA workers at a cost of 4.5 million dollars, and so named because of its proximity to the Harlem River, the Harlem River Houses stretched along Seventh Avenue between 151st and 155th Streets. Understandably, demand for an apartment in the project was staggering. When news of the project's opening was announced, between fifteen and twenty thousand families applied for the 574 available apartments.[9] They had good reason to be interested. Not only were the apartments clean, safe, and affordable, but the project itself offered quite an impressive number of amenities. There were, for example, a nursery school, a kindergarten, a health clinic, laundry rooms, four inside play areas for children, and two playgrounds outside, along with two capacious exterior wading pools. The development also featured a spacious central courtyard, as opposed to the small backyard common to most Harlem tenements. Moreover, colorful, elaborate murals graced many of the walls in the courtyards, and sculpture dotted the grounds. The apartments themselves were marvels for that period. Each came with a "modern" kitchen equipped with a refrigerator and a gas range, and every unit had its own bathroom with a ceramic-tile floor (a far cry from the usual Harlem apartment building where all the tenants on one floor shared a bathroom). Tenants of the Harlem River Houses would not freeze in the winter the way most of them had in their former buildings: the units in the development all had central heating. Above all, sunlight came through the windows of each and every apartment, something unheard of in Harlem's multitude of dark, dingy tenements. In fine, the Harlem River Houses, as Peter Marcuse has noted, "provided housing of a quality at least equal to that of the private middle-income housing of the time."[10]

Today, when almost without exception public housing developments nationwide have a horrid reputation as concentrated pockets of poverty, decay, and crime, it is important to keep in mind that the opening of the Harlem River Houses in 1937 was a momentous occasion, one heralded by Harlemites and New York City officials alike as a blessing. "This is the happiest moment I've had since I became Mayor," Fiorello LaGuardia declared at the dedication of the development. "Here indeed is a dream come true."[11] A dream come true is precisely how the Harlem River Houses were viewed by the 574 families selected as tenants. Although these chosen families would not begin moving in until August 31, an important ceremony was held on June 16, 1937, on the grounds of the nearly completed housing project. Under a contract drawn up two years earlier, the city of New York—the New York City Housing Authority, to be precise—had agreed to lease the Harlem River Houses from the federal government (the United States Housing Authority) and to operate and manage the development, giving regular reports to the government on the project's operation and tenancy. It was this official lease-signing that took place on June 16. The ceremony, which began shortly after five in the afternoon, received heavy press coverage and drew close to four thousand people, half of them from Harlem. Among the officials who participated in the ceremony were Mayor LaGuardia, who had helped spearhead the development since its inception; Langdon Post, arguably the most outstanding chairman in the history of the New York City Housing Authority; Howard Gray, director of the Public Works Administration's housing division; Walter White, president of the NAACP; and Charles Toney, prominent African-American municipal court justice. After speeches by each of these officials and following resounding applause from the massive audience, Mayor LaGuardia signed the lease, and the city of New York officially took charge of the Harlem River Houses. On August 31, a little over two months after the dedication and lease-signing ceremony, the first twenty-seven families moved into the development, followed a week later by other families, then later on by still others until all 574 families had settled in.

While many praised the Harlem River Houses as a blessing, nobody saw the development as the cure-all for Harlem's serious housing problem.

Commissioner Post, in his speech at the lease-signing, remarked that the new housing development "is obviously only a beginning when there are so many thousands still unprovided for."[12] Two months later in an article he wrote for the Urban League's journal *Opportunity*, Post reiterated that point, lamenting that "the project barely scratches the surface of the housing needs of New York's Negro community" and expressing his "regret that Harlem's first low-rent housing development is not ten times as large as it is."[13] Many others agreed. "Those 574 apartments . . . are just a drop in the bucket," one New York City alderman remarked a few days after the lease-signing.[14] Writing in the *New York Times* a week after the dedication ceremony, black columnist Henry Lee Moon observed that the Harlem River Houses "serve more as a model than as an answer to the acute housing needs of [Harlem's] quarter-million Negroes."[15] Despite the truth of such comments, historians and urban studies specialists have nonetheless concurred that the construction and opening of the Harlem River Houses marked a step in the right direction, and LaGuardia was no doubt on target when he pointed out at the lease-signing and dedication ceremony that the Harlem River Houses represented "574 more sanitary and cheerful houses than the government has built in the last 100 years."[16]

The opening of the Harlem River Houses did not go unnoticed by Wright. His feature story on the development appeared in the October 8 edition of the *Daily Worker* and is as thorough, accurate, and informative as any of the articles that appeared in mainstream newspapers. As he does in so many of his *Daily Worker* articles (his pieces on the death of the heroic William Campbell, for instance, or his article on the eviction of Esther Bostwick and her children), Wright humanizes the story. One way he does this is by spotlighting "a typical and lucky Negro family selected for residence"—a Mr. and Mrs. Brannum and their two young daughters. Wright interviews Mrs. Brannum, and through her eyes readers see in graphic detail "the hovels in which she has lived"—"the foul-smelling fire-traps" with their "menace of disease, crime and exorbitant rentals" that she and her family are now free of ("Opening of Harlem Project Homes Shows How Slums Can Be Wiped Out in New York").[17] Particularly chilling is her description of opening her icebox in a previous residence, and constantly finding a hoard of roaches inside. "And the roaches!," she relates with a mixture of disgust and dark humor. "Honest to God, when you opened that icebox door, those black things just stared at you and dared you to come in! They acted like they had Constitutional privileges, as though they had signed leases and had a legal right to be there."[18] She goes on to tell of the oppressive darkness of the windowless flats and of the intolerable lack of privacy and unhealthful lack of ventilation. Mrs. Brannum's testimony not only underscores how squalid living conditions in Harlem were for most residents, it also throws into stark relief the comfort, safety, and joy that the Harlem River Houses provided for 574 fortunate families. Recalling the darkness that her family is leaving behind, she speaks excitedly of the sunlight that will pour through the windows of her new apartment and of the fresh air that will replace the foul smells pervading the hovels they have escaped. (Not coincidentally, many newspaper stories on the Harlem River Houses noted the presence of sunlight and fresh air as one of the development's outstanding features. The *New York Times,* for example, pointed out, "Every room [in the project] looks out at the sky and all have cross-ventilation."[19]) There is no doubt that Mrs. Brannum was emblematic of the fortunate souls selected as tenants and that her excitement and joy were theirs.

Like many others (including Commissioner Post, Justice Toney, and Donelan Phillips, the president of the Consolidated Tenants League), Wright did not regard the Harlem River Houses as the ultimate solution to Harlem's housing crisis. Echoing New York City alderman Charles Lynch, who himself echoed a popular catchphrase of the day, Wright points out that "the new housing unit . . . is but a drop in the bucket" and issues a reminder that notwithstanding the 574 families that have been provided with the comfort and safety of "snow-white walls" and high ceilings, there are still over 56,000 Harlem families living in "begrimed firetraps."[20] Wright, though, was no killjoy, and he does not end his article on a negative note by minimizing the value of the Harlem River Houses. Instead, he closes by holding up the newly created project as evidence that, as the headline proclaims, slum housing in Harlem can be wiped out. There is a solution, he insists (the Harlem River Houses show as much), but the people must fight to help bring about that solution. Harlemites must "organize and demand of their government housing and more housing."[21] If the Harlem River Houses can be constructed, Wright posits, so can others just like them, and he closes by maintaining that the first step toward making such houses a reality is for "the millions of Mrs. Brannums in America [to] make up their minds that they want them for their children."[22]

Fortunately for the residents of the Harlem River Houses, living in the new development meant escape from the rent gouging that so many other African Americans in Harlem were experiencing at the hands of greedy landlords. Harlem's slumlords, though, were not the only ones guilty of gouging. The milk conglomerates, especially Borden, also stood accused of unscrupulous price hiking. In Harlem in the mid-1930s, the average price of a quart of milk was fourteen cents. In July 1937, Borden and Sheffield Farms raised the price of milk by one cent, then raised it again another penny in September, and then in November by still another penny. By today's standards, such a seemingly small price increase in a product does not appear excessive (present-day price increases, while never pleasant for the consumer, are so commonplace that they are all but expected). But to Depression-era consumers, particularly those in Harlem, such a price hike was onerous and viewed as nothing less than callous corporate greed. In response to these milk price increases, irate consumers protested. A number of consumer protection groups picketed the milk companies' corporate headquarters and launched a boycott of their products. The *Daily Worker* roundly condemned the price increases, comparing the milk companies to gangsters like John Dillinger and Lucky Luciano. Wright himself covered quite a bit of the story, chronicling the picketing and the boycotts in a number of informative pieces.

■

In his second inaugural address, delivered on January 20, 1937, President Franklin D. Roosevelt lamented to, and with, the American people that "millions of families [are] trying to live on incomes so meager that the pall of family disaster hangs over them day by day." Roosevelt went on to say, in now-famous words, "I see one-third of a nation ill-housed, ill-clad, ill-nourished." Roosevelt's words rang true, accurately capturing the state of the nation at the height of the Great Depression, that monumental upheaval characterized by historian Meyer Weinberg as "the greatest economic catastrophe [in] American history." Although the entire country writhed in torment during the depression, one of the hardest hit American communities was Harlem. With its pervasive poverty, astronomically high unemployment, and rampant hunger and homelessness, Harlem was left a shattered ruin by the Depression. Reprinted here, some of Wright's best articles for the *Daily Worker* focused on the plight of the quarter-million Harlemites suffering, to a greater or lesser degree, from the ravages of the Depression. Wright's stories on Harlem's bruised and battered souls are nothing short of Dickensian in their ability to engage readers, then and now.

In addition to—or perhaps because of—the poverty that black Harlemites were mired in, they often fell prey to gross indignities and various forms of social injustice. One acutely painful injustice that Harlemites suffered, along with the multitudes of other New Yorkers from other sections and of other races, was price gouging by the milk conglomerates Borden's and Sheffield's. And just as exorbitant rents and deplorable housing conditions evoked protests, so too did the milk companies' unconscionable price hiking. Other injustices ranged from white-on-black brutality and job discrimination to wretched health care and exploitation by landlords and storekeepers. Many of Wright's *Daily Worke*r articles chronicled this ongoing pattern of abuse and neglect in Harlem.

Perhaps the main reason that Harlem during the Depression stood out as the shame spot of New York, as Wright once characterized it, was that housing conditions there were so horrendous. Decaying, foul-smelling, and teeming with rats and roaches, Harlem's tenements were for the most part barely fit for human habitation. Yet to rent an apartment in one of these tenements, African Americans were forced to pay twice, and sometimes three times, as much as white renters in other sections of New York. Outraged at the squalid living conditions and exorbitant rent, many tenants in Harlem rebelled by launching rent strikes, demanding from their landlords building repairs and rent adjustments. Another response to the housing situation in Harlem came from the federal government and the New York City Housing Authority in their joint construction of the Harlem River Houses, a public housing development heralded by Harlemites and New York City officials alike as a blessing. Harlem's deplorable housing, the community's reaction to these living conditions, the government's response in the form of the Harlem River Houses—all received plenty of attention in Wright's Daily Worker articles.

■ ■ ■

Daily Worker, DECEMBER 16, 1937

Two Cops Slay Negro Boy—"Ran When Questioned"

TWO BROOKLYN POLICEMEN shot and killed a 17-year-old Negro boy Monday because "the boy ran when questioned," it was learned late yesterday.

The boy, William Shepard, was shot in the back and died at St. Mary's Hospital.

The policemen sought to justify their act by declaring that Shepard carried a bundle containing jewelry and a bunch of pawn tickets.

The shooting occurred on the eastbound platform of the Fulton St. elevated station. No concrete evidence has been brought forward to implicate Shepard in any robbery.

The policemen who shot the boy are Albert Meyers and Patrolman Cicio of Brooklyn headquarters. ■

Daily Worker, SEPTEMBER 5, 1937

2 Negro Women Attacked in IRT Subway

THE UPPER HARLEM SECTION of the Communist Party will send a delegation of workers to visit the homes of two women who assaulted two Negro women in the IRT subway last week, it was announced today.

The two Negro women, Zola King and Fritz Richardson, actresses employed by the Federal Negro Theatre, were on their way to work when they were accused of having stepped on the feet of Libby and Nettie Horowitz, of 166 Second Ave.

The incident occurred at the height of the evening rush hour just as the train pulled out of the Times Square Station. The two women showered abusive language on the two Negro women and told them that:

"If we had you in the South, we would have you lynched."

STIRS UP MEN

Immediately afterward Nettie Horowitz hit Fritz Richardson in the mouth, and when Miss Richardson tried to protect herself, Nettie Horowitz sought to stir up a mob spirit by shouting:

"Are you white men going to sit there and see nigger bitches beat up a white woman?"

Miss King and Miss Richardson left the train at King's Highway Station, in Brooklyn, and the two women followed and had them arrested, despite the fact that they had not started the fight.

All four of the women were locked up over night in the 71st Precinct Police Station, at Empire Blvd. and New York Ave.

ASK DAMAGES

When arraigned in court the next morning, Libby and Nettie Horowitz asked that the case be dismissed if Miss Richardson would defray damages of $35. They claimed that they had lost their temper and were sorry for the incident.

All four were dismissed, but Miss Richardson says she will not pay the $35 damages asked. She claims that inasmuch as she did not start the fight she should not be held accountable.

When the case came to the attention of the Communist Party it was decided that a delegation of workers should visit the homes of the two women and make an attempt to show them the unfairness of their action.

"It is our duty to lead the fight against white chauvinism and all the encroachments against the Negro people," declared Simon Marshall, assistant administrative secretary of the Upper Harlem Section of the Communist Party. ■

Daily Worker, SEPTEMBER 16, 1937

24 Negro Families Begin Rent Strike in Harlem

BECAUSE OF EXORBITANT RENTALS and unsanitary living conditions, 24 Negro families declared a rent strike today against the New York Lease Co., 2061 Broadway.

A continuous picket line was thrown in front of the building, located at 9 W. 137th St. In discussing the reasons for the strike, Mrs. Anita Towers, chairman of the strike committee, stated: "The apartments have not been decorated for years. In many rooms there are holes a foot wide in the ceilings and floors.

DEMANDS 30% INCREASE

"The landlord is demanding for these slum apartments a 30 per cent increase in rentals. For four-room apartments we are now paying $25 and he is demanding $33.

"All of the tenants have stopped paying rent and will not pay until the landlord either fixes the apartments or rescinds the increase."

The tenants throughout the building are indignant over the proposed increases. Many of them are aware of the recently-opened Harlem River Houses where rents are much lower and facilities much better.

DISPOSSESS NOTICE

In an answer to the striking action of the tenants, the landlord is serving dispossess notices. But the tenants are determined that they are going to ignore them.

"If he carries one of us to court for non-payment of rent, then he will have to carry us all," one of the tenants declared.

The apartments are ill ventilated; in many rooms there is no fresh air or sunlight at all. On wash days the areas are so crowded with clothes hung out to dry that a child cannot see the sun from where he is forced to play. ■

Daily Worker, DECEMBER 18, 1937

300 at Harlem ERB Sit In to Demand Rent, Food Budgets

THREE HUNDRED NEGRO and Puerto Rican men, women, and children marched into the ERB office at 124th St. and Lenox Ave. yesterday afternoon and took seats, declaring:

"We are here to stay until all discriminatory practices are ended and until rent and food budgets are increased to meet the rising cost of living!"

Sanitary facilities and toilets were barred by the police to the 300 Negro and Puerto Rican men, women and children who are engaged in a sit-in strike at the ERB station, 124th St. and Lenox Ave. in Harlem, according to late reports received last night.

Officials of the Workers' Alliance [Workers Alliance of America] declared that a mass meeting will be held in front of the station protesting this action.

The demonstrators brought food, blankets, and milk for their children with them, and came prepared to sit in the offices indefinitely.

Meanwhile, 35 pickets marched in front of the station carrying placards explaining the actions of their fellow workers inside.

MANY NEW APPLICANTS

The demonstration is being conducted under the joint auspices of Locals 30 and 38 of the Workers' Alliance, with Louis Campbell and Albert Martinet acting as organizers.

The chief demand advanced by the sitters-in is for the ending of all discriminatory and red tape practices of the station.

Owing to the widespread layoffs in industry, the station is swamped with new applicants. No increase in personnel has been made to meet these conditions, with the consequent result that many people in desperate need are unable to obtain even an investigation.

The officials of the Workers' Alliance are demanding that all applications be acted upon within 72 hours, that better clinic care be furnished the clients, and that all designations according to race and creed on applications be stopped.

"We have used very polite methods long enough," declared Louis Campbell, organizer. "This time we are going to sit it out with them until they act."

Typical of the suffering heaped upon families because of the bogged state of ERB stations is the following case. No. 717919. A.S., a woman client, was allowed $4.50 for room rent paid on a semi-monthly basis. The landlord increased the rent to $4 and insisted upon weekly payment.

The relief investigator notified the landlord that the station would not pay the increase and agreed that the client should be turned into the streets. It was not until six days later that shelter was found. ■

Daily Worker, NOVEMBER 8, 1937

A.L.P. Assemblyman Urges State Control of Price of Milk

"THE PRICE OF MILK SHOULD BE REGULATED by the State of New York!" Oscar Garcia Rivera, labor-supported Assemblyman-elect from the 17th A.D. [Assembly District] in Harlem, declared yesterday in an interview with the Daily Worker regarding the 1-cent per quart increase in the price of milk imposed by the Sheffield-Borden Milk Trust.

"The reaction of the poor families in Harlem is against this increase. It affects those who live in Harlem particularly," Rivera continued. "The milk companies are unfair to the people!"

Rivera, a progressive Republican, a winner in the recent elections, was endorsed by the American Labor Party, the Communist Party, and the Independent Puerto Rican Democrats.

STOP DRINKING IT

In a similar vein, Lillian Gaskin, Negro trade union leader and member of the New York County Committee of the American Labor Party, declared her opposition to the 1-cent increase in milk imposed by the Milk Trust.

"I think the only way to reduce the price of milk is to stop drinking it whenever and wherever possible," Mrs. Gaskin declared. "It should be used only in those families where children need it for their health. All adults in Harlem and over the city should boycott Sheffield and Borden, because their increase of milk prices is a crime against the children of Harlem.

"The city should control the price of milk. We need city-owned, milk-producing and milk-distributing plants," Mrs. Gaskin said.

DON'T GET ENOUGH TO EAT

What does this 1-cent per quart increase in the price of milk mean to a Negro family in Harlem?

Mount the steps at 14 E. 120th St. and knock. The door opens and you hear the shouts of children. Mr. and Mrs. Adolphus Green stand in the center of the front room and ask you what you want. You tell them that you are representing the *Daily Worker* and you want to know how the rise in the price of milk will affect their living. They ask you to come in and sit down; and then they begin to talk.

Here is a family of ten, the mother, father, and eight children: Adolphus, Jr., 15; Roy, 14; Willis, 12; Mary, 9; Felix, 8; Muriel, five and a half; Sylvia, four; and Gwendolyn, 14 months old.

They have been on relief for more than two years. The children, including the mother and father, are undernourished. In telling the ages of her children, Mrs. Green declared timidly:

"I'm always ashamed to tell people how old my children are, they are so small. They simply don't get enough to eat."

THEY STARVE SLOWLY

The Harlem ERB [Emergency Relief Bureau] allows Mrs. Green $103 per month for food, rent, gas, light, and soap. In addition, she is given $15 every three months for clothing and two or three quarts of milk per day.

Of this $103, $40 per month goes to pay the rent on a dark, seven-room flat. On the remaining $63 they starve slowly. The electric lights have long since been cut off.

The dieticians of the ERB have instructed Mrs. Green to use eight and a half quarts of milk per day for her children, but they made no provision for her getting them. Deducting the three quarts given daily by the ERB, Mrs. Green's milk bill would run $16.50 per month. She cannot pay this, so she limits her eight children to five quarts per day, paying for the two extra quarts out of her $63 monthly living allowance.

TARGETS FOR DISEASE

The two cents per day exacted by the Sheffield-Borden Milk Trust from Mrs. Green creates a mountain-like problem for her. It takes at least 60 cents per month from her, and many a day that 60 cents will mean the difference between stark hunger and skimpy meal for ten people.

It means that her children's weight will decrease; it means that during the coming winter they will be targets for rickets and tuberculosis. ■

Daily Worker, NOVEMBER 20, 1937

Baby Carriage Parade to Protest Milk Gouge

HARLEM THREW ITS SUPPORT behind the fight against the high price of milk yesterday when the Women's Commission of the Upper Harlem Section of the Communist Party called upon all organizations to participate in the "baby carriage" demonstration which will converge upon the City Hall at 11 AM today.

Under the leadership of Audley Moore, chairman, and Mrs. M. E. Boyd, secretary, the commission issued a statement urging all churches, lodges, and civic groups to send contingents of women, with their children, to present to Mayor LaGuardia a demand for the establishment of free milk plans and stations throughout the five boroughs.

Rose Nelson, secretary of the Progressive Council, which is cooperating with the League of Mothers' Clubs, hailed this morning's demonstration.

"Consumers must make their voices heard all over the city," she said. "There is no limit to the lengths the milk monopoly will go in their greed for profits if the people take it without protest.

"The present price of milk is a direct attack against the health of our city's women and children, and we must fight back until the milk trust is forced to supply this vital necessity at a price the people can afford to pay."

More than a thousand mothers under the auspices of the League of Mothers' Clubs are expected to bring their infants to City Hall to demonstrate against climbing milk prices. ■

Daily Worker, DECEMBER 15, 1937

Ban on Negro Doctors Bared at City Probe

BRAZEN ADMISSIONS of discriminatory practices against Negroes made yesterday by Miss Violet Cohen, head of the Manhattan Trade Schools, and S. S. Goldwater, Commissioner of the Department of Hospitals, featured the first day's hearings of the New York State Temporary Commission on the Condition of Urban Negroes.

The Committee for Better Schools in Harlem brought forth, through its chairman, Rev. John W. Robinson, and its vice-chairman, Emmett M. May, repeated evidences of discriminatory practices in school zoning which effectively shunted Negro students from four of the city's leading high schools.

The most arrogant and sensational testimony of the day came from Commissioner S. S. Goldwater, who sought to justify the lack of Negro doctors and nurses in New York City's hospitals on the grounds that they were "generally inferior to whites in training, quality, and personality." Then in the next breath he blandly declared that "to my knowledge no discriminatory practices exist in the hospitals of New York against Negroes."

BARRED IN SCHOOLS

The testimony of Emmett M. May showed that the Board of Education had so zig-zagged the zoning boundaries that Negro students were barred from the George Washington, Theodore Roosevelt, Evander Childs and Peter Stuyvesant High Schools.

The hearings, held in the Seventh District Court at 447 W. 151st St., began yesterday morning with Lester Granger, secretary of the Urban League's Workers' Bureau, directing, and Assemblyman Harold P. Herman presiding as chairman. The hearings will continue through Thursday and many witnesses will be called from all walks of Harlem life to testify on Negro conditions.

In the course of Emmett May's testimony it was brought out that in many of the text books used in New York elementary high schools insulting allusions were constantly made to the Negro people to make for contempt on the part of white students.

The testimony of Miss Ellen Phillips, superintendent of schools, disclosed that overcrowding [and] lack of proper equipment had so lowered the standard of many Harlem elementary schools that their reputation had become "unsavory." It was brought out that no elementary school had been built in Harlem since 1900.

HARD TO GET JOBS

Sidney Lake, principal of New York Industrial High Schools, declared in his testimony that it was a hard proposition for Negro boys to obtain jobs after graduating from industrial courses.

"The trouble at the bottom of it all is that Harlem is poor," he said.

He placed the responsibility for job discrimination against Negroes on the shoulders of industrial establishments, and spoke of the "individual ways unions have of not giving union cards to Negroes."

Miss Bell Hawley, secretary of the Advisory Board on Industrial Education and vice-president of the State A. F. of L., admitted that she advised Negro students to take "only those courses in which they might get jobs." Many industrial courses, such as those relating to beauty culture, are denied to Negro girls. She admitted reluctantly that she and the Board of Education had no right to do this.

HOSPITAL JIM-CROW

Discriminatory exclusion of Negro nurses and doctors seeking admission to the city's hospitals was bared by Ruth Logan Roberts, chairman of the Committee of Citizens, and Mabel Staupers, executive of the National Association of Colored Graduate Nurses.

It was pointed out that few city-run hospitals admit Negro nurses with any degree of frequency. They were excluded from others on the grounds that their "educational qualifications did not warrant their admission."

Dr. Theodore Gattings and Dr. Peter Murray, two leading Harlem Negro doctors, cited in detail the amazing system by which the Medical Board evaded its responsibility of appointing Negro doctors.

It was stated that a doctor had to have the approval of the head of his department before he was eligible for appointment as a "visiting doctor." Then his application had to pass the Medical Board, and finally the Commissioner of Hospitals. Inevitably Negro interns are never able to obtain the endorsement of the heads of their respective departments because of prejudice.

Today's hearings will deal exclusively with Harlem housing and many tenants and landlords will be called to testify.

The commission consisted of State Senators Howard, Fischel and Mahoney; Assemblymen Justice and Andrews; Henry Stern, Francis Rivers, Mrs. W. Ross Haynes, Henri Shields, Dean S. Yarborough, Lewis Mayers and Rev. Michael Mulvoy. ■

Daily Worker, JULY 20, 1937

Bar Negroes Relief after Pink Slip Cuts

DESTITUTE NEGROES who have been lopped off the WPA rolls in the pink slip drive are not finding it easy to obtain relief, it was disclosed today by Charles Tylor, vice-president of the Uptown Division of the City Projects' Council.

Delegations visiting ERB's in Harlem find that discriminatory practices are glaring when the rate of Negro applicants receiving relief are compared with applicants in other parts of the city.

MAPS PROTEST CAMPAIGN

Vice-president Taylor said: "The WPA has cut Negro personnel 50 per cent in most instances, which is much higher than in other parts of the city. And not only have they been unjust in firing Negroes from WPA jobs, but they are making Negro applicants wait till the starvation point before granting them assistance."

An example is at the ERB, precincts 26 and 28, located at 124th St. and Lenox Ave., where Supervisor Edward Wilson has to date granted relief to but one out of eight applicants. The City Projects Council, Harlem offices at 326 Lenox Ave., is now mapping plans for a vigorous campaign on behalf of Negro relief applicants. ■

Daily Worker, JULY 14, 1937

Butcher Slugs Negro Youth Asking for Change

BECAUSE HE WAS A NEGRO BOY and asked for his change after purchasing hot dogs, 14-year-old John Wilson was slugged and beaten yesterday by a Brooklyn store-keeper until rescued by four Negro women.

Bleeding profusely, John was rushed to a drug store for treatment. Leo Toscana, the [clerk], denied beating the boy when an indignant crowd of Negro men and women passersby jammed into his store to investigate.

Toscana had given the boy a piece of raw frankfurter as a bonus for spending his parents' money with him. More concerned with the taste of raw meat than with his money, the boy did not think of the 10 cents change from a quarter until he had almost reached home. When he returned for it, he was beaten.

The Y.C.L. [Young Communist League] branch of Stuyvesant Heights threw a picket line in front of the shop immediately after the incident and forced the shop to close its doors.

The Citizens Civic Affairs Committee, under the leadership of Alexander Clayborn and Eugene Wright, is pressing charges of assault against Toscana today at 9 A.M. in the Pennsylvania Avenue Court.

In their little dingy flat at 43 Kingston Avenue, Brooklyn, John Wilson and his wife, the boy's parents, sit distraught and bewildered. "I was just thinking of those Scottsboro Boys this morning," said Mrs. Wilson. "And now this comes to me, here in Brooklyn." ■

Daily Worker, JULY 15, 1937

Protests against Slugging Grow: Butcher Who Attacked Negro Boy Is Fired

LEON TOSCONA [Leo Toscana], employee of Philips' Butcher Shop, 1592 Fulton Street, Brooklyn, was released yesterday morning from the Pennsylvania Avenue Court on $500 bail for an assault committed yesterday upon John Wilson, 14-year-old Negro boy. The boy had gone into Philips' Butcher Shop to purchase 15¢ worth of hot dogs and forgot his change. When he returned for it, he was slugged and beaten.

The following sign appeared in the shop window yesterday morning:

"Because of yesterday's occurrences and complying with the demands of the Communist Party, the Young Communist League, the Citizens Civic Affairs Committee, we are closing this store until the people of this neighborhood decide otherwise. THE MANAGEMENT."

STORE CLOSED

Late Tuesday afternoon the Young Communist League forced the shop to close its doors by throwing a strong picket line about the place immediately after the assault.

Sensing the indignant attitude of the Negro and white workers of the neighborhood, Philips, owner of the store, approached the Communist Party, the Young Communist League, and the Citizens Civic Affairs Committee and made several proposals. He indicated willingness to dismiss the man responsible for the assault. He agreed to replace this man [with] a Negro butcher at union wage scales and promised that the two Negroes now employed in the establishment would not be discriminated against in any way.

At a meeting scheduled for tonight at 1600 Fulton St., held under the auspices of the Communist Party, the Young Communist League, and the Citizens Civic Affairs Committee, [Philips will reveal what action he is taking and will apologize] to the people of the neighborhood. The store will bear all of the boy's medical expenses and will send him to the country to recover.

The store will grant time on its radio program Sunday evening to the Communist Party, Y.C.L., and the C.C.A. to explain the case to the people of Brooklyn. ■

Daily Worker, August 26, 1937

Citizens Ask Committee to Probe Harlem

ALARMED AT THE MOUNTING TIDE of vice, crime, and starvation, citizens and organizations of Tammany-controlled Spanish Harlem are asking Mayor LaGuardia to appoint a committee of investigation, it was learned today.

The fight for the investigation is being led by the Harlem Civic Committee, a provisional group set in motion two weeks ago by the Workers' Alliance, La Vox, a Spanish newspaper, the Lower Harlem Division of the Communist Party, and various individuals. The committee has been holding meetings in the office of Oscar Garcia Rivera, at 113th and Fifth Avenue.

When originally organized, the committee petitioned Mayor LaGuardia for heavier police re-enforcements in the 17th A.D. This move was fought by several members of the committee and it was pointed out that residential segregation, discrimination, and other forces and not the lack of police caused crime and hard times.

The 17th A.D., the neighborhood in which Mayor LaGuardia lives and which he formerly represented in Congress, is now under the thumb of Tammany's man, Rep. James J. Lanzetta.

The area comprises some 68 densely populated square blocks and borders upon the ultra-exclusive Park Ave. district. Over 80 per cent of the population is unemployed and it is one of the most congested areas in Upper Manhattan. During recent years the rate of Negro influx has risen steadily. Rents are relatively 20 per cent higher here than elsewhere in Harlem. ■

Daily Worker, NOVEMBER 29, 1937

Few Harlem Tables Weighted by Turkey

THE MELLOW CHIMES OF CHURCH BELLS rang through the sunny air of Harlem Thanksgiving afternoon, but on many tables there were no turkeys and in many hearts there were no thanks.

Of course, there were turkeys, fat, browned ones stuffed with dressings, but they were in the show-windows of cafes. Groups of small boys gathered about the windows and talked excitedly, pointing their skinny fingers. But the cafes were not crowded; it takes money to buy turkeys in cafes.

VET DENIED RELIEF

In a chilly, furnished room at 225 W. 129th St., a 49-year-old World War vet sat and wondered if he would get any dinner at all, much less a turkey dinner.

"How about your turkey dinner today?"

"Turkey is turkey," he replied simply.

This vet, whose name is James Lewis, fought a year in France in 1916. With a sort of humble pride, he showed his papers of "honorable discharge." He's been out of work for three months. Time and again he's been to the relief agencies for help. The last time he went he was told to come back Monday.

"You see," they told him, "Mr. Lewis, Thanksgiving is a holiday and we won't be able to do anything till after the weekend."

A young class-conscious Negro chap was stopped on the street and asked:

"How about your turkey dinner, buddy?"

"I ain't got no turkey, but I know a friend who's got one. I'm going over to his house now; maybe I'll get some."

In a Jim Crow branch of the Salvation Army at 224 W. 124th St., more than 350 homeless Negro men had eaten free turkey dinners. They were sitting around on the stoop in the sun, smoking, drinking and talking.

"You fellows had turkey dinners?"

"Yeah. But we're gittin' beans tomorrow."

"Any white boys eat turkey dinners here with you today?"

An elderly black man looked in mock surprise. He pointed into the interior filled with Negroes.

"Yeah, see all them white folks in there," he said with soft irony.

NOT A SINGLE TURKEY

An entire building was canvassed at 311 W. 145th St. There wasn't a single turkey in all the 15 apartments. Why? The landlord had just slapped a $7 per month rent increase on each tenant.

In the last apartment visited, a group of Negro Communists were found. They had just come in from house-to-house canvassing. They did not say anything about being thankful, but from their attitude they seemed thankful to be off from their jobs, thankful for the opportunity to be free one day to ORGANIZE. ■

Daily Worker, DECEMBER 15, 1937

Gouging, Landlord Discrimination against Negroes Bared at Hearing

CHARGING IN SENSATIONAL TESTIMONY yesterday that the 250,000 Negroes living in Harlem are being victimized by unscrupulous landlords, Langdon W. Post, Tenement House Commissioner, cited appalling rates for crime, tuberculosis, juvenile delinquency, diphtheria and infant mortality among Negroes and told of the tragic cost in opportunity and efficiency which followed in the wake of such exploitation.

Mr. Post's testimony was given at the public hearings being conducted in Harlem at the Seventh District Court, 447 W. 151st St., under the auspices of the New York State Temporary Commission on Conditions Among Urban Negroes.

Amid gasps of horror from the crowded court room, Post declared that there were 19,517 instances of violations of the Multiple Dwelling Law to be found in Harlem.

"It is impossible to enforce this law," he said.

WORST IN CITY

"Generally speaking, conditions in Harlem in relation to housing are much worse than in other sections of the city," he continued. "Artificial conditions in the form of racial discrimination are the cause of this."

All efforts possible have been made, the ex-Commissioner said, to keep the Negro in Harlem.

"The conditions obtaining in Harlem were deliberately created by man, and are deliberately being kept so!

"It is claimed by some that such legislation is unconstitutional and is class legislation; but it is needed.

"There is racial discrimination, and we must not kid ourselves. The reluctance of landlords in other parts of the city to rent to Negroes is the cause of the congestion and crime in Harlem.

AN EMERGENCY

"If the landlords won't let the Negroes move out of Harlem, then the law must say to the landlord: 'You cannot gouge the Negro.'

"There is no doubt that we are faced with an emergency in Harlem," he concluded.

Preceding Mr. Post's testimony, many landlords representing Harlem property admitted under persistent questioning on the witness stand that they had gouged the Negro tenants.

D. B. Lucky, representing John Meenan, realtor, declared that his firm was "not exploiting, but just charging what the man next door charges to Negroes."

Lucky implied under questioning that it would be contrary to the ethics of his profession to charge lower rents to Negroes than other realtors were charging. The remark caused a scene of disorder which stopped the hearings for several minutes.

Earlier in the day the Consolidated Tenants' League, 209 W. 125th St., presented through its officers, Daniel J. Phillips and Vernal Williams, entered a plea to place "human rights above property rights."

A SOCIAL QUESTION

"Housing is not a legal but a social question affecting public policy," said Williams. "The law should make it a crime to deny citizens the right to live where they please on the basis of creed and color. Today housing affects the rights of the masses to happiness."

The New York Real Estate Board was greeted with approval from the audience for the role of its powerful lobby in Albany. It was stated that much progressive housing legislation had been spiked by the lobby.

The practice of Harlem landlords of inserting clauses in their leases denying jury trials to the tenants in litigation cases was denounced by Williams.

Roy Wilkins, editor of the *Crisis*, official organ of the National Association for Advancement of Colored People, testified regarding rent struggles at 409 Edgecomb Ave., a building which is owned by the Metropolitan Life Insurance Co.

URGES HEARINGS JAMMED

Wilkins advocated laws abolishing residential segregation; he said that such laws would be hard to enforce, but their educational effect would help to solve the problem.

Timothy Holmes, assistant educational director of the New York State Communist Party, in commenting upon the proceedings, declared:

"I think every Negro in Harlem that can get into that court room should be there and hear the incredible facts of his condition."

The hearings will be resumed today at 10 A.M. with Lester Granger, secretary of the Urban League's Workers' Bureau, directing. ■

Daily Worker, AUGUST 8, 1937

Harlem Cop Compelled to Apologize for Abuse

LIEUTENANT LANIHAN, IN CHARGE OF DETECTIVES at the twenty-eighth police precinct, 229 W. 123rd Street, apologized yesterday to Jeanette Cohen in the presence of representatives of the International Labor Defense and the *Sunday Worker* for the insulting conduct of one of his detectives towards a Negro and white couple in Harlem.

"We were in the wrong," Lanihan admitted grudgingly after he had been subjected to a verbal protest lasting for over an hour by Jeanette Cohen.

"I assure you it won't happen again," he added.

The interview between Lieutenant Lanihan and Jeanette Cohen was a result of a letter of protest sent by Jeanette Cohen to Mayor LaGuardia in relation to police insults and intimidation of Negro and white couples.

A week ago Jeanette Cohen and a friend went into the police station to inquire about a friend whose car had been wrecked. Because she was in the company of two Negro men, the detective used abusive language and pushed her upstairs where she was subjected to questioning and further insult.

The International Labor Defense impressed Lieutenant Lanihan with the fact that if such conduct was continued the detectives responsible would have to face charges. ■

Daily Worker, AUGUST 16, 1937

Harlem Crowd Shows Feeling on Chiseling

SO HIGH IS THE PITCH OF RESENTMENT in Harlem against exploitation by landlords, storekeepers, and businessmen that a small incident based on a misunderstanding resulted in a near riot Saturday morning on W. 125th St.

On the strength of a rumor that a Negro boy had been attacked by the management of the Betty Lee Shoe Co., 108 W. 125th St., a crowd of outraged Negro men and women collected and smashed the store's windows. Further violence was halted only with the appearance of the boy who pleaded with the crowd to go home.

Samuel Murphy, the Negro boy, had done some electrical work for the Betty Lou Shoe Co. A clerk sought to pay Murphy only $2 when the stipulated price was $2.50, and a scuffle ensued. The disputants were parted and Murphy went home with his money.

An hour later the management frantically called him to come back and prove to the indignant crowd that he was unhurt.

"I was glad they were there ready to protect me," said Murphy. "But it wasn't nothing."

Incidents of petty and large chiseling are so numerous and widespread against the Negro people in Harlem that the nerves of the people are strung tight, it was pointed out by leaders of the Communist Party in commenting upon the incident.

It was further declared that residential segregation, exorbitant rentals demanded by landlords, and a multitude of attendant causes which were the basis of the March 1935 flare-up are still in existence. ■

Daily Worker, AUGUST 13, 1937

Harlem Plans to Send 25 on WPA March

THE HARLEM CONTINGENT of the National Hunger March will leave New York Aug. 21 after a mass open-air rally and will speed toward Washington in a caravan of cars, Frankie Duty, president of the Harlem Council of the Workers' Alliance, 108 W. 133rd St., revealed yesterday.

The quota for the unemployed locals of the Harlem Workers' Alliance is 25. The reason for this small number, Miss Duty pointed out, is that the unemployed Negro workers are too destitute to send more.

The average number of Negroes pink-slipped off the WPA in Harlem is 70 per cent as compared with 30 per cent in other sections of the city.

Louis Campbell, organizer of the Harlem Council, will lead the Harlem contingent in the same militant manner in which he lead the last march to Washington when Hunger Hoover was in office.

The army of unemployed that is to converge upon Washington plans to stay there until Congress acts favorably upon the Schwellenbach-Allen Joint Congressional Resolution.

"We want our jobs back and not relief," Miss Duty declared. "The WPA should continue until private industry can absorb the unemployed."

The march is being publicized in Harlem through meetings and leaflets. The 10 locals of the Harlem Council have an unemployed membership of over 2,800.

"One of the most tragic aspects of the situation in Harlem is the dismissal of many West Indian Negroes. Many of the West Indian Negroes are heads of families, having married American women. Legally, they are not citizens and now that they are lopped off the WPA they have no place to turn."

About one-fourth of the Negro population of Harlem is West Indian. ■

Daily Worker, NOVEMBER 11, 1937

Harlem Rally to Protest Milk Gouge

HARLEM WILL GIVE ITS ANSWER to the Sheffield-Borden milk trust which imposed a one-cent increase in the price of milk last Sunday, by staging an open-air mass rally tomorrow night, at 8 o'clock, at the corner of 125th St. and Seventh Ave.

The rally will be held under the auspices of the Women's Commission of the Upper Harlem Section of the Communist Party, of which Audley Moore, a Negro woman leader, is chairman.

The organizational activities which the commission hopes to follow from this rally were explained by Miss Moore.

OUTLINE PLANS

"We are calling upon all Harlem organizations to support this important rally. We hope to organize out of this meeting a committee of women to see Mayor LaGuardia regarding some possible action by the City of New York against the Sheffield-Borden milk trust, which is guilty of super-exploitation.

"We will also ask the Mayor to establish emergency milk stations throughout Harlem so that our people, already over-burdened with high rents and other forms of oppression, will be able to get this basic food so urgently needed by our children.

"We are also calling upon the people of Harlem to petition Gov. Lehman to intervene in this serious situation by declaring emergency municipal distribution milk plants." ■

Daily Worker, October 17, 1937

Harlem Rent Strike Gains New Support

HARLEM'S MOST SENSATIONAL RENT STRIKE entered its second week today, when a mass picket line was thrown about the tenement at 312 Manhattan Ave.

The strike began on Oct. 1, when 90 per cent of the 55 tenants who live in the building declared a rent stoppage as a protest against the proposed rent increase. The strike has attracted unusual attention in Harlem, inasmuch as the building is owned by the Green-Wood Cemetery Co., 170 Broadway, a firm which controls a vast network of Negro-rented real estate in Harlem.

It is believed that if the management is successful in its demand for increases ranging from $3 to $10 a month at 312 Manhattan Ave. it will make similar increases in other sections of Harlem.

The striking tenants are calling upon all organizations and individuals in Harlem to pack the court room at 151st St. and Amsterdam Ave. on Monday, Oct. 18 at 9:30 A.M. when their dispossess notices are to be reviewed. ■

Daily Worker, November 17, 1937

Harlem Rent Strikers Win Agreement

TWO HUNDRED AND SEVENTY-FIVE NEGRO TENANTS living in 3 Harlem buildings—108 W. 141st St. and 133 and 149 W. 140th St.—won their week-old rent strike against the E. H. E. Realty Corporation, 615 Lenox Ave., it was announced yesterday.

A blanket agreement was signed yesterday by the landlord and the tenants limiting the rent increase to $2 instead of the $5 originally demanded. In addition, the landlords agreed to withdraw all eviction notices with the understanding that no eviction or dispossess notices would be served for organizational activities on the part of the tenants for a period of one year.

The landlord also agreed to install new ice boxes, stoves, decorate, and to give elevator services until 3 A.M.

On Friday, Saturday and Monday a mass picket line of 100 was maintained about the offices of the corporation; banners carrying slogans attracted wide attention. Some of the slogans read:

"We Refuse to Pay the Rent Increase!"

"Wages Are Low and Rents Are High!"

"We Demand Lower Rents in Harlem and More Jobs!"

After two hours of picketing Monday, the landlord called in Atty. Hampton Gill, legal representative of the strikers, and an agreement was signed.

Maurice Hubbard, organizer of the strike, declared in an interview with the *Daily Worker*:

"I think that this victory of ours demonstrates the correctness of our action. There is but one way to fight these rent increases, and that way is by organizing, striking, and compelling the landlords to arbitrate."

Maurice Hubbard is a member of the Musicians Union, Local 802, A. F. of L. ■

Daily Worker, October 19, 1937

Harlem Rent Strikers Win in Court Fight

THE 33 NEGRO TENANTS at 312 Manhattan Ave. won their rent strike yesterday morning when Judge Prince of the Seventh District Municipal Court handed down a ruling compelling the landlords to arbitrate.

As a result of the arbitration, a compromise was made which allowed the rents to remain at the old levels under the new leases signed for a period of one year.

The strike, which lasted for 18 days, was one of the most sensational ever held in Harlem and attracted wide attention.

BIG RENTING FIRM

The ruling of Judge Prince set a precedent inasmuch as it conferred upon striking tenants bargaining rights with the landlords.

The strike began on October 1 when 90 per cent of the 55 tenants declared a rent strike as a protest against a proposed rent increase. The Green-Wood Cemetery, 170 Broadway, owners of the building at 312 Manhattan Ave., is also the owner of a vast network of Negro-rented real estate in Harlem.

It is generally believed that if the management was successful in their efforts to increase the rents at 312 Manhattan, they would impose similar increases elsewhere.

RENT PLACED IN BANK

A strike committee, composed of [Lodie] Biggs, Harry Edwards, Mrs. David Catlin, Mrs. Warren Brown, Mrs. Dolly Nash, and Hampton Gill, elected one of their number to act as temporary rent agent during the process of the strike. The money which the tenants had been paying to the Green-wood Cemetery was paid to him to be deposited in the Dunbar National Bank.

A mass picket line under the leadership of James Green of the Harlem Tenants Association was thrown about the building at 312 Manhattan Ave. Saturday morning. Participating in the picketing were the American Labor Party, the International Labor Defense, the Workers Alliance, the Communist Party, and the Harlem Division of the City Projects Council. ∎

Daily Worker, OCTOBER 8, 1937

Opening of Harlem Project Homes Shows How Slums Can Be Wiped Out in New York

AT LONG LAST the Harlem River Houses are open for 574 Negro families!

The $4,219,000 federal-built, low-rent project, located at 2521 Seventh Avenue, sprawls in the October sun over some two square blocks on the banks of the Harlem River, in Upper Manhattan overlooking the Yankee Stadium.

All day long moving vans are backing up to the sidewalks and unloading furniture. It will not be long before all of the accepted quota of 574 families—selected out of 12,000 applicants—will have quit their foul-smelling fire-traps and will be enjoying for the first time in their lives decent living quarters free of the menace of disease, crime, and exorbitant rentals.

TYPICAL FAMILY

How do these Negro families feel about quitting the slums? What do they think of these new, beautiful apartments? And what are the chances of more housing units like these being built?

Let's talk to the Brannums, a typical and lucky Negro family selected for residence here. There are Mr. and Mrs. Brannum, and there are two girls, Barbara and Joan, four and three years old, respectively.

Mrs. Brannum was born in New York, but her husband is from Washington, D.C. Both of them, however, have lived in New York since childhood.

Brannum is a porter in a downtown dress factory; he makes a straight salary of $18 per week. For years he and his wife have been living in what Mrs. Brannum calls "railroad" flats, that is, the kind of flat that has no private rooms. If you want to go to the kitchen or bathroom, you have to walk through every other room in the house to get there.

LACKED SUNLIGHT

She had to burn the electric light all day long, for no sunlight ever got into the dark rooms of her old flat. And so many people lived in the building she was afraid to let her children go outside and play. And every month a landlord who lived somewhere downtown came knocking at the door, wanting money or threatening to leave a dispossess notice.

A year and a half ago Mrs. Brannum heard of the proposed Harlem River Houses and grew excited. She made her husband go down and make out an application for an apartment. He did, and his application was rejected.

When he inquired on what basis he was turned down, he was informed that no tenants would be accepted for 4-room apartments unless their weekly income averaged $20 or more.

"I told my husband," said Mrs. Brannum, "to go down and tell them he could work overtime at the factory and make that amount." He did and his application was accepted.

STILL TOO HIGH

In order that his children may live in this new housing unit, Mr. Brannum works long, hard hours; otherwise his income would be too low and he would be an undesirable tenant.

Though these apartments represent the lowest rents for the best apartments that can be found in Harlem, they are yet too high for Harlem's Negro workers whose incomes remain pitiably low.

If you would know how deeply grateful Mrs. Brannum is for the chance to live here even under these conditions, listen to her tell of the hovels in which she has lived.

DESCRIBES FORMER HOME

"The last place we lived in we had less room than we have now and we paid $30 per month for rent, or almost 50 per cent of our income. The children's room had one window which opened onto a foul-smelling airshaft.

"The building was old and full of insects of every kind. The icebox was built into the wall. It was impossible to keep ice for a single day. The children's milk always soured. And the roaches! Honest to God, when you opened that icebox door those black things just stared at you and dared you to come in! They acted like they had Constitutional privileges, as though they had signed leases and had a legal right to be there. . . [ellipses in original]

"But now!" Mrs. Brannum sighed. "When I wake up in the morning my whole apartment is flooded with sunshine! I can't tell you what it means! And I can look through every window and see the sky! Fresh air blows in all day and light everywhere! I dreamed about these apartments for an entire year!"

SCHOOL IN PROJECT

Out of Mr. Brannum's $25 salary—$18 per week plus $6 or $7 for overtime—he must pay $5.75 per week for rent, which demonstrates that even the Harlem River Houses are not enough to solve Harlem's urgent housing problem. Hundreds of more units such as this with lower rents are needed.

The project has three buildings—with apartments ranging from 2 to 5 rooms. Rents run from $4.75 for 2 rooms to $6.75 for 5 rooms per week. But even these low rentals are still in the "higher brackets" for most of Harlem's relief-supported thousands.

Before the furniture of these families was moved in, it was carted to a cyanide vault and fumigated with lethal gas to exterminate bedbugs, roaches, etc.

The unit possesses four penthouses and a nursery school which is under the supervision of the New York Kindergarten Society.

Children already living in the neighborhood will also be served by the Society.

N.Y. SHAME SPOT

Walking from room to room in Mrs. Brannum's apartment you see snow-white walls trimmed with grey steel molding. There is a huge clothes closet in each room and each room has wide windows. The layout of the apartment is such that each room is accessible from a small hallway. The ceilings are high.

Mr. and Mrs. Brannum have had to wait 17 long months to move in here; and there are thousands in Harlem whose appetites for better housing have been whetted by the sight of this lonely model housing unit set amid a thousand begrimed firetraps.

Harlem is New York's shame spot when it comes to housing. The present residences were built years ago for another race and another class of different economic status. The Negro, forced by proscription to live in certain sections of the city, had to take what he could when he fled the South seeking better conditions.

MANY VIOLATIONS

Residential segregation has caused Negroes to live as many as 620 to the acre in houses 85 per cent of which were built over 35 years ago. On many streets garbage is piled on the sidewalks; as many as 15 to 20 persons use one toilet, thereby creating conditions for the spread of disease.

In certain areas of Harlem over 20 per cent of the residences have been branded as "unlivable." No electric facilities. No hot water. Violations of the Multiple Dwelling Law are widespread.

With these conditions as a background, it can be seen that the 56,157 Negro families who live in Harlem are not adequately helped when 574 of their number are allowed to live in the Harlem River Houses.

AID TO KIDS

But the new building unit, although it is but a drop in the bucket, is making many Negroes conscious that it is possible to have better and cheaper houses to live in.

Mrs. Brannum is keenly aware of what this new apartment of hers means to her children and their future.

"I didn't have anything like this when I was a child," she said, pointing to the wide windows. "But I'm glad my children can escape what I've lived through.

"And there were so many people who wanted to get apartments here and who couldn't. There are simply not enough apartments to go round. People with small children, too, living in holes. . ." [ellipses in original]

Such houses can be built if the millions of Mrs. Brannums in America make up their minds that they want them for their children. If they organize and demand of their government housing and more housing, they can get it. ■

Daily Worker, SEPTEMBER 8, 1937

Harlem Women Picket Milk Co. Tomorrow

ONE HUNDRED HARLEM WOMEN, Negro and white, bearing aloft placards protesting the high price of milk, will converge and form a continuous picket line at 3 P.M. tomorrow at the Sheffield Farms Co., 632 W. 125th St.

The picketing will take place under the auspices of the Women's Commission of the Harlem Division of the Communist Party, of which Mrs. Helen Holman is director. The picketing will be led by Margaret Witherspoon, director of the Women's Committee of the Upper Harlem Section of the Communist Party.

The picketing will last from 3 PM to an undetermined hour and will be the first of a series of picket lines which will be massed in front of Sheffield and Borden offices and plants throughout Harlem.

PLAN MEETING

To mobilize women for the picket line, an open-air mass meeting will be held tonight at 125th St. and Lenox Ave. at 8 o'clock.

"We will attempt to educate and mobilize the women of Harlem in street meetings of this sort to curtail the consumption of milk until the Milk Trust brings down the price," stated Mrs. Holman.

Mrs. Holman expressed gratification over the enthusiastic response of Harlem housewives to the 10,000 leaflets issued last week calling for a curtailment of milk consumption. Mrs. Holman pointed out that the campaign was not being conducted against the companies' milk drivers, but against the companies themselves.

"It is not our aim to harm in any way the workers employed by these companies," Mrs. Holman declared. "We are out to show these profit-makers that they will lose more profit by trying to jack up the price of milk than they would if they were content to reduce the price and make a reasonable margin of profit." ■

Daily Worker, SEPTEMBER 4, 1937

Insect-Ridden Medicine Given in Hospital

INSECT-RIDDEN MEDICINE

That's what the Harlem Hospital gives to its Negro patients!

You go to a hospital with faith in your heart. When you tell your doctor what's wrong with you, you do so with infinite trust, placing your life in his hands. You feel that you have a right to do this, for do not the laws of the land and the ethics of the medical profession protect you? But if you should go to the Harlem Hospital, located at 136th St. and Lenox Ave., you will find that such faith is unwarranted.

On Aug. 31 Marjorie Hill, a Negro woman suffering with a severe chest cold, went into the Harlem Hospital for treatment.

HAD A COLD

A doctor asked her what was wrong. She told him she had a cold. The doctor did not examine her; he simply pulled forth his pad and wrote a prescription.

"Take this to the dispensary," he said, and turned to another patient.

Miss Hill carried her prescription, No. 21733H, to the dispensary and the clerk simply reached upon a shelf for a bottle of medicine and put it in her hands.

When she got home and started taking the medicine, she noticed sediment in the bottle. She poured it out to investigate and discovered that the medicine was mixed with flies.

Alarmed, she took the bottle to a private doctor who stated that the medicine was not fit for human use.

In an interview with the *Daily Worker,* the doctor stated:

"Things like this are common at the Harlem Hospital. The facilities are so poor and the need for medical attention so great that it is impossible to practice scientific medicine. There are not enough doctors or nurses. One doctor has to treat as many as one hundred patients an hour."

Hospitalization under capitalism reaches a low point when hospitals become the centers from which disease is spread!

Miss Hill, the victim of this outrage, lives at 155 W. 122nd St., in Harlem. ■

Daily Worker, AUGUST 23, 1937

Low-Cost Rent in Harlem Too High for Many

THE THOUSANDS OF NEGROES who live in Harlem's fire-traps and who pay from 40 to 50 per cent of their incomes for rent are beginning to believe that the New Deal can't fulfill its promises when it comes to supplying adequate low-cost housing.

To live in the Harlem River Houses, the newly-built Federal housing project at 2521 Seventh Avenue, a Negro family must have an income of $1,340.14 per year if the analysis by the Municipal Housing Authority last week means anything. For Harlem's poverty-stricken Negro thousands, this sum is in the "higher brackets."

The analysis revealed that but ten of the 574 families awarded apartments in the WPA-financed project had annual incomes below $900. Families occupying five-room units are paying from $2,000 to $2,150 per year. More than 11,500 families have made application for apartments and the average monthly rental per room is $7.10.

The entire project will be opened for occupancy soon and will house 1,829 persons—1,246 adults and 581 children. ■

Daily Worker, SEPTEMBER 11, 1937

Scores Picket Borden's Protesting High Prices

JOIN OUR STRUGGLE AGAINST SHEFFIELD AND BORDEN!

WOMEN OF HARLEM FIGHT AGAINST RICKETS AND T.B.!

HARLEM CHILDREN HIT HARDEST BY RISING MILK PRICES!

MILK DRIVERS DO NOT BENEFIT FROM PROFITS IN INCREASED WAGES!

ALL ORGANIZATIONS, SOCIAL, POLITICAL, AND CHURCHES SHOULD PROTEST TO BORDEN AND SHEFFIELD!

THESE ARE SOME OF THE SLOGANS which a score of Negro and white men and women paraded Thursday in front of Sheffield Milk Company, 632 W. 125th St. The picket line paced to and fro over the block, and hundreds of leaflets were passed out to passersby.

The picketing, sponsored by the Women's Committee of Upper Harlem Section of the Communist Party, was a protest against the sky-rocketing price of milk. The committee is making an effort to cut into the mountain-high profits of Sheffield and Borden (the Milk Trust) by advising milk consumers to use as little milk as possible, just enough for the children and the sick.

The demonstration was led by Elizabeth Witherspoon, director of women's work in the Upper Harlem Section. Miss Witherspoon indicated that this picket line was the first of a series to be held at the Sheffield and Borden plants throughout Harlem. ■

Daily Worker, OCTOBER 9, 1937

Mother, Three Children Are Evicted in Harlem

ARMED EVICTION is the order of the day in Harlem.

Under the threat of the guns and clubs of five mounted policemen and 13 patrolmen, marshalls threw the furniture of Mrs. Helen Boyd and her three children into the streets yesterday morning.

This was the third time Mrs. Boyd, who lives at 383 Lenox Ave., had been set on the street within a week. The presence of so many cops was to forestall the attempt of members of the Workers' Alliance to replace the furniture as they had done on two previous occasions.

About a month ago Mrs. Boyd's case at the ERB, 28th precinct, 124th St. and Lenox Ave., was closed on the pretext that her relief could not be continued until her husband was located. Mrs. Boyd's husband is at some unknown point in the South.

In response to a telegram of protest sent to Mayor La Guardia the first of the week, a check for $28 was sent to Mrs. Boyd. But she has been unable to obtain an apartment because Harlem landlords are refusing to accept relief tenants.

Under the auspices of the Workers' Alliance, several open-air meetings have been held to protest the treatment of Mrs. Boyd and her children. Plans are under way to throw a picket line about the offices of Samuel Pomerantz, the landlord, 307 Lenox Avenue.

The drastic curtailment of relief expenditures in Harlem has resulted during the past month in hundreds of evictions. A mounting feeling of desperation is common among Harlem workers, many of whom feel that relief conditions are reaching Hoover levels. ■

Daily Worker, AUGUST 4, 1937

Negro, with 3-Week-Old Baby, Begs Food on Streets

THIS ISN'T FICTION; these are not scenes from the novels of Charles Dickens. The sidewalks of Harlem are real and hard; and black people on those sidewalks are truly starving.

Trekking into the headquarters of the Workers' Alliance at 326 Lenox Ave. is an endless stream of black people looking for help. They come here because someone has told them that the Alliance will help. Usually their pride keeps them back until the last moment[;] then they make this their desperate "court of final appeal.

Here is a Negro woman, Mrs. Essie Bostick, the mother of five children. One is nine years old, the other is six years old, and the other is 3 years old, and another is 2 years old; and the last one is in her arms, just three weeks old.

SLEEPY

Mrs. Bostick's eyes are ringed and heavy with sleep. She stands leaning against a wall, holding her baby on her hip.

"I've been walking the streets for four days and four nights," she says wearily. "I've been begging for food wherever I could. When my children wanted water, I went into drug stores and cafes and brought it to them in a tin cup."

Mrs. Bostick's husband was pink-slipped off the WPA some eight weeks ago; rather than face the harrowing task of feeding five children with no job, he ran away and has not been seen or heard from.

Since her dismissal from the hospital three weeks ago, Mrs. Bostick has been trying to get the ERB District Office at 74 W. 124th St. to help her.

TORTUROUS SYSTEM

But the relief, with its torturous system of time-consuming red tape, told her to wait until her husband is located. Meanwhile, she and her five children walk the streets and slowly starve.

"My children haven't eaten today," continued Mrs. Bostick. "If it wasn't for my own milk, the baby would have starved. But how can I keep on feeding my baby at my breast when I don't eat?"

Mrs. Bostick is now spending her days waiting. She waits in the relief office. She sits on a bench with her five children and waits—waits for the ERB to feed her.

The relief committee of the Workers' Alliance is now handling her case. For the first time in a month Mrs. Bostick has been able to collect her distracted thoughts. She feels that now she has someone stronger than she to fight the thing through for her.

Standing in the doorway of the ERB station is a young Negro couple. The black girl holds a baby on her hip. You can tell that they are in their early twenties. While you talk to the young man and wife the nine-month old baby reaches hungrily for the buttons on your coat and tries to put them in his mouth.

SLEEP ON STREETS

The young man's name is Theodore Theus; his wife, Elizabeth, and Junior. They've been on the streets for three days, eating and sleeping where they can.

"Have you ever had orange juice for the baby?"

"No."

"Cod liver oil?"

"No."

"Ice, during the hot days?"

"No."

"Milk?"

"No; not now. Not since I stopped nursing him."

As you ask her about the items her baby needs her eyes assume a faraway look, as though you were speaking of things forever unattainable.

Theodore Theus used to work as a hotel clerk. The depression threw him on the streets of Harlem. He went on relief and then got a job under the WPA working for the city-owned water, gas and electric supply. Then, like thousands of others, he was pink-slipped off WPA. When rent day rolled around he was put out doors; he spent the last week-end on the streets.

The Workers' Alliance is handling their case as well as hundreds of others. The problem of relief is slowly assuming the proportions it had before the advent of work relief. In fact, it's now worse than ever to be out of work, for food is sky-high and a dollar doesn't go far.

If you are the type to weep, you can have a good cry over this and then feel good, "purged," you know. But tears can't stop starvation! ■

Daily Worker, November 5, 1937

Negro School Boy Attacked by Teacher

BECAUSE HE WHISPERED TO A SCHOOL CHUM the correct spelling of a word during a spelling bee, Edward Stewart, 2864 Eighth Ave., 11-year-old Negro boy student in P.S. 46, was struck in the head with a book thrown by a teacher last week, it was disclosed yesterday morning.

Fearing to tell of the assault, Edward asked his mother to allow him to remain home because he did not feel well. The boy had been operated on five months previously for a serious ear ailment, and as his condition grew worse, he finally told his mother of the clash with his teacher at school.

PRINCIPAL DENIES ATTACK

Yesterday morning Edward's mother, Sarah Stewart, reported the matter to the Grievance Committee of the Parent-Teachers Association for investigation and possible action.

When interviewed by the *Daily Worker* yesterday morning, Felix Arnold, principal of P.S. 46, 156th St. and St. Nicholas Ave., disclaimed any knowledge of the incident. When asked point blank if the child had been struck, he declared:

"Not that I know of."

One Mr. Soloff, the teacher involved and whose first name was withheld from publication by the principal, could not be reached for questioning.

Still another organization which is preparing to act in the case is the Permanent Committee for Better Schools.

In a statement issued yesterday morning, Theodore Bassett, chairman of its Grievance Committee, declared:

"In the course of our work last year it was shown that corporal punishment existed to a greater degree in Harlem schools than in other schools in other parts of the city. This recent case indicates the necessity of carrying on a campaign to eliminate this evil.

This condition reflects the attitude of Tammany Hall toward the Negro people."

Last year the Permanent Committee for Better Schools conducted a campaign which resulted in the removal of Gustav Schoenchen of P.S. 5 because of his brutal attack upon little Roy Shelton.

Bassett declared further:

"This case has been brought to our attention and will be thoroughly investigated and acted upon." ■

Daily Worker, November 23, 1937

Negro Tenants Win Rent Cuts in 8 Houses

THE NEW TENANTS' MOVEMENT, which was launched by the 312 Manhattan Avenue Tenants Association on Oct. 1 is rapidly gaining momentum in Harlem with the recent organization of eight apartment houses and victories in rent reduction for more than 500 Negro families, it was announced today by Lodie Biggs, secretary of the newly organized Harlem Tenants Association.

As a result of victories won over their landlord, the Green-Wood Co., 170 Broadway, a firm which controls a vast network of Negro-rented real estate in Harlem, the 312 Manhattan Tenants Association assumed the initiative and called a conference of Harlem tenants on Nov. 4 for the purpose of launching a Harlem-wide tenants' organization.

Out of this conference emerged a plan to coordinate the existing tenants' units and to encourage the formation of new ones. The plan differed from the old organizational setup in that the organizational basis came from the bottom.

A committee consisting of James Green, Cyril Phillips, Miss Lodie Biggs, Mrs. Maurice Hubbard, James R. Managautte, and Miss Juanita Hall was elected to investigate all other tenant group constitutions and map out policies and plans for permanent organization of the new body.

At another conference on Nov. 18 the organization became a permanent body under the title of the Harlem Tenants Association.

From Oct. 1 to Nov. 15 the following apartment buildings were organized: 108 W. 141st St., 133 W. 140th St., 140 W. 140th St., 306 112th St., 409 Edgecomb Ave., 9 W. 137th St., 207 W. 141st St., and 322 Lenox Ave., comprising more than 500 Negro families.

The Harlem Tenants Association, with temporary headquarters at 312 Manhattan Ave., Apt. 1G (MO 2-2992), is calling upon all Harlem renters to contact the Harlem Tenants Association for educational directives on organizational procedure. ■

Daily Worker, July 14, 1937

Negro Union Painters Seek Higher Wages

NEGRO MEMBERS OF THE BROTHERHOOD OF PAINTERS, District Council No. 9, A. F. of L., threw a militant picket line yesterday about the offices of Dr. Godfry Nurse, 186 W. 135th Street, Harlem Negro landlord.

Instead of the $3 they are now receiving, the painters are demanding $9 for a 7-hour day and general union conditions on the job. "And we are going to get it," said Bill Russell, militant Negro organizer of the painters' union.

"This picket line will stay here until he accepts our demands. This doctor should be ashamed of treating his own exploited group in this manner."

Negro school children passing the doctor's office and seeing the picket line threw taunts at the physician's offices: "Why don't you pay your men a union wage?"

The struggle parallels a similar fight of Harlem Negro newspaper men which took place in 1935. At that time the editorial employees of the Amsterdam News forced the owners of that paper to sign a union contract with the New York Newspaper Guild. ■

Daily Worker, DECEMBER 27, 1937

Negro, Who Escaped Lynch Mob in South, Ordered to Return by Harlem Relief Officials

HE FLED THE SOUTH TO SAVE HIS LIFE, and now the officials of the New York City ERB want to send him back to a certain death on the flimsy pretext that "New York cannot shoulder the burden of other states."

That, in short, is the story of John Jones, 39, Negro worker and farmer, who today sits in fear in a Harlem tenement flat at 35 Mount Morris Park, with a wife and nine children.

Because he defied the mob rule of Southern landlords, because he could not square the South's treatment of him with the demands of his conscience, John Jones had to flee the South in the dead of the night.

"They wanted to kill me because I was not afraid," said Jones.

STORY LIKE FICTION

His story reads like fiction. A little more than a year ago he lived in Oak City, North Carolina. He owned a little home, a cow, pigs, chickens, and a garden. His children were in school. His neighbors respected him. He was a "solid citizen."

One Saturday afternoon, together with his brother and a few more friends, he was standing in front of a grocery store, talking. A white man approached and asked:

"I want one of yuh niggers to buy me some whiskey."

The group of Negroes did not respond.

The white man demanded a second time that someone "get me some liquor and I'll pay you!"

Jones urged the man to "go ahead and don't try to get us into trouble."

One word led to another and a fist fight ensued. Jones beat the man and went home.

At ten o'clock that night he was awakened by a pounding on his door. His wife answered; he heard the voices of a mob and escaped through his window.

For weeks Jones dodged mobs that combed the countryside looking for him. To go home was to be caught. He spent many a night hidden in a ravine overlooking his home, watching the mob waiting outside for him. He could hear their shouts:

"If you see 'im, kill on sight!"

He went from one of his friend's homes to the other and finally begged enough money to catch a train for New York. His wife and his nine children followed him.

He is now receiving relief from the Non-Settlement Bureau, which wants him to return to face the Southern mobs. But a few days ago the Workers' Alliance stepped in and said, "No!"

"People in New York don't know what it means to live in the South," Jones said. "All I want is a chance to work and support my family."

With the Workers' Alliance at his back, Jones feels a little safe now. Whether he can escape the Southern landlords depends upon how strongly the workers of Harlem can bring pressure against the ERB officials to make them grant him refuge. ■

Daily Worker, DECEMBER 21, 1937

Pickets Ask Somervell Ouster for Negro Firings

BEARING ALOFT RED AND BLACK PLACARDS demanding the ousting of the Southern WPA administrator, Col. Brehon Somervell, and the reinstatement of dismissed Negro educational workers, 300 Negro and white pickets marched yesterday in front of the WPA headquarters at 70 Columbus Avenue.

The Negro teachers charged discrimination in dismissals and cited concrete evidence as proof.

It was asserted that on the Remedial High School Project, the entire Negro personnel of nine were fired. Likewise, on the Elementary School Project there are only three Negroes employed out of a total of 300.

It was maintained that of the total Negroes employed, 39 per cent were dismissed, whereas out of the total of whites only 25 per cent were dismissed.

ASK SAME RATION

Officials of the WPA Teachers' Union pointed out that owing to the deplorable conditions in Harlem, there are more Negroes proportionately on relief than whites, and the same ratio should be maintained on WPA jobs.

It was charged that Col. Somervell does not act on Negro applications, no matter how qualified the applicant. The Education Department of the WPA, which has charge of the Women and Professional Projects, sought to justify its exclusion of Negroes on the specious grounds that Negroes were less qualified than whites.

Gretel Spiro, organizational secretary of the Teachers' Union, 781 Broadway, Local 453, declared in a statement today:

"We believe that the ousting of the Southern-born Somervell will help to cure this situation. Our demand is for the expansion of the WPA educational program and for the inclusion of more Negro workers."

Many of the pickets who marched yesterday were from the Harlem office of the union, which is located at 306 Lenox Avenue. ■

Daily Worker, DECEMBER 9, 1937

Probe of Negro Conditions Opens Dec. 13

FOR THE SECOND TIME since the March 19 outbreak in 1935, a legal investigation will be conducted into the terrible housing and [unemployment] conditions existing among the quarter of a million Negroes living in Harlem.

The investigation will take the form of open hearings and witnesses will be subpoenaed from all walks of Negro life to appear and testify.

The hearings, conducted under the auspices of the New York State Temporary Commission on Conditions of Urban Negroes, will begin

Monday, Dec. 13, at 10 a.m., and will last four days, including Thursday, Dec. 16, at the Seventh District Court, 447 New Amsterdam Ave.

4 DAYS TOO SHORT

Owing to the desperate plight of the Negro in Harlem, the opinion has come forward from many quarters that the four days allotted to the hearings are totally inadequate. The commission, however, declares that it lacks the funds to continue longer.

Numerous letters from Harlem leaders and workers have been sent to Gov. Lenman in Albany urging him to extend the duration of the hearings so that the full extent of the unemployment, bad housing, and practices of discrimination against Negroes can be aired.

The commission has conducted similar investigations into the living conditions of Negroes in Hempstead; White Plains, Westchester County; Jamaica, Queens; Albany; and Buffalo. The investigation, which begins Monday, covering Brooklyn, Bronx, Richmond, and Manhattan, will be its final hearing.

$30,000 FUND

Authorization of the investigation was voted last spring by the New York State Legislature and a fund of $30,000 was appropriated for that purpose.

Lester Granger, secretary of the Urban League's Workers' Bureau, is the executive director of the commission.

It was pointed out in many sections of Harlem yesterday that the commission is opening its hearings at a time when New York City's Commissioner of Police, Valentine, is demanding that 4,000 additional cops be added to the force upon the assumption that "Negro criminality" necessitates it.

The call for more police grew out of the finding of the unconscious body of a 60-year-old public accountant, Charles A. Klein, in Central Park last Thursday night.

Recovering consciousness a few seconds before he died, Klein declared that he had been attacked by "two Negroes." His testimony, however, has been contradicted by two youths who claimed they saw Klein kill himself. ■

Daily Worker, SEPTEMBER 8, 1937

Harlem Rent Strike Ends; Tenants Win

A THREE-MONTH OLD HARLEM RENT STRIKE terminated today when the landlords, Fox and Gold of 580 Lenox Ave., agreed to compromise on their demands for a 20 per cent rent increase, it was revealed today by the Consolidated Tenants League.

The strike, which began in June, was declared because the landlords demanded increased rentals without a guarantee that the fire-trap tenements would be decorated.

"The landlords are demanding an increase in rent and they have not painted, fixed doors, or the dumbwaiter. The entire building is overrun with vermin and they have done nothing to make these apartments decent since white tenants moved out years ago," declared Thomas S. Stanley, chairman of the strike committee.

The building, located at 2048 Seventh Avenue, contains 13 apartments, all the occupants of which participated in the rent strike. The strike action of the tenants was under the auspices of the Tenants' Consolidated League, of which D. J. Phillips is president.

The terms of the proposed compromise could not be ascertained today, but Thomas Stietley declared that they would be based upon the proposals laid down by the strike committee. ■

Daily Worker, SEPTEMBER 2, 1937

Retail Clerks to Continue Picketing

LOCAL 338 of the Retail Grocery Clerks Union, CIO, will continue its picket line about six Harlem stores until union recognition, shorter hours, and wage increases are granted, Hammie Snipe, organizer of the strike committee, stated yesterday.

The picket line, 24 strong, has been in operation for two weeks against the following establishments: the American Food House, 2413 Seventh Avenue; G & P Store, 2452 Seventh Avenue; the Harlem Model Food Store, 2480 Seventh Avenue; Jack's Store, 2792 Eighth Avenue; James Butler Store, 2783 Eighth Avenue; and the Demus Store, 669 Lenox Avenue.

Associated Grocers, a merchant organization, broke its contract with its employees. On May 27, the Associated Grocers signed a contract with the CIO which covered much of the retail business establishments in Harlem.

VIOLATE CONTRACT

In August the Associated Grocers passed a resolution making it compulsory that all stores should close on Sunday. This brought about a split in the organization which served as an excuse for the merchants to violate their contract with their employees.

The merchants who withdrew from Associated Grocers signed agreements with Ira Kemp, racketeering union organizer, who immediately launched a campaign in Harlem. Further, Kemp sought to muscle in on stores already holding contracts with the CIO.

RAPPED BY LABOR GROUP

In retaliation for the CIO picketing six stores because of broken contracts, Kemp has placed picket lines in front of six CIO stores, thereby bringing further confusion into the already troubled union situation in Harlem.

The Negro Labor Committee, of which Frank Crosswaith is chairman, is now conducting an educational campaign to enlighten the workers of Harlem to the dangers involved in following Kemp's leadership.

The picketing is being conducted by a strike committee composed of Harry Gordon, F. Barcourt, Jack Harding, Julia Sums, and Hammie Snipe, organizer. ■

Daily Worker, DECEMBER 26, 1937

Santa Claus Has a Hard Time Finding Way to Harlem Slums

"MERRY XMAS—ROOMS FOR RENT—WHITE ONLY!"

In a holly-bedecked window on 39 W. 120th Street, in Harlem, the above sign was displayed all day Christmas.

So even Christmas comes to segregated Harlem with irony. It seems that the slogan of "Peace on Earth, Good Will Toward Men" loses some of its magic when it reached the Negro area.

Harlem's Christmas was poor and quiet. All the brightness and tinsel represented a sacrifice on the part of parents who felt honor-bound to fulfill the expectations of their children. Some way or other Santa Claus found the courage to leave a few paltry toys even in sub-basement flats which violated the Multiple Dwelling Law.

When heads of families were questioned regarding how they found means to create such a gay atmosphere amid squalor, they replied:

"They wanted things so bad we just couldn't disappoint them. I reckon we'll be two months catching up with our bills. Lord, I'll be glad when Christmas is over."

A survey revealed that the ERB officials made no extra allowances for children in large families, and there were but few tables on which turkeys and cranberries were served.

At 18 W. 118th St., four flights up, is a typical Harlem tenant family. Though there was not much food in Mrs. Lily Grover's home, there was the inevitable Christmas tree. Mrs. Grover's husband deserted her over two years ago and she is raising her three children in a three-room flat on a $50 per month relief allowance.

After subtracting $25 for her monthly rent, she managed to eke out enough pennies above her other expenses to give one toy to each child. Ernet Grover, 8, Raymond, 5, and Doris, 3, had no conception of the sacrifice which gave them their toys and they were happy.

Mrs. Grover made her children go out of the room before she told of how she made Christmas for them. She did not want them to know how hard it was for Santa Claus to stop at their home.

She did not want little Raymond, who has a chronic case of bronchitis, to know that his milk allowance was cut in order for Santa to stop.

"And he's not getting enough milk now," said Mrs. Grover. "The only hope for him to recover, so the doctors tell me, is for him to outgrow his bronchitis."

Though the sun was shining Christmas Day, none of it reached Mrs. Grover's dark apartment. The hallways smelled of stale air. Mrs. Grover knows that more than milk is needed in her budget to give Raymond a chance of life. But houses are scarce in Harlem and Mrs. Grover, like a quarter million other Negroes, can't move out.

The mother was enthusiastic about the high hopes she had for her eight-year-old daughter, Ernet, who has maintained a B rating in all of her grades up to 3B.

"Ernet sings, dances, and speaks on the stage well," said Mrs. Grover. "But I can't for the life of me figure out how I can give her the chance I know she needs."

The newspapers carried slogans of "Peace on Earth, Good Will Toward Men," and for Mrs. Grover and millions like her that would mean that the conditions of life for one should be the conditions of life for all. ■

Daily Worker, OCTOBER 13, 1937

She Lay Dying, but They Would Not Give Her Aid

FOR THE WANT OF CARFARE she walked 16 blocks to a clinic; for the want of food and care she had heart trouble, and for the want of a doctor and attention, she died.

That is the story of 65-year-old Florence Christopher, a Negro woman who dropped dead from heart failure yesterday morning at the 28th precinct E.R.B. station in Harlem, 124th St. and Lenox Ave.

Though ill with heart trouble, Florence Christopher left her home at 24 W. 140th St., walking in the face of a cold wind to keep a 10 o'clock appointment at the eye clinic. She knew that if she missed her appointment, she would perhaps have to wait a month before she could get another one. This eye clinic in the 28th precinct station is the only one in Harlem that serves E.R.B. patients.

She entered the station and began to climb the steep stairs to the eye clinic. When her foot was on the second step she fell.

NO AID!

While she lay ill on the floor, no staff worker was allowed to touch her. It is one of the rules of the relief station. Almost a half hour passed between the time she collapsed and the time a doctor arrived and pronounced her dead.

Then for an hour and five minutes, from 10:15 to 11:20, her body lay behind a flimsy screen on a wooden bench, waiting for the Harlem hospital to send an ambulance that never came.

Scores of workers passing in and out of the station gave horrified glances at the dead body. Finally, a couple of cops threw a dirty burlap bag over her and shoved her into a police wagon and took her to the morgue.

Florence Christopher might be alive now if she had had the proper attention, but there are no first-aid facilities or rest-rooms for relief clients in the ERB stations in Harlem. The final shock that killed Florence Christopher might have come from any one of the hazards which the Negro unemployed must endure at the hands of an underpaid relief staff and inadequate service.

RED TAPE

There is a ponderous machinery of red tape with which the ERB dispenses its puny favors. This is enough to incite fatal nervous tension in patients. Clients are given what is known as the run-around until they are distracted. Relief offices are hot, close and crowded. Daily there are cases of fainting.

Almost everything that happened to dead Florence Christopher yesterday morning was a silent indictment of the terrible conditions under which Negroes live in Harlem.

In relation to their desperate conditions, the Negroes are given less than any other section of the city for relief purposes. The city's budget does not permit the building of first-aid stations in relief offices. The biggest slice of the city's budget will go to the bankers in Wall St. ■

Daily Worker, JULY 20, 1937

Store Clerks Demand End of Jim Crow

THE NEGRO AND WHITE WORKERS of the Department Store Employees' Union, CIO, are demanding that the Weinstein Concession of Kantor's Department Store sign contractual agreements which specifically embody a clause calling for non-discrimination between Negro and white workers, it was learned today.

The strike, conducted by Local 1250, has been under way since July 13. A strong picket line has been maintained continuously in front of the store at 218 W. 125th St., under the direction of James Webster, Negro organizer.

SPLIT ATTEMPT FAILS

Throughout the strike the management has sought by intimidation to split the Negro and white workers.

The Negro workers were called into private conferences at which the management offered to bargain with each separately. When that failed, agents were sent to the homes of the Negroes to offer them higher wages if they would scab. But the Negroes refused consistently and declared:

"We'll deal with you only through the union!"

NEGROES LEAD STRIKE

The contracts which the workers are seeking to effect call for shorter hours, job security, higher wages, and non-discrimination between Negro and white. And the general attitude in the strike is: "We'll hold out till they sign!"

Two Negro women, Annette Nickolwhite and Delphine McCleary, along with Leach Day, a Negro worker, are in the forefront of the strike, in which there are several white women jointly participating. ■

Daily Worker, AUGUST 14, 1937

Strikers Seek Reduced Rent in Harlem

A RENT STRIKE was declared yesterday in Harlem by the Negro tenants living at 306 W. 112th St. against the landlords of the Elliott Management Corp., 205 W. 145th St., and a picket line was thrown around the building at 4 P.M.

A majority of the 20 families living in the building are participating in the rent stoppage in an effort to halt the landlord's demand for exorbitant rental increases for ill-lighted, ill-ventilated apartments with little or no accommodations. Negro tenants have been asked to pay from $15 to $20 more for the same apartments which white tenants occupied just two months previously.

"It's outright chiseling," declared Pierce Smith, one of the striking Negro tenants. "Being Negro, we are confined to the ghetto of Harlem to live. The landlords take advantage of this residential segregation and exploit the Negro people to the limit!"

DISCRIMINATION

It was learned in addition that there now exists flagrant discrimination in the prices of apartments having equal accommodations.

At a meeting of tenants held Thursday night various rents were compared and the tenants were amazed at the difference paid by each for different apartments. For example, tenants having five rooms pay $47 per month for the same apartment for which some are paying $42.50.

The increases demanded by the Elliott Management Corp. run from $8 to $20 per month.

A meeting will be held Sunday at 3 P.M. to convince a few reluctant tenants who have refused to strike that their rights are being violated by these conditions.

The strike and picketing are being held under the auspices of the Consolidated Tenants' League, 209 W. 125th St. ■

Daily Worker, NOVEMBER 6, 1937

Tenants Plan Big League in Harlem

HARD ON THE HEELS of the victory won over their landlord, the [Green-Wood] Cemetery, 170 Broadway, a few weeks ago, the 312 Manhattan Ave. Tenants Association is launching a drive to organize Negro tenants throughout Harlem, it was announced yesterday.

At a conference held at the Prince Hall Masonic Temple, 235 W. 120th St., Thursday night, plans were mapped to build "one big tenants' league in Harlem."

Hampton H. Gill, the association's legal representative, and Robert Custis, of the State Commission on Urban Conditions Among Colored People, were the two main speakers.

Custis urged the 20 individuals who attended the conference to aid in gathering facts relating to the housing situation in Harlem.

At present the association is engaged in supporting the tenants of 108 W. 141st St. in their struggle with the E. H. Realty Corp. to compel lower rents. ■

Daily Worker, November 8, 1937

Tenants Push Fight on High Harlem Rents

WAGING A DETERMINED FIGHT against Harlem landlords to resist rent increases, the tenants at 108 W. 141st St. have engaged Attorney Hampton Gill, who won a victory in the courts for the 312 Manhattan Avenue Tenants' Association a few weeks ago, to carry their own struggle into the courts, it was learned yesterday.

The landlords, the E. H. Realty Corporation, are demanding $5 per month increase, a price which the tenants have refused to pay.

Immediately upon organizing a few days ago, the tenants received dispossess notices. To avoid bargaining collectively or arbitrating rental scales, the Harlem landlords have devised a technique of serving dispossess notices at the least sign of dissatisfaction among tenants.

TENANTS ORGANIZING

The validity of the first of the dispossess notices will be tested in the Municipal Court, Part One, Tenth District, 1 W. 125th St. at 9 A.M. today.

A picket line is being planned for the home of the senior member of the corporation, Joseph Sheinsinger, 832 Manida St.

Meanwhile, the tenants of three buildings owned by the E. H. E. Realty Corporation, 101, 133, and 149 W. 140th St., are being organized to resist rent increases. Maurice Hubbard, member of Local 802, A. F. of L., Musicians' Union, is leading the organizational drive. ■

Daily Worker, December 16, 1937

Utilities Admit Bars to Negro on Jobs

HIDING BEHIND THE SMOKE-SCREEN that the public does not want to come in contact with Negroes, New York utilities heads admitted yesterday in testimony to the Commission on Conditions Among Urban

Colored People that they have systematically excluded Negroes from all responsible positions in transportation and public service industries.

The testimony was given by the executives of the IRT, BMT, and the Manhattan and Bronx Telephone Companies in a crowded court room at 447 W. 151st St., with Lester Granger, secretary of the Urban League's Workers' Bureau, acting as director.

"You can't give the proper kind of telephone service if Negro and white girls work together," declared Walter D. Williams, general traffic manager of the Manhattan Telephone Co., under persistent questioning.

VIOLATES STEVENS LAW

Williams reluctantly stated that out of 4,500 telephone operators employed by his company, there were no Negroes. He admitted that he thought Negroes were very competent to fill these jobs, but felt that it was contrary to precedent "to hire Negroes for these positions."

Peter Lowrie, manager of the same company in the Bronx, stated that although 11,000 clerks were employed by his company, there were no Negroes.

Before a Negro and white audience that constantly murmured its disapproval, George Keegan of the IRT and W. S. Menden of the BMT, stated that out of 10,655 employed in both companies, there were but 917 Negroes.

The executives hedged, stammered, evaded, and lied outright when reminded that their practices violated the Stevens Law, which expressly forbids discrimination on the basis of race, creed, or color.

Among the companies which gave like testimony were the New York City Omnibus Corp., the Third Avenue Railway, and the Fifth Avenue Coach.

MEANY TESTIFIES

When pressed to explain wholesale discriminatory practices prevalent in A. F. of L. locals, George Meany, president of the state A. F. of L. had no solution to offer the commission to end the exclusion of Negroes from many important industries. He did not favor state laws prohibiting Jim Crow locals.

Countering the testimony of Meany, A. Philip Randolph, president of the Brotherhood of Sleeping Car Porters, recommended state legislation prohibiting franchises to those public utilities who refuse to employ Negroes. He further advocated laws which would make it an illegal act for trade unions to discriminate against citizens on the basis of race or color. ■

Daily Worker, DECEMBER 4, 1937

Weisbecker Strike Strong in Harlem

THE STORMY WEISBECKER STRIKE entered its third week yesterday with 20 C.I.O. pickets, members of the Retail Employees of America, marching to and fro in front of the store with placards demanding union recognition, a living wage scale, and the abolition of job discrimination.

The store, a food market situated at 268 W. 125th St., in the heart of Harlem's business area, has operated for 54 years.

Ten pickets, eight of whom were Negroes, have been arrested during the course of the strike and charged with "disorderly conduct."

REFUSED CONFERENCE

Some two weeks ago the union, having organized a majority of the workers at Weisbeckers, sought a conference with the management and was refused. The union then filed application with the State Labor Relations Board contending for the right to bargain for the employees.

The management countered with the contention that the union did not represent a majority of the employees and that the signatures of its workers had been forged. The management, however, refused to submit its payroll to the State Labor Relations Board to check the authenticity of the signatures.

The State Labor Relations Board called an election, the result of which gave the C.I.O. 205 votes as compared with 95 for the company. ■

Daily Worker, September 3, 1937

Women in Harlem Assail Milk Boost

"BUY AS LITTLE MILK AS POSSIBLE, just enough for the children and the sick!"

This is the answer of the women of Harlem to the Milk Trust. Rather than have the Milk Trust steal milk from their children through exorbitant prices, they have decided not to drink milk and to buy just enough of this basic food to keep health going.

Indignant because the price of milk has been increased the second time within a few weeks, Negro housewives throughout Harlem are organizing to move against Harlem's high cost of living. So desperate and deep has been the concern over the soaring toll of infant mortality, malnutrition, rickets, and tuberculosis that a Harlem-wide conference of housewives is being planned for October.

BAND TOGETHER

Many women, under the leadership of Helen Holman, director of women's work in the Harlem Division of the Communist Party, have banded together and issued 10,000 leaflets calling upon housewives to boycott as much as possible the Milk Trust (Sheffield and Borden).

They are demanding that the delivery of milk to the home be stopped until the increase is rescinded; they are informing the milk companies' drivers that they will not resume taking milk until the price comes down.

"We are asking women to buy their milk from the stores and then entirely from independent companies," stated Mrs. Holman. "We are also instructing them to buy grade B milk instead of grade A, for there is no real difference in quality between the two brands. Grade A simply serves as a source of bigger profit to the Milk Trust.

"Women are deciding to register their protest against the Trust in a manner that will hurt them, that is, we are going to cut down their profits."

BIG PROFIT

Mrs. Holman stated that the combined net profits of Sheffield and Borden amount to over $21,000,000 per year.

Letters are being sent to Gov. Lehman and the Commissioner of Agriculture demanding that the investigation of the Milk Trust be pushed vigorously.

Using the mass indignation against the prohibitive price of milk as a point of departure, the women are set to launch a campaign against the whole system of chiseling and cheating in Harlem stores.

"Some of the flagrant abuses to be found in Harlem stores are adjusted scales to short weigh," said Mrs. Holman. "Harlem is the cesspool into which the rotten, stale and inferior foods are dumped and sold at the same and sometimes higher prices than first quality foods are sold at in other sections of the city."

NEGLECTS INSPECTION

Mrs. Holman further stated that the city apparently neglects to inspect the food sold in Harlem, thus leaving storekeepers free to unload goods that are putrid.

"These conditions constitute a menace to health and are very often the direct cause of epidemics of dysentery and typhus," continued Mrs. Holman. ■

Daily Worker, AUGUST 23, 1937

WPA Official Charged with Negro Bias

GLADYS WILLISTON, NEGRO ACTRESS employed by the Popular Priced Theatre, a WPA unit, 152 W. 54th St., has presented evidence of discrimination against Negro actors and actresses before the board of appeals of the Federal Theatre, it was learned this morning.

The decision of the Board of Appeals is not yet known. The bulk of the evidence was directed against Ida B. Sullivan, a wardrobe mistress also employed by the Popular Priced Theatre. Six other workers, it was asserted, testified in support of Miss Williston's charges.

In order to discourage as many Negroes as possible from working in WPA theatres, a campaign of sabotage and abuse was launched against the Negro actors and actresses with Ida B. Sullivan at its head.

CHARGED WITH INSULTS

The evidence comprising a sheaf of typewritten paper notarized and sealed reads like occurrences in the deep South. On several occasions the woman was charged with addressing men employed in the capacity of doormen and cleaners as "Sambo," "Rastus," and any other name that would insult a Negro.

Whenever articles were missing in any part of the theatre, the wardrobe mistress would create the impression that they were stolen by Negroes. Further, she hummed insulting songs.

Whenever protests were made against such conduct, Ida B. Sullivan sought to besmirch the character of the accuser, a retaliation characteristic of Southern landlords who wish to mete out injustice to Negroes with impunity.

Substantiating the charges of Gladys Williston are Edward Blake, Eleanor Benedikt, Mary Leuzzi, Ruth Pinn, Edith Fabian, and Jonnie Belle Mitchell, all employees of the Adelphia Theatre. ■

Daily Worker, JULY 8, 1937

WPA Slashes Are Bar to Harlem Homes

CAUGHT IN THE AVALANCHE of WPA dismissals, numerous Negro applicants for apartments in the new federal-built Harlem River Houses fear that their dreams of moving out of the community's slum-areas will go up in smoke.

The exact extent to which the recent wholesale slashes of WPA personnel [are] affecting the successful 574 applicants to the Houses could not be fully ascertained from official sources yesterday—but it was grudgingly admitted by those in authority that it was "somewhat a factor." Some of the prospective tenants have been waiting to occupy the Houses for more than two years.

At least two units in the mammoth project, comprising 24 apartments, will be ready for occupancy the first week in August. Three apartments furnished by downtown apartment stores were open for exhibition. They have the facilities Harlem tenants hope for: Full of light, sunshine, good ventilation, and well arranged. Furnishings are estimated to run from $295 to $400 for 3- and 4-room apartments.

There is at present a waiting list of 11,534 applicants for the 574 apartments, indicating that this project does not even begin to fill the urgent need of Harlem housing. The project, however, with its relatively lost-cost rentals, is creating a yardstick by which Negro tenants are measuring the exorbitant rentals exacted by Harlem landlords for thousands of apartments not fit for human habitation.

A Negro woman inspecting the neat and spacious apartments and comparing them with Harlem's fire-traps remarked: "They look just like the pictures in the magazines, don't they?" A young, fairly well-dressed Negro man was discussing with a friend the possibility of his taking an apartment for his family now that he had failed to pass the civil requirements of the ERB. "There's hardly any use in my looking at these," he said resignedly. Still another woman was concerned because her sister had recently lost her job, thereby reducing her family income below the requirement standards set by the project's administrators.

Though the Harlem River Houses represent a good step forward, in some measures it brings into relief the obstacles which prevent workers generally from raising their standard of living: [l]ow wages, job insecurity, and the fact for that every decent apartment available there are thousands of workers who need them but who can't pay the price. ■

SECTION TWO

THE WINDS OF WAR

Once more
The guns roar.
Once more
The call goes forth for men.
Again
The war begins.

LANGSTON HUGHES, "SOME DAY"

The kinds of boycotts and strikes that Wright wrote about in his *Daily Worker* articles were decidedly signs of the times in Depression-era America. But though the United States in the thirties was agonizing in the grip of the Great Depression, one consolation was that it was not yet embroiled in war. In 1937, Pearl Harbor—and America's entry into World War II—was still four years away. There was peace of a sort. Despite bread lines and soup kitchens and unemployment lines, there was the absence of war. Such was not the case in Europe, however. One of that continent's hot spots was Spain. There a brutal civil war raged that was to claim several hundred thousand lives and devastate much of the country. The Spanish Civil War, which was in effect a revolution against the Spanish government, began in July 1936 and lasted for almost three years. The two opposing sides in the war were the fascist Nationalists, who sought the republic's overthrow, and the Loyalists, who fought to preserve the republic. The war evoked an international response. Nazi Germany threw its support to the rebel Nationalists, who in October 1936 had chosen Francisco Franco as their leader. The Nazis' counterpart in Italy, the Fascists, likewise supported Franco and the Nationalists. On the other hand, Mexico and the Soviet Union came out strongly in support of the Loyalists, as did the United States.

In America, Loyalist sympathy was quite high, and in few places was it higher than in Harlem. As Mark Naison has noted, there was "an enthusiastic support network in Harlem for the Loyalist cause," with "many black intellectuals adopt[ing] the Spanish cause with great fervor."[1] A number of African American doctors and nurses, Naison points out, traveled to Spain and volunteered their medical services.[2] Many African Americans enlisted in the Abraham Lincoln Brigade, a battalion of American volunteers that fought alongside the Loyalists, some returning home wounded and some dying in battle. Noted American writers also did their part for the Loyalist cause. Ernest Hemingway and Langston Hughes served as war correspondents in Spain, Hemingway reporting for the news service NANA (the North American Newspaper Alliance) and Hughes reporting for the Baltimore-based *Afro-American.* Unlike Hemingway and Hughes, Wright did not travel to Spain to cover the war. He simply did not have the financial backing to do so. (Twenty years later, though, he would visit that country and write about its culture, traditions, and beliefs in a book he would title *Pagan Spain,* published in 1957.) While Wright did not journey to Spain during the war, he nonetheless, like a host of other American and European writers, fervidly supported the Loyalists. "I am wholeheartedly and militantly pro-Loyalist," he declared, "and for the national freedom of the people of Spain."[3]

Partly because he was stateside and partly because he adopted a different journalistic approach, Wright's coverage of the war differed from that of Hughes and Hemingway. Eyewitnesses to the death and destruction rampant in Spain, these two important contemporaries of Wright wrote graphic, firsthand accounts of the war. Hughes, for instance, in his series of articles for the *Afro-American,* penned powerful descriptions of the air raid in Barcelona that "kill[ed] almost a hundred persons in their homes and wound[ed] a great many more," of the multitudes of Spanish "houses

. . . in ruins, gutted by bombs."[4] He wrote of the "[air raid] siren screaming its long, blood-curdling cry . . . and the walls of the building shaking. BOOM! Then the dull roar of a dying vibration. And another BOOM!"[5] With bombs falling all around him in Madrid, Hughes was there. "Today the Fascists are shelling Madrid again," he wrote on November 20. "The shells from their big guns exploding as they strike and the sound of crumbling plaster can be heard quite clearly as I write. In fact, 'clearly' is not the word. Loud and near would be a better description of the sounds."[6] There was no mistaking that Hughes's reporting was direct from the front lines.

Wright, on the other hand, brought the war experience home to his readers not by detailing battles and carnage but by focusing on men and women who in one capacity or another played vital roles in the war. Some of these figures were soldiers, others were civilian observers, and still others were stateside activists with a personal stake in the war's outcome. Each had something important to convey about some aspect of the war, and through Wright's articles their voices were heard. Though lacking the gunpowder smell that characterizes Hughes's and Hemingway's accounts from the front line, Wright's articles on the conflict nonetheless contribute significantly to a clearer understanding of the Spanish Civil War—especially how the Loyalist cause was relevant to the black struggle for freedom in America.

One such article that addresses the war's relevance to African Americans is Wright's interview with Walter Garland, a twenty-three-year-old New Yorker who served with the Loyalist forces. Convinced that fascism, if allowed to spread unchecked in Spain, would ultimately engulf blacks in America, Garland enlisted in the Abraham Lincoln Battalion of the Twenty-fifth International Brigade in Spain. He soon distinguished himself for his courage on the battlefield, advancing from the rank of private to section leader and then to lieutenant in charge of a machine gun company. Wright's profile of Garland, which appeared in the November 29, 1937, *Daily Worker*, is noteworthy for the nexus it clarifies between fascism abroad and racism in America. Wounded twice in battle, Garland proudly tells Wright that he and many other US and West Indian blacks are fighting the fascists in Spain so that "maybe [African Americans] won't have to go through . . . what the Spanish people are going through now."[7]

Another figure Wright spotlighted in connection with the war was activist Louise Thompson. Intelligent and articulate, Thompson was intolerant of oppression in any form and was deeply committed to social activism. (She remained a stalwart member of the Communist Party until her death in 1999 at the age of ninety-seven.) In the mid-1930s Thompson went to work for the International Workers Order, and as part of an IOW delegation she traveled to war-ravaged Spain in August 1937. Her departure for Spain received front-page coverage from the *New York Age* in its August 28 issue, which included a picture of her waving good-bye as her ship sailed for Europe. In Spain Thompson observed firsthand the extent to which the conflict had devastated the country and its people, and she also witnessed the bravery of the Loyalist forces fighting Franco. A few days after her return ship docked in New York the next month, Thompson sat down with Wright for an interview. His lengthy article on her appeared in the September 29 *Daily Worker* and is noteworthy for a number of reasons. One is that, through Thompson, Wright is able, just as he had done through Walter Garland, to foreground the relevance of the Spanish Loyalists' fight against fascism to the African American struggle against racism in the United States. Quoting Thompson, who quotes Walter Garland, Wright's article identifies Franco's fascists as "the counterparts of those who have been grinding . . . down [African Americans] back home."[8] Wright himself did not need to be convinced of the relevance of the Loyalist fight to the black struggle in America. Nor did other politically astute Harlemites, a prime example of whom was James Jones, the prominent black doctor in Harlem whom Wright quotes in his brief article "Negroes Form Committee to Aid Spain." "We regard the cause of Republican Spain," Dr. Jones declares, "no less than that of the cause of Black Americans."[9] Wright would have agreed heartily. But as a news correspondent—and a realist—Wright knew that not everyone was like Harlem's Dr. Jones, that not everyone grasped the relevance of the one struggle to the other. Such was Wright's social conscience that he believed it was part of his mission as a journalist to enlighten those who did not see such a connection. Wright's interview with Thompson thus afforded him the perfect forum. Fascism, his article makes clear through Thompson, is essentially another manifestation of racism, and what the Spanish Loyalists are battling against in Spain, he argues, is actually quite similar to what blacks are fighting against in America.

Wright's article on Thompson is also intended to instill pride in African Americans by underscoring the heroism of many of the black volunteers fighting in the International Brigades. Thompson is generous with her praise for these volunteer soldiers, singling out for special commendation Garland, Harry Haywood (whom Wright knew—and despised—from his Chicago days), and Harlem native Vaughn Love. Thompson is particularly eager to emphasize that these black troops, unlike most of the black soldiers who had fought in World War I, are not consigned to menial labor ("work battalions") but are instead engaged in actual combat. Indeed, the headline of Wright's article nicely captures Thompson's emphasis on black bravery: "American Negroes in Key Posts of Spain's Loyalist Forces."

Another reason for the article's importance is that it sheds light on an aspect of the war that many, especially African Americans, found puzzling and not a little unsettling: fighting on the side of Franco's Fascist rebels were tens of thousands of soldiers from Spanish Morocco, Spain's Army of Africa, known to many, including Wright, as "Moors." Voicing a concern that no doubt gnawed away at Wright himself, Thompson maintains in her interview that the Moroccans fighting on the side of the rebel Nationalists "have been misled . . . [and] tricked into the ranks of the fascists by Franco."[10] "[T]he story of [Moroccans] fighting against the Loyalists," Thompson argues, "is [the] story of how the fascists have duped and defrauded a terribly exploited people."[11] In his coverage of the war for the *Afro-American,* Langston Hughes made much the same point a month later. North Africans, Hughes remarked, were either conscripted or enticed by false promises of good money, only to be "paid off in worthless German marks" or placed on the front lines where they became instant casualties.[12]

Thompson could not have agreed more. That Hughes and Thompson arrived at such similar conclusions regarding Franco's treatment of the Moroccans indicates not so much that they were kindred spirits or collaborative journalists (the two were, in fact, close friends and even made joint broadcasts over Radio-Madrid) but points to the accuracy of their individual investigative reporting. In all, Wright's article on Thompson brought the war home to readers in several significant ways.

Wright gives further attention to American citizen involvement in the war in "Harlem Spanish Women Come Out of the Kitchen," an article dated September 20, 1937. The women profiled in the article are members of La Pasionaria, an East Harlem organization of Spanish women dedicated to the Loyalist cause. The group was named in honor of Basque-born Dolores Ibárurri, revolutionary champion of Spanish freedom, herself known as La Pasionaria, and, as Francesca Patai has characterized her, a "world-renowned embodiment of resistance to tyranny."[13] It is impossible to overestimate the depth of Ibárurri's commitment to the Loyalist cause during the Spanish Civil War or the extent of the leadership and inspiration she provided, not only to Republican Spaniards but to antifascist forces around the world. Impassioned orator whose speeches were broadcast over Radio-Madrid and reprinted in millions of leaflets, charismatic organizer whose leadership galvanized a nation, fervent believer in and tireless worker for women's rights, one of the founders of the Spanish Communist Party—Ibárurri was all these and more. As her biographer Robert Low points out, she "was the personification of the Spanish Civil War . . . [and] seemed to represent the very essence of beleaguered Spain. . . . [She] was Boadicea, Joan of Arc, Mother Courage rolled into one (she was even compared to Saint Teresa of Avila)."[14] Ibárurri adopted the pseudonym La Pasionaria (Passion Flower) in 1918, using it when she wrote articles for such leftist newspapers as *La Bandera Roja, Mondo Obrero,* and *El Minero Vizcaíno.* The sobriquet adhered, becoming as much a part of her identity, her revolutionary persona, as her signature black dresses. What was arguably her most famous radio speech, delivered on July 18, 1936, the very day that the Spanish Civil War began, included the defiant words that were to echo across Spain: "*No pasaran! Los Fascistas no pasaran!* (The Fascists shall not pass!)" The phrase "No pasaran!" quickly became the battle cry of the Loyalists, inspiring and rallying the Republican freedom-fighters, as well as the volunteer troops of the International Brigades, to revolutionary "acts of resistance seldom paralleled in modern history."[15] "It is better to die on your feet than to live on your knees," she exhorted the Loyalists in another one of her famous radio speeches, and in yet another broadcast she reminded Spanish women, "It's better to be the widows of heroes than the wives of cowards." With her zeal, eloquence, and charisma, "[i]t was no wonder," remarks Low "that the legend of La Pasionaria flourished around the world."[16]

It was in honor of this living legend, this "feminine heroine . . . who succeeded in a particularly masculine-dominated society," as Low puts it, that a zealous group of women in Spanish Harlem organized themselves into a unit and proudly adopted the name La Pasionaria.[17] In keeping with its namesake's beliefs and teachings, the group consisted of wives and mothers, like La Pasionaria herself, who were progressive-thinking, active participants in the antifascist movement on the home front. Several of these women, Wright would point out in his article, had husbands fighting on the battlefields in Spain. Wright's article on these women more than does them justice, detailing their activities in support of the Loyalist cause. Some of these activities include mundane, yet important, fund-raising efforts. Wright relates, for instance, how some of the women boldly venture into rowdy bars to collect dimes that will help fund the Communist Party's Building Drive, while others solicit contributions for the party and the *Daily Worker* in various stores and cafés. They are also active, Wright reveals, in protesting against the price increase put into effect by the Sheffield and Borden Milk Trust—a hike that brought about waves of protest from other activists and consumer groups (many of which Wright covered for the *Daily Worker*). The women are just as active, he further reveals, in recruiting new members for their branch and in rallying support for Jose Santiago, the political candidate whom they are backing for election as New York City assemblyman.

Wisely Wright anticipates a question that he suspects will probably arise: how are these women's activities related to the war in Spain? There is indeed a connection between the two, Wright explains. "There is in them all," he points out, "a firm and passionate belief in the heroic role played by the Communist Party of Spain. They know that the Party they are helping to build is international; they know that by building the Party in America they are also helping their husbands in the trenches in Spain."[18] Work that was certainly directly related to the war was the women's collection of over fifteen pounds of tin foil that would be shipped to Spain and converted for use as ammunition.

Wright, however, does not gloss over the fact that many of these women must attend the group's meetings and conduct their activities without their husbands' knowledge. Not because their husbands are anti-Loyalists (far from it) but because in the culture of these women there is the residual belief by males that such hands-on political activism is "man's work," something too macho for women. (As Robert Low has reminded us, the term *machismo* is Spanish.[19]) Wright stresses that these women are "descendants and relatives of forebears who kept them firmly relegated to the home."[20] The irony, of course, is that the group is named in honor of the very woman who placed a premium on female participation in the war—the same woman who organized and led women's brigades during the siege of Madrid. As if to underscore the group's liberated spirit, Wright's article is headlined "Harlem Spanish Women Come Out of the Kitchen." Wright undoubtedly intended for the emphasis to be placed squarely on the prepositional phrase *out of the kitchen*. As it has always been, so is it here: the kitchen symbolizes domestic confinement, the stereotypical female role in society and the family: woman as the cook for and feeder of man. The women of La Pasionaria, though, Wright sees, have taken courageous steps to shatter the culturally ingrained image of the Spanish woman as cookie-baking female. These women, through their "passion and their work," Wright concludes, "have leaped in the span of one short year from the kitchen into the arena of international politics."[21]

Also active in that international arena was social worker Thyra Edwards, whose wartime humanitarian efforts Wright reported on in his article

"Negro Social Worker Hails Housing, Education in Spain." While today Edwards is not as well known as the irrepressible Louise Thompson, her activism, her work as a labor union organizer and lecturer, and her commitment to justice for the oppressed working class distinguished her during the 1930s and 1940s as "one of the most important Black social work pioneers of the twentieth century."[22] Educated in Chicago and Gary, Indiana, Edwards won a fellowship from the American Federation of Labor (labor leader A. Philip Randolph was her sponsor and mentor) to study in Denmark. Her area of specialization was social work, a comparatively new field at the time, and she gave her life over to it with a zealous, all-consuming dedication. Edwards's primary interest within the field of social work was child welfare (she founded her own children's home in 1928). She was also a staunch advocate of the Loyalist cause and saw no disconnect between social work (a so-called "women's profession") and Loyalist support. "Edwards's brand of social work embraced the world," sociologists Elmer and Joanne Martin have remarked.[23] In fact, one of Edwards's most firmly held convictions was that "a chief role of the social worker was to fight against oppression in all forms and to promote social justice and equality."[24] Further, like a host of others, she recognized the importance of African American support for the Loyalists in their fight against the fascists. "[T]he Spanish people," she wrote in October 1937, are "symbolic of all the rest of us. And certainly there isn't going to be any freedom and equality for Negroes until and unless there is a free world."[25] As did so many others—black and white, American and European—Edwards journeyed to Spain during the war, traveling as a delegate of the leftist Social Workers' Committee to Aid Spanish Democracy. While there, just as Louise Thompson and Langston Hughes had been, Edwards was an eyewitness to the death and destruction throughout war-torn Barcelona, Madrid, and other cities. What Edwards found more tragic than the sights and sounds of battles was the plight of hundreds of thousands of children orphaned, homeless, starving, and even wounded as a result of the war. Children had always been Edwards's greatest love, and thus it was only natural that her utmost concern should be those multitudes of innocent children caught up in the war. Most of her time in Spain was spent working in children's colonies, helping to organize and staff them and setting up relief stations.

Just he had done with Louise Thompson before her, Wright contacted Edwards for an interview after her return from Europe. In Wright's published article that followed, Edwards, consistent with her concern for child welfare, keeps the plight of Spain's traumatized children at the center of almost every point she makes. She praises the Loyalists not only for their efforts at "colonizing children far from the places of combat" but for doing so "on a scale never heard of before."[26] Spain's efforts to keep these children "out of the range of fascist guns and planes" by colonizing them, she points out, is "[b]y far the most interesting and heroic social work being done among the Loyalists today."[27] She goes on to call for something bold, at least for the period: the involvement of African Americans in colonizing the war's child-victims. "What I want to see above all," she declares, "is the establishment of one of these homes by American Negroes."[28] Although during the 1930s African Americans had severe problems of their own to grapple with, Edwards maintains that such an undertaking would be a highly appropriate black response to fascism. "I can't think of anything more fitting," she tells Wright, going on to explain that "in this way the American Negro could actively participate in this world-wide struggle for the preservation of democracy in a world where democracy is under attack everywhere."[29]

Other issues also emerge in the article—housing and education, for example. Edwards reports that in the midst of the devastation and death in Spain, the Loyalists are building and staffing schools and launching vast housing programs. She clearly sees this as a vibrant expression of their assurance of victory over the fascists and as a testimony to their commitment to a democratic future. In hindsight, Edwards's optimistic prediction of a Loyalist victory, voiced at the end of the article, proved wide of the mark: in 1939 Franco's rebel Nationalists defeated the Loyalists, ushering in a fascist regime that remained in place for the next thirty-six years.

Another activist who, like Edwards, was devastated by the fascist victory in Spain was English novelist Ralph Bates, whom Wright centered on in a *Daily Worker* article that appeared a few days after his interview with Louise Thompson. Like Ernest Hemingway, Bates was an established novelist who sided passionately with the Loyalists. Bates, though, went further than Hemingway in espousing the Loyalist cause: he enlisted in the Anglo-American Fifteenth Brigade of the International Brigades, serving at the rank of captain. Bates's decision to fight against Franco and the rebel Nationalists did not stem solely from his hatred of fascism. Although born and raised in England, Bates had been living in Spain for nearly fifteen years when the war broke out. During those years, he had fished with the fishermen of the coastal village he called home, helping them to unionize. For a time he was also a factory worker. He later moved to the Pyrenees and spent his time writing, scaling cliffs, and tilling fields alongside farmers. In fine, Bates loved Spain and its people. As Ben Ray Redman remarked in 1939, Bates's attachment to the country was profound: "In literature and life [he gave] himself to Spain and made Spain his own."[30] The Spanish returned Bates's love, nicknaming him El Fantastico in tribute to his boundless energy and zest for Spanish life. Accordingly, Bates's support of the Loyalists was motivated as much by patriotism as it was by his abhorrence of fascism. It was while he was living in the Pyrenees that the war broke out. Wasting no time, he organized Basques into antifascist guerrilla groups. Before long he enlisted in the International Brigades, where he soon became an invaluable leader on the Anglo-American Fifteenth Brigade.

While Bates was in New York on a lecture tour in the fall of 1937, Wright interviewed him for the *Daily Worker,* and the resultant article, "Ralph Bates Tells of Spain's Fight for Strong Republican Army," is another jewel in Wright's cluster of articles on the war. Bates goes into great detail (some might say too much detail) explaining why the Republican Caballero government had not been successful in its efforts to defeat the rebel Fascists and why that government's replacement, the Negrín administration, was making greater progress in the war. Bates also makes it a point to clarify the Communist Party's role in the war, a role he defines as "that of an awakener and organizer of the masses."[31] Though Bates's explanations are occasionally a bit technical, they nonetheless offered to readers of the day a clear and informative look at the progress of the war from the perspective of a man who fought with the sword as well as the pen.

Although the Spanish Civil War was arguably the most written-about military conflict of the 1930s, Japan's war on China also grabbed headlines around the globe. In July 1937 Japan began a brutal, full-scale war on China, a war that has since become known as the Second Sino-Japanese War. (Though a war in every sense of the word, it remained an officially undeclared war until 1941.) World opinion at the time was that Japan's attack on China was unwarranted aggression, and even today most historians agree with that. The major newspapers and magazines across America and the world covered the Asian conflict in detail. So did the *Daily Worker,* running scores of feature stories about the war. Wright himself wrote five pieces related to the conflict.

Much like his coverage of the Spanish Civil War, Wright's brief pieces on the Asian conflict did not detail battles and bombings; instead they revealed what was being done in Harlem and around New York in reaction to the war. One way, he relates, that activists in Harlem and throughout the New York area found to protest Japan's war on China was to urge a boycott of Japanese products. Accordingly, picket lines sprung up around stores selling such goods. Newspapers such as the *Daily Worker* and journals like *New Republic* ran advertisements and editorials urging such boycotts. To the gratification of activists, quite a number of these boycotts were successful. Dozens of stores in the New York City area capitulated and removed Japanese-made goods from their shelves. Pharmacies, five-and-dimes such as W. T. Grant's, clothing stores, and even some branches of the famed giant F. W. Woolworth chain cooperated by refusing to stock and sell goods made in Japan. On several occasions activists also picketed the Japanese consulate in midtown Manhattan, and on that Wright also reported.

Many African Americans, no doubt, wondered what a war of Asians against Asians thousands of miles away had to do with their own plight. One purpose that Wright's pieces served was to answer this question, and one article that answered it was headlined "Harlem Group Pushes Aid for China," published September 22, 1937. In it, Wright quotes African American activist Vivienne France, who is striving to forge "a solidarity between the people of Harlem and those of China." "What Japan is doing in China," France argues, "is what fascist Italy did to Ethiopia and what Italy and Germany are doing today to Spain. It is fascist aggression pure and simple."[32] And fascist aggression, Wright knew, was the mirror image of racism (a point that was made in his articles on the Spanish Civil War). Though generally brief, Wright's pieces on the Japan-China conflict proved informative then and now.

■

While the United States in the thirties was mired in poverty and despair, one consolation was that it was not a nation at war. The same could not be said for many parts of Europe and Asia, however. In Spain a ferocious civil war raged between fascist rebels seeking to overthrow the Republic and freedom-loving Loyalists defending it. The Spanish Civil War was a cataclysm that evoked an international response, with Nazi Germany and Fascist Italy siding with and aiding the rebels and countries such as the Soviet and the United States supporting the Loyalists. The stakes were high. In a radio speech delivered in Madrid in 1937, Langston Hughes warned of the dire consequences of a fascist victory in Spain. "If Fascism creeps across Spain, across Europe, and then across the world," he predicted, "there will be no place left for intelligent young Negroes at all. In fact no decent place left for any Negroes—because Fascism preaches the creed of Nordic supremacy and a world for whites alone." Wright believed this as deeply as Hughes did, and in several of his articles for the *Daily Worker* he drew attention to the importance of the Loyalists' fight against the fascists, foregrounding the relevance of that fight to the African-American struggle against racism in the United States. Those articles, reprinted here, remain among his most enduring.

Another conflict that generated international concern was Japan's war on China. Almost unilaterally the global community viewed Japan's invasion of China as unwarranted aggression, and protests against Japan went up from around the world. One form those protests took was boycotts of Japanese products. Such boycotts were especially widespread and effective in New York City, and Wright's *Daily Worke*r articles covering them, though generally brief, proved informative.

■ ■ ■

Daily Worker, DECEMBER 9, 1937

12 Harlem Shops Sign to Ban Fascist Goods

WITH AGREEMENTS OF 12 STORES to their credit, the Committee for the Boycott of Fascist Goods entered the third week of picketing activities against Harlem business establishments yesterday. Armed with rubbers and umbrellas to protect them against the cold, 30 Latin-American men and women of Lower Harlem continued to march in front of the F. W. Woolworth Store, 113th St. and Fifth Ave., in an effort to force the management to discontinue selling Japanese silks and products made in Italy and Germany.

Of all the stores picketed so far, Woolworth has refused to comply with the demand to stop carrying or selling Japanese products.

Despite two weeks of intense picketing in intense cold, the morale of the picketers is high. Most of the Puerto Rican workers participating have no organizational affiliations.

CAMPOS AIDS PICKETS

Lucas Rodriquez, secretary, and Alberto Lugo, chairman of the Committee for the Boycott of Fascist Goods, stated yesterday morning that Francisco Campos, 600 W. 162nd St., Washington Heights, had made donations of money to keep the picket line going. Also, letters of solidarity had been received from many sections of the city.

The Valencia Bakery, 1365 Fifth Avenue, had for the past week been giving free lunches to the picketers.

The five following stores were the last ones to sign agreements not to carry fascist-made goods on their counters or in stock:

The Whitehouse Drug Store, 1337 Fifth Ave.; the Morton Pharmacy, Inc., 1706 Madison Ave.; the Adrian Ruiz Store, 1370 Fifth Ave.; Lopez Pharmacy, Inc., 1355 Fifth Ave.; and the Louis Barrett's Store, 1674 Madison Ave. ■

Daily Worker, July 23, 1937

100 Negro, White Women Picket Italian Consulate

AT THE HEIGHT OF YESTERDAY'S NOON HOUR scores of women, Negro and white, picketed the fascist Italian Consulate, 626 Fifth Avenue, bearing aloft red and black placards protesting Mussolini's atrocities in Ethiopia and his invasion of Spain.

A dozen or more cops bullied the crowds to keep moving in an effort to drive many sympathizers away. Many hundreds saw the slogans telling of fascist Mussolini's butchery of women and children in Ethiopia.

The picket line was sponsored by the Harlem Women's Peace Committee, the American League Against War and Fascism, the Progressive Women's Council, the American Friends of the Chinese People, the United Aid for People of African Descent, and many other civic, church, and social organizations.

3 STATES REPRESENTED

The women, representing organizations of three states—New York, New Jersey, and Connecticut—converged upon the fascist Italian Consulate and formed a picket line which chanted antifascist slogans for an hour amid the noon-day crowds of Fifth Avenue.

Thousands heard: "Drive Mussolini out of Ethiopia"; "Thirty Thousand Killed by Mussolini's Terror"; "Stop Fascist Destruction of Women and Children in Spain and Ethiopia"; "Free the Scottsboro Boys!"; "No American Aid for Italian Invaders."

Incensed at the widespread unfavorable publicity, a representative of the fascist consul contemptuously tore to pieces a statement presented by a women's delegation protesting Mussolini's atrocities in Ethiopia. Among the women who presented the demands were Mrs. Julia Church Kolar, a member of one of America's oldest families; Miss Helen Holman, secretary of the Harlem Women's Peace Committee; Jeanette Turner, representing the American League Against War and Fascism; Rose Nelson, of the Progressive Women's Councils; Esther Carroll, of the American Friends of the Chinese People; and Maggie Gibson, of the United Aid for People of African Descent.

100 IN LINE

A hundred women marched in the picket line and hundreds more gathered at the corner of 51st and Fifth Ave. at 1 P.M. and participated in an open-air meeting where the fascist Italian Government's brutal attitude toward women was dramatized in speeches.

Miss Holman revealed the demands presented to the Consulate were the following: that there be immediate cessation of the barbarous, bestial and murderous attacks upon the Ethiopian people and that there be an immediate cessation of hostilities against the Spanish people and prompt withdrawal of Italian fascist forces from Spanish territory.

Among the speakers at the open-air rally were Julia Church Kolar and Miss Helen Holman.

Following the demonstration a mass meeting was held last night at the St. James Presbyterian Church at 141st St. and St. Nicholas Ave. ■

Daily Worker, SEPTEMBER 27, 1937

Big Harlem Rally for China Tonight

WITH THE RALLYING CRY that neutrality aids invasion, thousands of Harlem workers, Negro, Chinese, and white, will gather tonight at 8 P.M. to protest Japan's undeclared war against China.

Sponsored by a score of Harlem leaders, the open-air street rally will attract the night crowds at Harlem's busiest intersection—125th St. and Seventh Ave. The demonstration is being staged under the auspices of the American Friends of the Chinese People and the American League Against War and Fascism.

In discussing Harlem sentiment against Japan's aggression, Miss Vivienne France, of the United Aid for Peoples of African Descent, declared:

KNOW FASCISM

"The oppressed of Harlem know what fascist aggression means. We watched Mussolini's invasion of Ethiopia in 1935. We watched fascist Germany and Italy invade Spain in 1936. Now in 1937 Japan has begun her long planned attack upon China.

"Because of the acute conditions in Harlem and the sympathy of the Negro people for the Chinese, we in Harlem will show the rest of the country the way in stopping fascism."

The Rev. Shelton Hale Bishop, pastor of the St. Philip's Episcopal Church, in commenting upon tonight's meeting, declared:

"The Sino-Japanese controversy precipitates the American pacifists into difficult positions. But in the last analysis, their sympathy can only be for the nation which suffers from aggression."

TOTTEN, FORD TO SPEAK

One of the outstanding speakers at the rally will be Ashley L. Totten, secretary-treasurer of the Brotherhood of Sleeping Car Porters. Another will be James W. Ford, organizer of the Harlem Division of the Communist Party.

Two additional features of the rally will be the speeches of the Rev. William Lloyd Imes, pastor of the St. James Presbyterian Church, and G. T. Linn, representing the American Friends of the Chinese People. ■

Daily Worker, DECEMBER 2, 1937

Boycott Is Spreading in Harlem's Stores

THE DRIVE AGAINST FASCIST-MADE GOODS was spreading in Harlem stores yesterday as Committee for the Boycott of Fascist Goods wrung agreements from three additional stores and threw a picket line in front of another Woolworth store at 126 Lenox Ave.

After removing from their counters and shelves all goods made in Japan, Italy, and Germany, the managers of the following stores indicated their willingness to sign agreements not to sell or carry in stock fascist-made merchandise: Benny's Store, 1 E. 114th St.; El Siglo Store, 1369 Fifth Ave., and Gilman's Store, 1368 Fifth Ave.

Meanwhile picketing in front of the Woolworth Store at 1360 Madison Ave. entered its third day. This is the only store so far picketed by the committee which has refused to comply with the demands to withdraw fascist-made goods.

TO BROADEN SCOPE

Plans are already under way to broaden the scope of the boycott campaign. Representatives of Latin-American working class organizations have conferred with the Harlem branches of the Workers alliance and the City Projects Council with a view to the establishment of joint picket lines composed of Negroes and Puerto Ricans in front of stores throughout Harlem.

Throughout the day open-air meetings are being held in front of stores where speakers inform the Harlem public of the reasons for boycotting Japan, Italy, and Germany.

ASK VOLUNTEERS

The Committee for the Boycott of Fascist Goods, with headquarters at 1668 Madison Ave., issued a call yesterday for volunteers to aid in establishing new picket lines. Lucas Rodriguez, recording secretary, and Alberto Lugo, chairman, are in charge of the boycott activities and will give educational guidance to those wishing to participate.

Lucas Rodriguez and Alberto Lugo, in a statement to the *Daily Worker* yesterday declared:

"The picket lines we are establishing are almost 100 per cent effective. The managers of stores are made to realize that the population of Harlem does not want fascist-made goods. We shall continue picketing until we have compelled every store in Harlem to dump Japanese silk."

Prominent in the work of the committee are Joseph Caballero and Gaspar Delgado, of the American Labor Party, and Ceofollo Ruiz. ■

Daily Worker, October 30, 1937

Fifty Fascists Attack Women's Picket Line

WITH SHOUTS OF "GET OUT," fifty attachés of the fascist Italian Consulate, 626 Fifth Ave., assaulted a delegation of three Latin-American women yesterday when they called to protest Italy's invasion of Spain.

The women, Lucy Gonzales, organizer of the La Pasionaria Branch of the Communist Party; Reva Gilbert, organizational secretary of the Lower Harlem Division of the Communist Party; and Maria Gomez were thrown to the floor, trampled and kicked.

The delegation represented a picket line of fifty Negro, Latin American, and Italian women who paraded in front of the Italian Consulate for more than an hour with placards demanding the withdrawal of Italian troops from Spanish territory.

In reciting what happened to the delegation, Lucy Gonzales declared:

"We had no sooner entered the hallway than fifty men rushed us and knocked us to the floor. We set up a holler and more came running out of doors from all sides and kicked us.

"It was easy to see they had planned it. The fact that we were women had no effect upon them. The attitude of those men toward us confirms our conception of fascists as vicious and brutal people!"

Reva Gilbert and Lucy Gonzales sustained severe bruises about the shins and stomach from the blows and kicks administered by the Italian henchmen of the Consulate.

The picket lines of fifty women, which began its picketing and chanting at 1 P.M., carried placards reading: "We Demand Immediate Withdrawal of Italian Troops from Spain!" "Stop the Murder of Women and Children in Asturias!" "Butcher Mussolini, Hands off Spain!"

Six police patrolled the streets in front of the Italian Consulate to keep thousands of passersby from blocking the sidewalks.

Immediately following the picketing, Reva Gilbert announced that plans were under way for a larger picket line in the near future.

The demonstration was conducted under the auspices of the Lower Harlem Section of the Communist Party, with Upper Harlem and East Harlem participating. ■

Daily Worker, SEPTEMBER 22, 1937

Harlem Group Pushes Aid for China

TO BUILD UP SOLIDARITY between the people of Harlem and those of China, plans for a huge open-air street rally for Sept. 27 were announced today by representatives of the Friends of the Chinese People, the American League Against War and Fascism, and the United Aid for Peoples of African Descent.

Vivienne France, executive secretary of the United Aid, in commenting upon the preparations, stated:

"To date almost a score of Negro leaders representing the outstanding organizations in Harlem have agreed to show their solidarity with the Chinese people in their hour of need.

"We feel that it is particularly fitting that we hold such a meeting now in view of the spreading of much insidious propaganda by Japanese militarists to the effect that the present war against China is for the sake of protecting the colored races of the world against the whites.

"We know that in some parts of America Japanese agents are seeking to convince Negroes that they are the 'protectors' of the colored races. Nothing could be further from the truth.

"What Japan is doing in China is what fascist Italy and Germany are doing today to Spain. It is fascist aggression pure and simple."

DEPLORE "NEUTRALITY"

Miss France went on to say that many Negroes deplore the American government's neutrality policy which in effect is an aid to Japan's aggressions.

The street rally will be held on Sept. 27 at the northeast corner of West 125th St. and Seventh Ave.

Among the individuals who have agreed to sponsor and support the rally are: A. Philip Randolph, international president of the Brotherhood of Sleeping Car Porters; Dr. Catherine Lealtad, of the National Negro Congress; Dr. P. M. H. Savory of the United Aid and the Amsterdam News; the Rev. Adam Clayton Powell, Jr., of the Abyssinian Baptist Church; Frank Crosswaith, of the Negro Labor Committee; and many others.

Among the speakers to address the meeting will be many Negro and Chinese leaders. ■

Daily Worker, JULY 26, 1937

Harlem Party to Protest Japan's Action

TO PROTEST JAPAN'S UNDECLARED WAR against the Chinese people, the Harlem Division of the Communist Party will demonstrate in front of the Japanese consulate, 500 Fifth Ave., Thursday at 5 P.M.

The Party called upon all of its members, sympathizers, and other thousands of lovers of peace to give their active support to this protest. To publicize the demonstration, the Party is issuing leaflets.

The Harlem Division of the Communist Party, 2038 Fifth Ave., issued a call which read in part:

"We call upon Negro and white and all defenders of liberty in the world today to demonstrate against Japan's military aggressions in China." ■

Daily Worker, SEPTEMBER 20, 1937

Harlem Spanish Women Come Out of the Kitchen

EACH WEDNESDAY AT 1 P.M. some 70 women in Spanish Harlem lay aside their aprons, turn off the gas in their cook stoves, tell their children to be good (or sometimes they take them with them), and go to a small, dingy meeting hall at 84 E. 111th Street.

They are not going to a women's sewing circle, or to a temperance meeting, or to a Bible class. These dark-haired, bright-eyed women are about much more serious business. They are members of the Communist Party, and the ideal in their hearts is La Pasionaria, the heroine of the Loyalist Spanish masses.

AID SPANISH PEOPLE

Some of these women are elderly; some are young; almost all of them have children; and eleven of them have husbands in the Loyalist trenches. They meet in the daytime because it is the best time for them to go to meetings: the husbands of some of them would not like it if they knew or thought that they were doing Communist work.

They assemble in the room and wait for their comrades. The room is quiet. Soon there is heard a faint humming; it grows louder, then finally breaks into song. NO PASARAN! More come in, bringing their children whose grubby hands are filled with tin foil.

Luz Salazar, president of the La Pasionaria Branch of the Communist Party, rises and announces the beginning of the meeting. In rapid succession four songs are sung: No Pasaran, Cuatro Milpas, Bandera Roja, and the Internationale.

LEADS IN DRIVE

Felicita Prieto is designated as chairman and Luz Salazar rises again to give an organizational report. She concludes by conducting a minute check-up on assignments in the Party Building Drive. La Pasionaria Branch is in competition with Branch 1 of the Lower Harlem Section and a keen interest is manifested in each comrade's reply as to what she has done.

As woman after woman arises to explain the extent of her activities for the past week, there emerges a picture of their passion and their work.

La Pasionaria Branch is leading the other branches in the Lower Harlem Section in the Party Building Drive. Of the 800 signatures they are to collect to place their candidate, Jose Santiago, to put him on the ballot, over 300 are already in. One hundred and ten dollars of their $150-quota is in. In an effort to double their membership, they have recruited during the past two weeks 25 new members.

These women are poor and could not make substantial contributions to the Party's financial drive, so they took their *Daily Worker* dime-books into the streets, into stores, cafes, bars, and business establishments and raised $110 in dimes.

They tell some entertaining tales about their Party adventures. When they go into bars to collect dimes, the men try to get them to drink, stipulating that they will give a dime only if they drink a beer with them. The woman replies that she wants both of the dimes, for the Party needs them. The man agrees but still demands that she drink a beer. She demands still another dime for her dime-book.

PROTEST FOOD CUTS

On one occasion a group of these undaunted women went into the Tammany headquarters in Harlem to collect dimes for the *Daily Worker*. They were ordered out. They refused to go, demanding the right to talk to the workers. Despite the harsh attitude of the officials, they collected seven dimes.

How do they recruit? It is through such campaigns as these. This coming Thursday night at 8 P.M. they are holding an open-air mass rally at the corner of 111th St. and Madison Ave. in protest against the sky-rocketing price of milk and food. They will get out leaflets calling upon the mothers and wives of the neighborhood to voice their resentment against Sheffield and Borden (The Milk Trust).

DANCE SEPT. 26

On Sept. 26, Sunday, they will dress in the costumes of their native land and hold a dance at 1168 Madison Ave., the Lower Harlem Section Headquarters. The proceeds of this affair will go to the Party's Building Drive.

There is in them all a firm and passionate belief in the heroic role played by the Communist Party of Spain. They know that the Party they are helping to build is international; they know that by building the Party in America they are also helping their husbands in the trenches of Spain.

So far they and their children have gathered more than 15 pounds of tin foil to ship to Spain for munitions.

When they speak of husbands who are "somewhere in Spain," they do so with a slight sigh and avert their eyes. But their sacrifice is a willing and passionate one. Are they not following La Pasionaria?

This unit has been in existence less than a year. These women, descendants and relatives of forebears who kept them firmly relegated to the home, have leaped in the space of one short year from the kitchen to the arena of international politics. ■

Daily Worker, JULY 31, 1937

Harlem to Hold Peace Parade on Wednesday

THE GLARE OF 500 TORCHES on 100 cars carrying flags, banners, posters, and streamers will be the spectacle Harlem will watch at 9:30 P.M. Wednesday, when the American League Against War and Fascism stages its preliminary peace parade.

From a mobilization point at 145th St. and Lenox Ave., the parade will wind southward between Seventh and Lenox Aves., covering Lower and Upper Harlem, and ending at 118th St. and Lenox Ave., where an open-air meeting will be held.

The purpose of the parade, the American League Against War and Fascism disclosed today, is to mobilize and popularize the Peace Parade to be held on Aug. 7.

Numerous Harlem organizations are endorsing the demonstration. Among the individuals who have pledged support are: Rev. Lorenzo H. King, of the St. Mark's M.E. Church; Dr. Charles A. Pettioni, of the West Indian Federation of America; Archbishop Ernest, of the African Orthodox Church; James Hubert, Executive Secretary of the New York Urban League; and the Rev. Drs. Adam Clayton Powell Sr. and Jr.

Among the speakers are: Frank Ibanez, of the Bakers Union local 87; Halton Henry, of the Brotherhood of Sleeping Car Porters; Tim Holmes, for the American League Against War and Fascism. ■

Daily Worker, SEPTEMBER 29, 1937

American Negroes in Key Posts of Spain's Loyalist Forces

BECAUSE OF DISTINGUISHED RECORDS of bravery and heroism, Negro members of the Abraham Lincoln Brigade in Spain have been promoted to leading military positions in the Loyalist armies, Louise Thompson, Negro secretary of the English Division of the International Workers Order, declared yesterday after a three-weeks' tour of war-torn Spain.

Miss Thompson, who is also a leading figure in the National Negro Congress, arrived in New York Saturday aboard the S.S. *Paris*. In addition to her trip to Spain, she spent five weeks in France. As a representative of her organization which has collected $30,000 to aid Loyalist Spain, she was enthusiastically greeted through Spain by American volunteers and the Spanish people.

"But my greatest interest was in the American Negro volunteers fighting in the International Brigades and in the Moors fighting with the Fascist Franco. I wanted to see with my own eyes the difference between these two dark-skinned people fighting on opposite sides of the struggle," said Miss Thompson.

BROADCAST FROM MADRID

On August 27, Miss Thompson, together with Harry Haywood, Langston Hughes and Walter Garland, made a special radio broadcast in Madrid for the benefit of American Negro fighters.

"These Negro soldiers are not in the work battalions as was the case of the Negroes who fought in France during the World War. They occupy any military position for which they are qualified."

Do any of these Negro volunteers regret having gone to Spain to lay down their lives for Spain? Miss Thompson answers by giving the exact words of Walter Garland, Negro volunteer from New York, who said:

"You know, we Negroes who have been in Spain are a great deal luckier than those back in America. Here we have been able to strike back, in a way that hurts, at those who for years have pushed us from pillar to post. I mean this—actually strike back at the counterparts of those who have been grinding us down back home."

This 23-year-old Walter Garland, Miss Thompson informed, has now a rank of lieutenant and has been stationed for the past five months at the American Military Training School. He was wounded three times in action and spent 130 days of unrelieved hell in the trenches when he went into action for the first time in his life.

Another Negro fighter in Spain from whom Miss Thompson brought greetings to his Negro and white comrades in America was Harry Haywood, who has the rank of captain and is the political commissar in the George Washington Brigade.

FRANKSON PRAISED

Miss Thompson also told a story of an African lad who had gone to Spain to study and got caught in the mesh of war. She told of how he gladly set aside his books and took up arms against fascism.

"He said that he could not afford the lose the opportunity to do his bit toward defeating fascism and making Spain and the world so that not only he, but the millions of his fellow countrymen in Africa would have a chance at an education," said Miss Thompson.

Still another heroic figure from whom Miss Thompson brought greetings is Vaughn Love of Harlem, who is now in an officer's training school. Love saw his first action at [Brunete], a twenty-one day stretch of fighting in which he distinguished himself for conspicuous bravery.

Then she told the story of a Negro machinist over whom numerous Loyalist brigades have been in competition to get his services. This is Oliver Frankson, chief of mechanics at Auto Park, the transport base of the International Brigade. It is claimed, Miss Thompson reports, that Frankson is largely responsible for the continuous flow of food and goods into Madrid even after many lines of communication had been cut off by the fascists. He performed miracles of mechanical work upon trucks and autos partially destroyed by fascist shells.

Then she told of Oscar Hunter, a boy from the stockyards of Chicago, who is now political commissar at Murcia. Oscar Hunter studied at Hampton Institute in the South and is known among the Loyalist peoples as the man who can get things done.

She gave accounts of many others, all playing vital roles in defense of Spanish liberty.

DISCUSSES MOORS

One of the most interesting parts of Miss Thompson's interview with the *Daily Worker* was her remarks regarding the Moors fighting with Franco. It was reported that there were some 30,000 of them in Franco's lines.

Those whom Miss Thompson saw in hospitals in Madrid could not tell their story, for they could not speak Spanish. But enough is known of them to know that the story of their fighting against the Loyalists is a story of how the fascists have duped and defrauded a terribly exploited people.

The most remarkable spirit Miss Thompson encountered among the Spanish people was the deep understanding of why Moors, Germans, and Italians were fighting against them. So high has become the political consciousness of the civil population that when Italian, German, or Moorish prisoners are brought into towns, they are greeted by, "Love Live the Italian Peoples!" or "Long Live the German Peoples!" or "Long Live the Moorish Peoples!"

"They know," said Miss Thompson, "that these people have been misled. They bear toward them no ill-will."

To help settle the problem of the Moors there has been formed the Hispano Moroccan Anti-Fascist Association. This organization spreads posters throughout Loyalist territory informing the people of the true state of affairs. Its appeal is two-fold: one of its purposes is to convince the Moors that the Government of Loyalist Spain is their friend; the other purpose is to combat the antagonism of the Spanish people toward the Moors who have been tricked into the ranks of the fascists by Franco.

CONGRESS DELEGATE

On the question of the unity and morale of the Spanish masses, Miss Thompson said the following:

"Loyalist Spain is truly united. Everywhere I went was a feeling of deep confidence that they could defeat the fascists. This was true of young and old, and those whose sons and husbands were at the front, or those who had lost their sons and husbands in battle.

"The military equipment of the Loyalists may not be what the military equipment of the fascist countries are, but the Loyalists have something which no fascist university can give: and that's the courage that they are fighting to free a great and beautiful land which is their home."

During her five-week stay in Paris, Miss Thompson was, along with Max Bedacht and William Weiner of the International Workers Order, a delegate to the World Congress Against Racism and Anti-Semitism.

At this congress there were 327 delegates, representing 93 organizations from 26 different countries. It is estimated that these delegates represented some 40,000,000 people.

The manifesto issued by the congress reads in part:

"This world assembly urges you to reject the bloody lie of racism, that of theoreticians as well as that of dictators."

At its closing sessions the congress established an International Coordinating Committee with headquarters in Paris. The task of this committee is to keep in contact with all national committees in other countries and to call world congresses.

Miss Thompson will make a public report on her trip Saturday at the Royal Windsor Palace (formerly St. Nicholas Arena), 66th St. near Columbus Ave., when a memorial meeting for I.W.O. members will be held. ■

Daily Worker, SEPTEMBER 25, 1937

Negro Pastor Assails [Tokyo] Aggression

REFLECTING THE AROUSED MORAL CONSCIENCE of the Negro church in Harlem, the Rev. Shelton Hale [Shelton Hale Bishop], pastor of the St. Phillip's Episcopal Church, declared this morning in an interview with the *Daily Worker* that:

"The Sino-Japanese controversy precipitates the pacifists into difficult positions. But in the last analysis, their sympathy can only be for the nation which suffers from aggression."

Rev. Bishop made this statement after endorsing the proposed street rally which will take place in Harlem Monday night at 8 P.M. at the corner of West 125th St. and Seventh Ave.

"CHINA NEEDS OUR HELP"

Commenting further on what he believed should be the attitude [of] the Negro in Harlem toward the situation in China, the Reverend stated:

"Our sympathy for China should be so intense that it should move all of us to extend every effort to stop the aggression and to aid the sufferers.

"China needs the moral and the material support of the democratic nations of the world, and those of us who sense her plight must give her every peaceful support."

The American Friends of the Chinese People and the American League Against War and Fascism announced today that an additional sponsor had lent support to the Monday night street rally. Vito Marcantonio, national president of the International Labor Defense, gave his hearty endorsement. ■

Daily Worker, NOVEMBER 12, 1937

Negroes Form Committee to Aid Spain

A GROUP OF LEADING PHYSICIANS and liberty-loving Negroes of Harlem have constituted themselves into the "Negro People's Committee for Medical Aid to Republican Spain" and hopes soon to send a bullet-proof ambulance and a corps of doctors and nurses as a gift to the Loyalist cause, it was announced today.

Dr. James J. Jones, chairman of the committee and one of Harlem's leading doctors, explained the aims of the committee as follows:

"This gift of ours is in appreciation for the great aid democratic and progressive mankind have given to the struggle for freedom of the Scottsboro boys and to the Negro people generally.

"We regard the cause of Republican Spain no less than that of the cause of Black America.

SPEEDY ACTION URGED

'The Negro People's Committee for Medical Aid to Republican Spain' calls upon all progressive Americans to emulate this action of ours and respond to the Loyalist appeal."

The organization of this committee was the result of the death of a number of American Negroes in Spain, particularly that of Milton Herndon, brother of the heroic Angelo Herndon. [Editor's note: Angelo Herndon was a nineteen-year-old African American Communist activist who was arrested in Fulton County, Georgia, in 1932 and charged with attempting to incite an insurrection after leading a protest march. He was convicted and sentenced to twenty years in prison. His case, like that the Scottsboro case, garnered national attention, and the US Supreme Court overturned his conviction after five years of appeals by his legal defense team.]. The idea that more concrete aid from many sources should be sent in the name of the American Negro has crystallized and taken concrete form.

Following hard on the heels of Roosevelt's anti-isolationist speech in Chicago, many Negroes have begun to see the futility of "neutrality" and are anxious to align themselves with internationally progressive and democratic nations. ■

Daily Worker, November 1, 1937

Picket Lines Win Withdrawal of All Goods Made in Japan

A WEEK'S PICKETING by the American League Against War and Fascism has resulted in the withdrawal of all goods labeled "Made in Japan" by the management of the Woolworth Store at 557 Sutter Ave. in Brooklyn.

Pressure from the picket line forced the management to announce on Saturday that all Japanese goods had been withdrawn from the counters and removed from stock.

A subsequent investigation of the store's stock by the Chinese Committee of the American League Against War and Fascism substantiated the management's claims.

In a declaration issued yesterday from the League's offices at 333 Sheffield Ave., Brooklyn, it was revealed that the League would launch a campaign to remove Japanese goods from all stores in the East New York area. ■

Daily Worker, November 30, 1937

Pickets Force Stores to Ban Japan Goods

A MASS PICKET LINE of 50 Latin-American men and women stretching for more than four blocks along Madison Ave., from 112th to 115th Sts. forced three out of four stores to remove all Japanese, German, and Italian made goods from their counters and shelves yesterday.

The picketers carried red and black placards and shouted anti-fascist slogans to thousands of passersby who blocked the sidewalks.

The stores which complied with the demands of the picketers were the Fifth Avenue Fair, 1362-66 Madison Ave.; W. T. Grant Store, 1352 Madison Ave.; and the Adolph Parker Store, 1380 Madison Avenue.

The only store refusing to comply with the demands of the picketers was the F. W. Woolworth Store, 1360 Madison Ave.

UNITED COMMITTEE

The picket line was conducted under the auspices of the newly-formed Committee for the Boycott of Fascist Goods, which maintains headquarters at 1668 Madison Ave.

During the early afternoon the managers of Grant's, Parker's, and the Fifth Avenue Fair called at the headquarters of the Communist Party and in an interview with the organizational secretary, Reva Gilbert, offered to compromise by promising not to purchase fascist-made goods in the future.

The compromise was rejected and Reva Gilbert demanded removal of all fascist-made goods from counters and shelves. ■

Daily Worker, October 1, 1937

Bates Tells of Spain's Fight for Strong Republican Army

"THE VICTORIES OF THE SPANISH REPUBLICAN ARMY during the summer months of 1937 are not the result of the imposed will of any one political party: these victories represent an upsurge coming from below. The present Negrin Government is the political expression of the Spanish people's will to win," declared Ralph Bates today in an interview with the *Daily Worker*. Ralph Bates, author of *Lean Men, The Olive Tree*, and *Rainbow Fish*, is an outstanding English novelist who has spent several years in Spain.

He arrived in the United States a few days ago fresh from his post as captain in the International Brigade and he spoke of conditions in Spain from firsthand knowledge.

DESCRIBES PARTY'S ROLE

Owing to widespread confusion as to the role of the Communist Party of Spain, Mr. Bates was emphatic in pointing out that the role of the Party was privately that of an awakener and organizer of the masses.

"What really happened was that the Communist Party made the will of the people articulate. It helped to convert sporadic, spontaneous, and courageous action into planned, disciplined military tactics," Mr. Bates explained.

"The best possible way to get a picture of what happened is to review the state of affairs under the Caballero Government," Mr. Bates continued. "There existed no organized army. In the early phase of the war, defense was conducted by spontaneously organized groups of trade unionists, political parties, factories, and syndicalists.

A REGULAR ARMY

"There were times when certain sections of the front were under as high as six conflicting commands. There was no central military authority. Despite the splendid show of courage manifested by troops who fought with sticks, rifles, [and] shotguns, this type of militia could not conduct an effective offensive against the swelling armed legions of fascists from Italy and Germany.

"The problem that faced the people of Spain was that [of] lifting the conscience of the People's Front from a mere political level to a military one.

"You might call the first period of defensive fighting of the Loyalists a Romantic Period. Then things began to happen. The Fifth Regiment was formed, modeled on the plan of a regular army under a centralized command. The Communists played the leading role in organizing this regiment. Its first battalion was a thousand strong and was called the Battalion of Steel.

"Soon others were formed. By October of 1936 some 70,000 well-trained men were in arms in Madrid. The same process was taking place in other cities, bringing the total strength of the Fifth Regiment to 115,000.

MILITIA MILITARIZED

During this intensive organizational period the Communist Party launched a campaign for a regular army of the people, an army of national liberation. On October 9 the Government issued a decree militarizing the militia; on October 10 Lister and Contreras announced the formation of the first mixed brigade, composed of the Fifth Regiment, the Loyal Republican Guard, and others."

Mr. Bates was emphatic in pointing out what happened after the formation of the Fifth Regiment.

"This army was handed over to the Spanish Government lock, stock, and barrel. The Communists supported this move. They were not agitating for a separate, Communist commanded army. And in turning over the Fifth Regiment to the Government, they called for like action throughout Spain. They were answered in every walk of Spanish life.

"From below there rose companies, then battalions, then brigades, and finally army corps.

YANKS IN TRENCHES

"An example of this miracle can be seen in the action of 200 women in the north region of Madrid. Voluntarily, this small group organized and washed the clothing of the soldiers who were at the front. This lasted from November of 1936 to February of 1937; then the women handed their organized laundry over to the Government; thus it became a part of the military service.

"At an accelerated pace this process went on in industry and agriculture until the early months of 1937. Meanwhile the fascists were recruiting in ever larger quantities arms and men from abroad.

"And what did the Spanish people do in this situation?" Mr. Bates asked. "What did they demand of their Government?"

"They demanded that the Government double, triple its efforts. They demanded supreme command under democratic control. They demanded the building of large reserves to allow the proper replacement of men exhausted at the front.

"As an example of how necessary the building of reserves was, look at this astounding fact. The 15th International Brigade, composed of American volunteers, remained in the trenches with but a 2-day break for a period of four months.

"The people demanded the launching of a summer offensive. And what did Caballero do?

CRITICIZES CABALLERO

"No supreme command was organized. The summer offensive was not prepared. Nor did Caballero report to his own cabinet the situation. His ministers did not have a knowledge of what was happening in the country. Emphatically, he did not build up adequate reserves, a thing which was the crying need at that moment.

"The result was that the demands of the People's Front led to the downfall of the Caballero Government. This downfall came in May after the disgraceful uprising in Barcelona. For this the minister of the interior under Caballero, Ganarza, must take full responsibility.

"There is the charge that personal intrigue and ambition caused Caballero's downfall. That is not true. An examination of all the activities and speeches of the People's Front parties preceding Caballero's downfall show that they had in mind but one aim: the building of a rearguard and the military might of the people to repel the fascists. And it was precisely this that the Negrin Government did on coming into power.

ACHIEVEMENT OF PEOPLE

"During the first week of the Negrin Government, over 100,000 men were called to the colors. The reserves were built up. The Supreme War Council met repeatedly, and elaborate preparations were set in motion.

"Look at the history of the Spanish Republican Army since Negrin came to power!" Mr. Bates exclaimed. "The magnificent Brunete offensive, the first Loyalist offensive made by the Government during the war, was launched.

"In August the opening of a powerful offensive on the Aragon front began. And think of the last drive in Jaca! For the first time the Spanish Government is able to conduct operations on all fronts according to necessity and pain," Mr. Bates pointed out.

"This is the achievement of the Spanish people after they'd been allowed to express themselves," said Mr. Bates. ■

Daily Worker, November 12, 1937

Negro Social Worker Hails Housing, Education in Spain

THE SLOGAN OF LOYALIST SPAIN today is, "We would rather die in the ranks of the Loyalists than live in the slime of fascism!" Thyra Edwards, noted Negro woman social worker and a delegate of the Social Workers Committee to Aid Spanish Democracy, declared yesterday in an interview with the *Daily Worker.*

She is one of the vice presidents of the National Negro Congress and chairman of the Committee on Women's Work in the Congress.

Miss Edwards arrived in New York Monday aboard the S.S. Normandie after spending several months traveling in the Soviet Union, England, France and a month studying housing, education, and the colonization of children throughout Loyalist Spain.

"There are but two places in all Europe where you can feel that new life is centralizing and crystallizing toward new goals," Miss Edwards said. "Those two places are the Soviet Union and Spain. The rest of the countries of Europe are either static or terrified with the fear of war.

VAST PROGRAM

"That confusion is absent from Spain. Even though in the midst of war, the Loyalists are going about the tasks of launching vast housing programs, building new and extended systems of education, and colonizing children far from the places of combat on a scale never heard of before."

Miss Edwards said that the people are undertaking these programs on a volunteer basis and with the enthusiasm of a people who long wanted an opportunity to do them.

"By far the most interesting and heroic social work being done among the Loyalists today is the colonization of some quarter of a million of Spanish children," she said. The program was begun under the Negrin Government by the Ministry of Education."

Miss Edwards recounted her impressions of Spanish refugee children living in England and the great difficulties and hardships visited upon them there.

TARGET OF ATTACKS

"Firstly, inadequate records were kept of the children, and many were cut off from their families. Secondly, there was the demoralizing situation of their being made to feel that they were objects of charity in foreign countries. Thirdly, the Catholic Church, especially in England, launched a vicious campaign of abuse against these children, branding them as urchins of the streets and as not being worthy of the help given them.

"It was for this reason that the Ministry of Education under the Negrin Government set up what is known as the Delegation of Colonies for the purpose of establishing homes for these children right in Spain, in the mountains and out of range of fascist guns and planes.

"Most of these children are being evacuated from Madrid, Barcelona, and Valencia. In Madrid alone the evacuation of 250,000 children must take place. Proportionate numbers must be taken from Asturias and other regions.

USE PALACE

Miss Edwards spent considerable time at Con Toni Gros, a children's home far up in the Pyrenees Mountains. This home, Miss Edwards said, was like so many others, housed in an abandoned palace amid dramatic natural scenery.

"In visiting these children homes, I never visited so many palaces and former summer villas in all my life," said Miss Edwards.

The North American Committee to Aid Spanish Democracy maintains several of such homes in Spain. The American Youth Committee maintains the Thomas Jefferson Home; Anna Louise Strong maintains such a home in Puigcerda, in the Pyrenees Mountains, a farm colony for boys.

"Those outside of Spain who no longer have opportunity of helping can contribute funds through the Paris Coordinating Committee, the foreign arm of the Delegation of Colonies," continued Miss Edwards. "The need is still great, as but 50,000 of 250,000 have been colonized so far. There are thousands of palaces and summer villas available; the great problem is getting money to support them.

DEMOCRATIC IDEAL

"Detail[ed] budgets are already worked out; a record of all available sites and sizes of houses has been compiled. Groups wishing to support one of these homes have the right to name it after some democratic hero of their own country. For example, the Thomas Jefferson Home."

Miss Edwards said that growing out of this work is the dissemination among Spanish children of the international democratic ideals of liberty-loving nations.

"What I want to see above all," Miss Edwards spoke further, "is the establishment of one of these homes by American Negroes. We could name it after one of our own great fighters for liberation: Sojourner Truth, Harriet Tubman, or Frederick Douglass.

"I feel that in this way the American Negro could actively participate in this world-wide struggle for the preservation of democracy in a world where democracy is under attack everywhere. At the present I can't think of anything more fitting."

WELL-STAFFED

She stated that these homes were staffed with registered public school teachers, men and women of the highest standards. In many cases teachers followed their pupils to the homes from whatever school or town they lived in.

Simultaneously with colonization, the school system of the Loyalists is being extended and new schools are being built and opened. Many of the teachers who went to the front during the early days of the war are now being recalled to man these schools. As a result of the increased efficiency of the Loyalist Republican Army, the Government feels that these forces can and should be spared from military duty. The aim of the Government is to have its social program keep pace with the winning of the war.

Parallel with education and colonization is the launching of a vast housing program. Even during war time, housing is being pushed in such cities as Madrid, Barcelona, and especially in Valencia. This housing program takes care of two burning needs, said Miss Edwards. Firstly, it replaces those houses destroyed by the fascist shells. Secondly, it is the beginning of a long-term housing program to raise the standards of living of the Loyalist masses.

She said most of this work is being done by volunteers, teachers, dentists, intellectuals, students, and professional women.

In concluding, Miss Edwards said that she could not see how the "fascists can beat the spirit of Loyalist Spain!" ■

Daily Worker, JULY 26, 1937

Torchlight March Called August 7 by Harlem Group

A FLARING TORCHLIGHT PROCESSION—a lurid symbol to remind the Negro of the horror of war—will wind its way through Harlem's streets Wednesday night, Aug. 4.

The parade will start at 7:30 P.M. at 145th St. and Lenox Ave. It is designed to mobilize mass support and popular enthusiasm for the mammoth anti-war parade and demonstration to be staged Aug. 7.

Scores of organizations in Harlem are cooperating—civic, fraternal, church, and labor groups. The United Aid for the Defense of Ethiopia and the American League Against War and Fascism are sponsoring the demonstration. ■

Daily Worker, NOVEMBER 29, 1937

Walter Garland Tells What Spain's Fight against Fascism Means to the Negro People

AFTER BRAVING FOR A YEAR the inferno of fascist fire, Lieutenant Walter Garland, just recently returned from Spain, told just what the heroic fight for Spanish democracy means to the Negro in America.

In an exclusive interview with the *Daily Worker* yesterday Garland revealed the courage and understanding of today's American youth who went to Spain and helped create the "miracle of Madrid."

Twice wounded in action, the 23-year-old Negro from Brooklyn rose in the short space of a year from the rank of private to that of a lieutenant in charge of the American Training Base in Loyalist Spain.

AT NEGRO CONGRESS

Until a year ago Walter Garland lived a life of "quiet desperation" in Brooklyn, earning his living in the orchestration department of the NBC studios on the Lucky Strike program. Of five children, two girls and three boys, he was the oldest son. Though his father is living, his mother died before he could hardly remember. Garland was hardly out of grammar school before he had to go to work and help carry the family responsibilities.

But the National Negro Congress, especially the Brooklyn Division which he joined shortly after its formation, gave Garland new perspectives and most important of all, courage and a method of action.

The first and most important discovery of Garland's life was his recognition that what was happening to him was what was happening to all the oppressed the world over, whether in Ethiopia, Spain, or China.

TO MEET THE ENEMY

Distressingly he had watched fascist Mussolini butcher the unarmed Ethiopians. He reasoned that it would only be a matter of time before these brutalities descended upon the Negro in America, unless the spread of fascism was halted. And Garland did the only thing that a man who saw as he saw could do: HE WENT TO MEET THE ENEMY!

In January he arrived in a democratic Spain with her back to the wall, a Spain desperately trying to stave off the hordes of fascism until it could organize its industries, government, and army.

"They put us through about four weeks of intensive training and shipped us to the Madrid sector," said Garland. "This was my first taste of war. Franco was trying to encircle Madrid, to cut it off from the rest of the nation.

TO SAVE MADRID

"You can imagine what effect the capture of Madrid would have had on the Loyalist population. We wanted to save Madrid at all costs.

At that time the Loyalists had no trained reserves to relieve us. We stayed in the trenches for 130 days."

Garland went into the front lines as a private but was soon promoted to Section Leader.

"Most of the officers of the old Spanish Army, being sons of the rich, had gone over to the Insurgents. When there was any occasion to fill a vacancy in the ranks, men were moved up from the bottom.

"One of the reasons for this," said Garland, "was to build a people's army to ensure loyalty to the workers' cause."

HIT ON 8TH DAY

On his eighth day in the front lines, Garland was wounded—a bullet through the stomach. Luckily, his cartridge belt deflected the force of the bullet and the wound was not fatal.

He spent eight weeks in a hospital at Chenchun and was then sent to an officer's training school. He emerged as a lieutenant and was placed in charge of training a machine-gun company.

In June of 1937 Garland took his company into a reserve position on the Jarma Front and stayed a month. Then, in the broiling heat of July, he was ordered to Brunete.

"It was a desperate period," said Garland. "We didn't have much time; the fascists were pressing us. In order to get into position as fast as possible, I took my men over an exposed area. All but two of us got over safely. One of the boys got hit and I tried to drag him to safety and got a fascist bullet in my hand. It wasn't much of a wound, but it was enough to keep me out for 12 days.

BACK JULY 18

"On July 18 I went back into the trenches and stayed till the end of the Brunete campaign."

Garland came out of the inferno of Brunete a hero of Loyalist Spain. His quick adaptation from civilian to military life, his understanding of the world-wide issues involved in the struggle, was the reflection of the ultimate hope of a Loyalist victory.

Garland estimated that more than 100 American and West Indian Negroes are now fighting in the ranks of the Spanish Loyalists. He stated that the heroic records of many of these men were due to the fact that there existed no discrimination toward them.

NAMES NEGRO HEROES

"They gave all of us a chance to put out abilities to use," Garland said. "For instance, a young Negro from Brooklyn, Burt Jackson, was promoted to a lieutenancy and is now in charge of the Loyalists Topography School. There is Oscar Hunter, who is a political commissar. Abe Lewis, another American Negro, is quartermaster at a training base.

"The Spanish Government is stronger today than ever. It is going to win. The capitalist press in this and other countries usually play up the gains of the fascists. That's where their interests lie. But the interests of the Negro and other oppressed groups lie with the Loyalists," Garland continued.

On the home scene what interests Garland most is the development of the People's Front Against War and Fascism in America—comprising the Negro people and progressives of all other races.

"The National Negro Congress is certainly doing fine work," he said. "The hope of the Negro lies through its activities. There's one thing that every Negro ought to do. He ought to get into the National Negro Congress and fight reaction in all of its forms. If they do, then maybe we won't have to go through with what the Spanish people are going through now." ■

Daily Worker, JULY 22, 1937

Women Picket Italy's Consulate Tomorrow

TOMORROW AT NOON the Harlem Women's Peace Committee, in conjunction with several other anti-fascist women organizations, will throw a picket line of women around the Italian Consulate, 625 Fifth Ave., in commemoration of Emperor Haile Selassie's birthday and as a protest against fascist Italy's subjection of the Ethiopian people.

The American League Against War and Fascism, the Progressive Women's Council, and several other organizations are co-operating. The picket line will last throughout the noon hour and will be followed by an open-air meeting.

Leading the picket line will be Julia Church Kolar, a member of one of America's oldest families, Olive Terrel, and others. Two Ethiopian refugees will also participate.

Helen Holman, Negro woman leader and secretary of the Harlem Women's Peace Committee, reported the progress of the plans for the picket line as follows:

"We are finding women, Negro and white, in all walks of life willing to show their solidarity in defense of the trampled Ethiopian people. Those who were not successful in persuading their organizations to participate are participating individually." Rev. Imes of St. James Presbyterian Church, Negro leader and chairman of the United Aid for People of African Descent, heartily endorsed the picket line. He stated in part:

"This is a courageous move on the part of women. It is heartening to see them take their place in the front ranks in the fight against reaction."

The Harlem Women's Peace Committee appeals to all women, Negro and white, to help swell their ranks tomorrow in front of the Italian Consulate. ■

SECTION THREE

HEROES SUNG AND SILENT

The hero is the living light-fountain, which it is good and pleasant to be near.

THOMAS CARLYLE

The war in China and Spain was fought with bullets and bombs fired and exploded thousands of miles away from American soil. But in America in the 1930s a different kind of warfare was being waged in another kind of arena—not by soldiers but by an athlete, and not in trenches but in a square ring with a canvas floor. The warrior-hero was Joe Louis, and his battlefield was the boxing ring. Nicknamed the Brown Bomber, Louis was one of the most popular and respected prizefighters in boxing history, and he was far better known by most Americans in the thirties than fascist-fighting soldier-heroes like Walter Garland and Milton Herndon. Born in poverty in 1914 in east-central Alabama, Louis began boxing professionally at the age of twenty, winning his first professional bout in the first round by knocking his opponent out of the ring. "All my life my hands felt important to me," Louis once revealed in an interview. "They felt big, strong, and they seemed to want to do something special."[1] And something special was exactly what Louis's hands did. In the ring, those hands as fists pummeled opponent after opponent into oblivion, establishing him as "the hardest punching heavyweight of all time," as one sports writer declared.[2] In 1937, Louis began his reign as the heavyweight champion of the world by defeating James Braddock for the title.

Louis, however, was much more than a boxing champion—he was a symbol, a living embodiment of black achievement, black dignity, and black power (thirty years before that term became a charged rallying cry). He was, in a word, a hero. Unlike America's first black heavyweight boxing champion, Jack Johnson, whose outrageous behavior alienated and angered white America (and a sizable portion of black America as well), Louis was lionized by both whites and blacks. Especially by blacks. "Joe was the first real symbol the Negro ever had," recalled one of Louis's friends in an interview with sportswriter Gene Smith. "And every time he knocked some guy out, every Negro had this tremendous feeling of personal satisfaction."[3] Legendary singer Lena Horne once summed up perfectly what Louis meant to African Americans: "Joe was the one invincible Negro, the one who stood up to the white man and beat him down with his fists. He in a sense carried so many of our hopes, maybe even dreams of vengeance."[4] This was precisely how Wright viewed Louis and how he portrayed him in several of his best articles.

Though Louis would go on to fight seventy-one professional bouts, continuing into the early 1950s, winning all but three of them, two of his most important matches were fought in the thirties. One of these was against Max Baer in September 1935. Louis at the time had been boxing professionally for less than a year and a half and had won all of his previous bouts, defeating each of his twenty-one opponents handily, most by a knockout or technical knockout. For his part, Baer was not one of the "bums" that many heavyweight champions-to-be have to fight on their way to the top. He was a former heavyweight champ himself. "At his best moments," historian Gerald Astor remarked, "Baer was an excellent fighter with an ability to hit very hard."[5] He was such a hard hitter that in 1930 his blows killed one of his opponents, Frankie Campbell, and two years later they put another challenger, Ernie Schaaf, in a coma. Further, he could take as much punishment as he could inflict: he had never been knocked out, or even down. Though he had a reputation as an incorrigible ladies' man and a light-hearted jokester—many even called him clownish—Baer was a formidable opponent, and his fight with Louis in September 1935 drew 95,000 people to Yankee Stadium.

Going into the bout, Louis was the odds-on favorite, and he lived up to all expectations. He was in control of the fight from the first round, pummeling Baer's head and body with one ferocious blow after another, flooring him twice in the third round. Baer did not last long. Louis was declared the winner in the fourth round when Baer did not get all the way up to his feet after a barrage of blows by Louis sent him reeling to the floor. After the fight, reporters asked Baer why he did not get up and fight on. Baer's answer was a classic: "I could have struggled up once more," he said, "but when I get executed, people are going to have to pay more than twenty-five dollars a seat to watch it."[6]

While to Baer the bout may have seemed more like an execution than a prizefight, to millions nationwide, especially African Americans, the match was a rousing, satisfying event. Having witnessed it from a ringside seat at Yankee Stadium, *New York Times* sportswriter James P. Dawson raved about the match. "There was drama in the finish," he exclaimed, "and sensation in the fight that lived up to the best traditions of the ring from every viewpoint. It was the kind of battle the occasion demanded, the ultimate in competition."[7] Although Wright did not witness the fight (he was still in Chicago at the time), he did witness black Chicago's celebration of Louis's victory and wrote about that euphoric outburst in an article titled "Joe Louis Uncovers Dynamite." Unquestionably one of the best articles Wright ever penned, it appeared in the leftist journal *New Masses*.

The dominant metaphor that Wright uses in the article is water. He compares African Americans, with their pent-up frustration and anger, their balked dreams, and their thirst for equality, to a dammed-up body of water. Louis's victory over Baer, Wright argues, cracked that dam and released the water, if only for a little while. Wright masterfully dramatizes the water's release, depicting it as emerging by degrees—first a trickle, next a flow, then a gush, and finally a tidal wave that threatens to engulf all in its wake. Wright introduces the water metaphor at the very outset of the article. After hearing on the radio of Louis's stunning fourth-round victory, "Negroes [on Chicago's South Side] poured out of beer taverns, pool rooms, barber shops, rooming houses and dingy flats and *flooded* the streets."[8] This "fluid mass of joy," Wright rhapsodizes, ultimately becomes a "tidal wave," coursing headlong through the city, even briefly changing its elemental form and becoming "a cyclone sweeping through a forest."

Near the end of the article Wright switches metaphors and sets up an important comparison that initially appears wrong-headed. He likens the jubilant crowd to the hydra, the ferocious, many-headed serpent from Greek mythology. The comparison at first glance seems odd, for in literature, mythology, and even scripture, snakes (or serpents) are invariably symbolic of evil that threatens or destroys. In Virgil's *Aeneid,* one of the greatest works in Western literature, monstrous twin serpents kill Laocoön as punishment for his questioning of the "gift" of the Trojan Horse. In Genesis 3:1–6 it is a serpent (the most famous one in history) who convinces Eve to eat, as John Milton sings in *Paradise Lost,* "the Fruit of that Forbidden Tree, whose mortal taste / Brought Death into the World, and all our woe." Even Wright's contemporary Zora Neale Hurston makes use of the snake as a symbol of evil and death in her magnificent short story "Sweat." Wright, of course, was quite aware of the snake's symbolic import: in his short story "Big Boy Leaves Home" (1935), he depicted the snake as emblematic of death. Wright well knew the conventional associations surrounding the snake.

In "Joe Louis Uncovers Dynamite," Wright works an interesting and effective variation on the snake's traditional symbolic meaning. He compares the exultant black masses to the dreaded mythological hydra not to suggest that the "joy-mad" black celebrants are evil (far from it) but to underscore that they have long been viewed as such by whites, and now, empowered by Louis's victory, they have become, in the eyes of white Chicagoans, that serpentine menace they have always been regarded as. The Brown Bomber's victory, Wright insists, has indeed roused them from their "coil," and like the monstrous hydra they are "darting forth [their] tongue," ready to strike. Wright's use of the hydra is also significant because, as he knew well enough from his Bulfinch, if one of the hydra's heads were to be cut off, two other heads would grow back in its place. Wright, then, uses the hydra to suggest the resilience and indestructibility of the black masses: if one is cut down, another—*others*—will take his place. Wright does not abruptly drop the serpentine image in his readers' laps: earlier in the article he prepares for the metaphor's inclusion by describing the crowd as "form[ing] long writhing snake-lines" as it weaves its way "in and out of traffic."[9]

Although coiled and ready to strike, the crowd—an extension, Wright suggests, of African Americans throughout the nation—relents and falls back. The hydra retreats to the "dark hole" it had "popped out of"; the water ebbs and flows back to its source. This falling back (of both the serpent and the water) is wholly in keeping with the essay's title, and, more important, with Wright's intent in the essay. That intent is embedded in the title. Joe Louis, it proclaims, has *discovered* dynamite—he has not ignited it. The difference is crucial. At the end of the essay, the dynamite has not been set off, has not exploded. Just as the water recedes, flowing back to confinement behind the dam without causing damage, and just as the hydra slithers back to its lair without inflicting injury, so too does the dynamite remain inert. By its very nature, Wright is arguing, the dynamite that the Brown Bomber has unearthed is clearly volatile—it simply does not explode. This time. But the potential is there, just as it is there for the water to drown out everything in its path and for the hydra to strike. That is precisely the point Wright is making in the essay: Joe Louis's victory has not only inspired and emboldened African Americans, but it has revealed to them (and to the rest of America) their enormous, untapped potential for righteous activism. Such potential must be channeled constructively, Wright advises at the end of the essay, reverting to the water metaphor and to the image of dynamite unearthed and, for now at least, unexploded: "[H]ere's the wild river that's got to be harnessed and directed. . . . Here's a fleeting glimpse of the heart of the Negro. . . . Here's the real dynamite that Joe Louis uncovered!"[10]

Clearly, then, Wright saw Louis's victory over Baer as one that was as meaningful to black America as it was to Louis himself. But as important as Louis's bout with Baer was, even more significant was the fight he would have three years later, a bout that promoters and the media billed as the fight of the century. It took place on June 22, 1938, and was far and away the most momentous one of Louis's career, earning him increased national and international fame. His opponent was Max Schmeling, Nazi Germany's *Wundermensch.* Hitler himself had wined and dined Schmeling and touted him as the incarnation of Aryan strength and superiority. On the other hand, Americans and most of the free world had come to regard Louis as the symbol of democracy and freedom, an angelic warrior battling the fascism and tyranny symbolized by Schmeling. "There was no question," Louis biographer Chris Mead points out, "that the American public attached a strong symbolic importance to the second Louis-Schmeling fight and accepted Louis—a black man—as the representative of American strength and virtue."[11] Accordingly, the Louis-Schmeling fight took on an almost apocalyptic tone. In the months leading up to the bout, another Louis biographer, Richard Bak, remarks, "Fight talk and war talk were interchangeable," and the bout became increasingly politicized. President Franklin Roosevelt even invited Louis to the White House and told him, after feeling his muscles, "Joe, we need muscles like yours to beat Germany."[12] Louis thus found himself a hero not only to blacks but to *all* Americans.

For Louis, though, the fight was also very personal. Two years earlier, in June 1936, Schmeling had knocked out Louis in the twelfth round of their first fight. Louis never forgot that loss. He brooded, even obsessed, over it. He was determined to redeem himself, to exact vengeance, a determination that became his ruling passion for two years. Shortly before his rematch with Schmeling, Louis told a columnist for the *New York Daily Mirror,* "I am out for revenge. . . . I've waited two years for this chance, and now my time has come."[13] But he was never allowed to forget that on his shoulders "he carried the hopes of everyone against Hitler's master race—black, white, Christian, Jew."[14] On the very day of the fight he stated to a reporter in a nationally syndicated article, "Tonight I not only fight the battle of my life to revenge the lone blot on my record, but I fight for America against the challenge of a foreign invader, Max Schmeling. This isn't just one man against another or Joe Louis boxing Max Schmeling; it is the good old U.S. versus Germany."[15] In their rematch, then, Louis was out for self as well as country, for blood as well as a national victory.

He got both. Held at Yankee Stadium on June 22, 1938, in front of 70,000 frenzied fans, the fight of the century was, in the words of ringside commentator Bob Considine, "short, swift, merciless, complete."[16] Louis won by a first-round technical knockout after flooring Schmeling three times. The fight, as one longtime boxing commentator summed it up well, was "the most concentratedly destructive 124 seconds in two centuries of ring history."[17] Louis's victory over Schmeling, Bert Sugar argues, "was a major moment in the history of sports and the sociological history of our culture."[18]

Along with a multitude of other writers, Wright was present at the fight, and his coverage of the bout appeared in the *Daily Worker* on June 24. A prefight article ran in the paper's June 22 morning edition, the same day of the bout. A third Wright article on the fight appeared a week and a half later (July 5) in *New Masses*. All three are crackling good pieces and stand as some of the best work Wright ever did as a journalist. If Wright had been so inclined, he might have made a decent sportswriter, albeit one with a distinctly political bent.

By the time of Wright's articles on the Louis-Schmeling fight for the *Daily Worker,* he was no longer working for the paper, having resigned six months earlier. He was thus reporting as a guest contributor. Even though, as Ralph Ellison reveals, many of New York's rank-and-file Communists, especially those on the *Daily Worker* staff, "sneered at [Wright's] intellectuality, ridiculed his writings, and dismissed his concern with literature and culture as an affectation," the newspaper was all too happy to feature his articles on the fight.[19] Wright, after all, was just beginning to make a name for himself in the literary world, something he had long dreamed of and the main reason he had come to New York. His collection of short stories, *Uncle Tom's Children,* had been published that spring by one of the country's most prestigious publishing houses, Harper and Brothers, and was receiving highly favorable reviews. Knowing this, the *Daily Worker* saw no reason not to capitalize on its former newsman's burgeoning fame.

Too, Wright was still a Communist Party member (it would be another four years before his break with the party), and that plus his name recognition would ensure a hefty readership for the paper's coverage of the fight. And no doubt very few on the *Daily Worker* staff did not know of his 1935 article on the Louis-Baer bout.

Accordingly, on June 22, 1938, the day of the Louis-Schmeling rematch, the *Daily Worker* announced to its readers on the front page that Wright would cover the hours-away heavyweight championship bout for the newspaper as a "guest contributor." The announcement flatteringly referred to Wright as the "distinguished young Negro writer . . . author of *Uncle Tom's Children* . . . [and recent] winner of the Story Magazine award." It went on to remind its readers that Wright had been "a former member of the *Daily Worker* staff" and had been "in charge of the *Daily Worker* Harlem Bureau." It closed by stating that Wright's articles on the fight would be written "exclusively for the paper." Prominently set off, the *Daily Worker*'s announcement appeared in a two-by-four-inch bordered box adjacent to an article by Wright on the upcoming bout, headlined "Why the Eyes of the People Turn to the Ring For the Title Bout at Yankee Stadium Tonight."

Spirited and engaging, the article seems partly designed to stoke the already fever-pitch interest in the fight. It was also a kind of journalistic appetizer intended to whet readers' taste for the main course, the blow-by-blow, analytical coverage of the eagerly anticipated face-off. Worth noting is that Wright touches, albeit lightly, on a point he would develop fully in his post-fight articles, one that he had already treated at length three years earlier in "Joe Louis Uncovers Dynamite": the Brown Bomber's symbolic import to Americans, particularly to black Americans. There is also unintentional humor in the article. In what has to be the biggest understatement he ever made, Wright predicts that if Louis keeps his promise to pulverize Schmeling, the bout "should be a great fight."[20] By no means filler, the piece ably captures "the wild elation of millions" anticipating that imminent bout.

As promised in the *Daily Worker*'s June 22 announcement, Wright's "exclusive" on the fight appeared in the newspaper on June 24. Even though news of Louis's victory was by then a day and a half old, Wright's article on the fight must have seemed like manna to readers starving for all they could digest on the bout. The *Daily Worker* knew this, for sharing the front page with Wright's story were two other articles on the fight, one by Wright's friend and mentor Ben Davis, Jr., and the other by staff writer Lester Rodney. Of the three pieces, though, Wright's is clearly the best. For more than half of the article, he gives a highly dramatic, almost blow-by-blow description of the bout. In 1938, well before television became a familiar part of everyday life, this was exactly what readers hungered for—all the savory details of Louis' s victory. Wright certainly did not disappoint them. In testosterone-charged prose that even the best writers at *Ring* magazine would envy, he provides a graphic, enthralling account of the now-historic match. Every jab, every uppercut, every overhand blow is described with cinematic clarity, allowing a kind of virtual view of the fight. Wright's awareness of (and disdain for) what Schmeling represents also surfaces at several points in the article, especially in his description of the pummeling the German heavyweight receives not long before Louis is declared the winner: "[S]till another right [by Louis] found the fascist chin. Maybe Hitler's Aryan Gods saved Schmeling from the next whizzing left hook, but all the pagan Gods of Dr. Goebbels could not have saved him from the next left hook, which staggered Schmeling and rocked his very senses. Hitler's wilted pet looked like a soft piece of molasses candy left out in the sun."[21]

But the article goes beyond merely narrating the blows. The headline "And Oh—Where Were Hitler's Pagan Gods?" indicates the tone and direction of the article's second half. After rousing coverage of the ring action, Wright concentrates on the "fistic and political significance" of Louis's victory—to Americans in general and to African Americans in particular. With his stunning victory over Schmeling, Louis had belied fascism's toxic doctrines of white supremacy and racial inferiority. "Louis' triumph," Wright posits, shattered "Hitler's pretensions of Aryan superiority" and was a clarion call to "native lovers of democracy to be true to democratic ideals."[22] Among those who most clearly understand this, Wright points out, are the quarter-million blacks "who live within [Harlem's] narrow confines." They are the ones, he emphasizes, who realize best "in terms of their daily American life what this [victory] meant."[23] That understanding is manifest in their post-fight behavior:

> "Knowing full well the political effect of Joe's victory upon the popular mind of the world, thousands yelled: 'Heil Louis!' . . . And Harlem ridiculed the Nazi salute of the outstretched palm by throwing up their own dark ones to show [how] little they feared the humbug of fascist ritual.[24]

In its frenzied elation and newfound empowerment, Harlem becomes "a huge wave of exultant humanity."[25] Taking a quick look back at his "Joe Louis Uncovers Dynamite," and glancing ahead to his lengthier, more intricately woven article "High Tide in Harlem," Wright goes on to describe Harlem's celebration of Louis's victory, "the largest and most spontaneous political demonstration ever seen in Harlem."[26] That demonstration, Wright undoubtedly knew, was not limited to Harlem. Black communities throughout America went "joy-mad," to use Wright's expression, over the Brown Bomber's first-round win. But it is on Harlem that, as an eyewitness to the celebration, he concentrates, and it is on Harlem's "exultant humanity" that he lavishes some of his best writing in the article.

A little over a week after his article on the Louis-Schmeling rematch, Wright's "High Tide in Harlem" appeared in *New Masses,* the journal that three years earlier had featured his essay "Joe Louis Uncovers Dynamite." Since *New Masses* was a magazine whose editors actively encouraged creative writing, Wright was free to give full vent to his linguistic creativity. And that he did. The result was a mini-masterpiece: insightful and thought-provoking, image-rich and exceptionally well written, one of the two best articles Wright composed during the thirties, second only to "Joe Louis Uncovers Dynamite."

Despite its title that suggests that water will be the main image used in the piece, the article's dominant metaphor is puppetry. Throughout the article Wright compares Louis and Schmeling to a pair of puppets, each saddled with "a configuration of social images whose intensity and clarity had been heightened [by] . . . skillful and constant agitation."[27] In the hands of a lesser writer, such a comparison would be almost insulting. In truth, when viewed from afar—from, say, the last dozen or so rows in Yankee Stadium—the two boxers must have looked like puppets. (In 1938, it must be remembered, there were no mammoth-sized television screens positioned around the stadium to capture and transmit coverage of an event to those in the "nose-bleed section.") Wright's comparison is visually accurate and thus not inappropriate. He goes on, however, to fully develop the comparison, investing it with weight, substance, and clarity. As a symbol of Aryan muscle and might, Schmeling easily lent himself to Wright's depiction of him as a puppet manipulated by Hitler and the Third Reich. Louis likewise was ripe for caricature, this solemn and stalwart emblem of the ideals of liberty and justice. But Wright's argument is not that Louis and Schmeling are wooden, soulless figures, devoid of will and individuality. Rather, his overarching intent in using the puppet metaphor is to illustrate that the supporters of the two boxers—the boisterous crowd in each man's corner—have become so entangled in the politics underlying their man's cause that they have come to view and treat him more as a marionette than as an individual. The puppet imagery, thus, says more about the fighters' supporters and spectators than about Louis and Schmeling.

But one massive group of Louis's supporters that Wright does not characterize as puppet masters is America's black populace. African Americans, as Wright points out, "took Joe into their hearts." He was "their champion," an idol whom they revered and held "in a state of deep awe."[28] Indeed, Wright devotes much of the article to capturing precisely what Louis's victory meant to them—how it affected Harlem's black community and, by extension, African Americans throughout the country. In sweeping, graceful prose, Wright conveys the unadulterated joy and sheer exhilaration that possess Harlem after Louis's victory:

> In Harlem . . . a hundred thousand black people surged out of taprooms, flats, restaurants, and filled the streets and sidewalks, like the Mississippi River overflowing in floodtime. With their

> faces to the night sky, they filled their lungs with air and let out a scream of joy that it seemed would never end, and a scream that seemed to come from untold reserves of strength.[29]

Wright also makes it clear that although Louis was white America's Golden Boy, "a public idol . . . respectfully enshrined in the public's imagination," he was even more precious to African Americans, to whom he was "the living refutation of the hatred spewed forth daily over radios, in newspapers, in movies, and in books about their lives."[30] By focusing on Louis's symbolic value to black folk and on the "high tide" in the wake of the Brown Bomber's victory over Schmeling, Wright was treading on ground he had covered the previous month in his *Daily Worker* article on the bout. As such, "High Tide in Harlem" is an expansion—a creative, exuberant expansion—of some of the important points Wright made in that piece but could not develop and expand due to the limitations of a newspaper. It is also a backward glance at the approach he took three years earlier in his article on Louis's victory over Max Baer, "Joe Louis Uncovers Dynamite." There are even brief reversions to the water imagery he used so effectively in that 1935 gem. For example, the exuberant Harlemites are compared to "the Mississippi overflowing in floodtime" and to "the sea," thereby crystallizing the "high tide" that gives the article its title. As a commentary on one of the most important prizefights in boxing history and in the political life of a nation, "High Tide in Harlem" is work of the highest caliber. What is perhaps even more significant is that in its depiction of Harlem as a microcosm of black America, the article is as much a paean to the spirit and untapped power of African Americans as it is a tribute to the magnetism and heroism of the Brown Bomber.

All told, Wright's essays and articles on Joe Louis in *New Masses* and the *Daily Worker*—his prose panegyrics to the Brown Bomber—are sterling examples of creative nonfiction at its best, and they stand as insightful treatments of an iconic figure, a sports legend whose significance transcended the boxing ring and yet whose victories in that ring instilled pride and hope in black folk while at the same time inspiring all Americans. A few years before Louis's death, sportswriter Michael Katz, then of the *New York Times,* observed that the Brown Bomber was "one of the greatest athletes in history and one of this country's greatest heroes."[31] Wright would have heartily agreed, as his essays and articles on Louis attest.

Heroes, however, were not always boxing icons like Joe Louis, Wright knew. Nor were they always activists like Louise Thompson or soldiers like Walter Garland and Milton Herndon. Often they were ordinary people who did extraordinary things. Wright devoted some of his most heartfelt writing in the *Daily Worker* to one such person, a man who emerges as one of the most memorable figures that Wright ever featured. His name was William Campbell. He was a white truck driver, and his story remains the stuff of drama. One cold afternoon in early December 1937, Campbell rescued two black children from a burning apartment building in Harlem. After saving the children, and believing that there were others still trapped inside the blazing tenement, Campbell dashed back in. He kicked in a door and went down into a smoke-filled basement in search of tenants. A back draft caught him, and he perished in the flames. His body was so badly charred that firefighters who found his corpse after they extinguished the fire mistook him for a black man. (The *New York Times* story on the fire referred to him as a "Negro.")

The children Campbell rescued were Mary Jane Gills, age two, and her one-year-old brother John.

Campbell's sacrifice took on an added poignancy with the revelation that he himself was the father of two children not much older than the two toddlers he had rescued. Campbell's widow fainted after identifying his charred body. Later, grief-stricken, she was not at all surprised that her husband would have done such a thing. He was by nature, she revealed in an interview with Wright, a compassionate, selfless man who worked among and cared about African Americans—and this at a time when such was simply not the norm for a white man from the Bronx. Admittedly, Wright was not the only journalist who covered the story. New York's two African American newspapers, the *New York Age* and the *New York Amsterdam News,* also devoted attention to the fire and the rescue (the story appeared in both papers on December 11), as did the *Times,* the *New York Herald-Tribune,* and the *New York Journal and American,* all in their December 5 editions. What distinguishes Wright's treatment of Campbell's heroism is the sensitivity, the humanity, in his approach to the tragedy. He moves beyond the standard who, what, and where of the five other papers' stories to capture (and almost dramatize) the significance underlying Campbell's fatal self-sacrifice. Wright also did what none of the other journalists did: as part of his four-article coverage of the tragedy, he reported on Campbell's funeral and even interviewed both the truck driver's widow and the mother of the children Campbell had rescued.

Ever perceptive, Wright saw Campbell's feat as more than "breaking news" or a human interest story. To Wright, Campbell exemplified the vision of life that the Communist Party—and he himself—had held up as the ideal: color-blind humanity reaching out to and aiding others in need. Here was a white man, Wright realized, who without hesitation had laid down his life to save the lives of two black children who were strangers to him. That kind of selflessness and caritas, Wright perceived, was nothing short of awe-inspiring, and he believed that Campbell's story was one worth sharing, even trumpeting, not one deserving the scant treatment Wright must have believed the other five newspapers gave it. Trumpet it is exactly what he did: Wright had four articles on Campbell published in the *Daily Worker.* These represent first-rate journalism, well worth reading, then and now.

Because of his admiration for heroes both celebrated and unsung, Wright was not a little dismayed when he learned that racial bigotry had reared its ugly head to dishonor some true American heroes—the country's black war veterans. These veterans, Wright discovered and reported on, were being excluded from southern chapters of the American Legion. Like so many before and after him, Wright was appalled that black soldiers, who had fought valiantly for the United States and its democratic ideals, should return to civilian life only to face racial bigotry and discrimination—variations of the oppression they had fought against on the battlefield abroad. In his classic autobiography *Along This Way,* first published in 1933, James Weldon Johnson reflects back on the high expectations of black veterans returning home from World War I and the ill treatment meted out to them. Johnson writes: "The colored people throughout the country were disheartened and dismayed. The great majority had trustingly felt that, because they had cheerfully done their bit in the war, conditions for them would be better. The reverse seemed to be true."[32] A year after the end of the war, race riots spearheaded by white mobs broke out in many cities across America. Johnson would call it the Red Summer. In 1937, when Wright began writing for the *Daily Worker,* conditions for black veterans had not changed much. This discrimination, which continued to poison national life, was Wright's focal point in his article headlined "10,000 Negro Vets in New York Silent, but They're Talking Up at Home."

The occasion that prompted that Wright article was the American Legion's huge gathering in New York City for its annual convention in September 1937. Over 250,000 Legionnaires from branches all over the country converged on Manhattan for what the *Herald-Tribune* called "the biggest national get-together the city has ever seen and the largest the Legion has ever staged."[33] From their arrival on Sunday, September 19, to their departure five days later, the Legionnaires, as one account in the *New York Times* put it, "turned the city up-side down."[34] Every New York newspaper gave the Legionnaires' convention heavy coverage, reporting on their every move, from their meetings and conferences to their parades, even down to their antics and pranks in Times Square. (The Legionnaires' shenanigans included deluging the midtown area's streets with paper-bag water bombs and squirt guns, dropping exploding firecrackers by the hundreds from the windows of their hotel rooms or setting them off continually in the streets, firing salute shots into the air, pulling up traffic signs out of their concrete bases and rolling them onto the trolley tracks, stopping automobiles and pouring beer into their radiators—turning midtown Manhattan into what the *Times* called "the Legionnaires' playground."[35] The highlight of the convention, all agreed, was the Legionnaires' mammoth parade, described in advance by the *Herald-Tribune* as "[o]ne of the greatest parades in New York's history."[36] Reporting after the fact, the *Herald-Tribune* called it a gargantuan spectacle that "dwarfed all of [the Legion's] previous annual parades."[37] Cascading up Fifth Avenue with three hundred thousand marchers, the parade began at 9:00 A.M. on Tuesday, September 21, and lasted for eighteen hours. Two and a half million people lined the parade's fifty-three-block route, the overwhelming majority of them staying until the end of the parade, at three on Wednesday morning. At noon, near sunset, and again around 11:00 P.M., one hundred army fighter planes staged an aerial salute to the Legionnaires as their parade flowed on, seemingly without end. Although that Tuesday was not an official holiday, it might as well have been: public schools were closed, as were all city and state offices as well as most businesses in midtown Manhattan. For eighteen hours absolutely no traffic was allowed anywhere near the parade route.

Even the African American *New York Age* reported on the convention. "New York City Welcomes Legionnaires," the newspaper's top headline read on September 25. There followed a front-page article spotlighting the presence of black Legionnaires, ten thousand of them, who attended the convention and marched in a contingent in the parade up Fifth Avenue. To its credit, the newspaper questioned the Legion's publicity director, Harold Philips, about the number of African Americans attending the convention, the treatment accorded them, and other issues. The director's reply wavered between denial of discrimination and evasion of the issue. In the same edition of the *Age*, an editorial pointed out that despite the Legion's stated commitment to "a program of Americanism" and to upholding the constitutional rights of all citizens, the organization "has not always taken a firm stand against racial and religious intolerance."[38]

But where the *New York Age* treaded lightly and diplomatically on this issue, Wright stormed in, and in his gem of an article he lays bare the racial discrimination in many of the Jim Crow units within the Legion. Wright's home state, Mississippi, is one of the worst offenders, he reveals, followed by other southern states. Through factual evidence and reliable testimony, Wright exposes the falsity of Legion officials' claim that the organization does not discriminate against black veterans. (Wright seems to have spoken with the same Legion official that the reporter from the *New York Age* did, Harold Philips, whose pat response seemed to be, "Why, there is no discrimination . . . in the American Legion."[39]) What is unique and noteworthy about Wright's story is that it dives beneath the hoopla, beneath all the chaotic merrymaking and lengthy speeches at Madison Square Garden, to reveal an ugly truth: black veterans are systematically excluded from southern American Legion posts, despite disclaimers by white Legionnaires that no such discrimination exists.

The opening of the article is a hook meant to snare the reader's attention and a near-perfect summation of Wright's general argument in the piece: "At every feast it seems that there must be a skeleton."[40] It is a delicious line. The feast in this case is the mammoth-sized convention, by turns raucous and solemn. On the other hand, the skeleton is emblematic of those guests at the feast who have been starved to death. Wright's juxtaposition of the feted and the famished—the white veterans honored and praised and the black veterans ignored and discriminated against—is a masterful stroke. Such a contrast—starvation in the midst of plenty—is at the very heart of the article. Wright interviews some of the starving guests. At first they are reluctant to open up to him out of fear, but gradually they let down their guard and pour forth their stories. What they reveal is that their participation in the war fought "to make the world safe for democracy," as Woodrow Wilson put it, has not made *their* world any safer or more democratic than it was before they risked their lives Over There. They go on to reveal to Wright their struggle to integrate various Legion posts, their efforts to aid in the ongoing Scottsboro case, their frustrations and discouragements, and even their surprise and pleasure at the relative freedom they find in New York, freedom they do not have in their hometowns in the South. It is this behind-the-scenes perspective that lifts Wright's coverage of the American Legion convention far above that of the mainstream press.

As bleak a picture it paints of the American Legion's dealings with black veterans, the article nonetheless closes on a note akin to guarded optimism. Some strides are indeed being made, Wright quotes black veterans as declaring, but the wheels of progress turn ever so slowly, too slowly, and doubt and frustration have taken root in them. The article closes with a warning to the powers that be. "These veterans," Wright concludes, "are ripe for more forthright action than many realize. . . . [D]on't forget that some of these black men seized armories in the South directly after the war to protect themselves."[41] Wright's conclusion is reminiscent of W. E. B. DuBois's oft-quoted statement in "Returning Soldiers," his editorial in the May 1919 issue of *The Crisis*: "[B]y the God of Heaven, we are cowards and jackasses if now that the war is over, we do not marshal every ounce of our brain and brawn to fight a sterner, longer, more unbending battle against the forces of hell in our own land. We return. We return from fighting. We return fighting. Make way for Democracy! We saved it in France, and by the Great Jehova, we will save it in the United States of America, or know the reason why."[42]

Although Wright disagreed with DuBois on several matters, he and DuBois were of one mind on the issue of returning soldiers, and Wright's *Daily Worker* article on the starving black doughboys at the feast is as effective in drawing attention to injustice and unrest in America as was DuBois's rousing editorial eighteen years earlier.

■

In his treatise *On Heroes, Hero-Worship, and the Heroic in History,* Victorian essayist Thomas Carlyle defines the hero as "a light of inspiration" and "spiritual Captain of the people." He further insists, "We cannot look, however imperfectly, upon [the hero] without gaining something." Throughout the course of *On Heroes,* Carlyle repeatedly emphasizes the value of the hero to society's well being. Although Wright would not have agreed with many of Carlyle's beliefs or much of his politics, he would have agreed with Carlyle on the definition and value of the hero. Nowhere is Wright's admiration for heroism and heroes more apparent than in his coverage of legendary boxing champion Joe Louis. To millions of Americans, black and white, Louis was heroism personified. In 1938, in what was then billed as the fight of the century, Louis fought and defeated German powerhouse Max Schmeling, a boxer most Americans regarded as the embodiment of fascism. Three years earlier, in a bout that was nearly as momentous, Louis had also fought and defeated the flamboyant and dangerous former heavyweight champion Max Baer. In two of his finest essays (both published in *New Masses*) and two of his best *Daily Worker* articles, Wright wrote about Louis's victories over Baer and Schmeling.

Wright also focused attention on a different kind of hero than Louis, an unsung hero who died saving children from a burning building in Harlem. He was William Campbell, a white truck driver, and in four captivating newspaper articles, Wright trumpeted Campbell's heroic rescue and elegized his tragic death in the fire.

Finally, in one of his finest pieces, Wright homes in on still another kind of heroism, that exhibited by the thousands of African American war veterans attending the gargantuan American Legion convention in New York in September 1937. He exposes the rank discrimination these former soldiers have suffered despite having served their country so honorably. Still captivating over seventy-five years after it was written, the article effectively complements Wright's pieces on Joe Louis and William Campbell.

■ ■ ■

Daily Worker, September 23, 1937

10,000 Negro Vets in N.Y. Silent, but They're Talking Up at Home

AT EVERY FEAST it seems that there must be a skeleton.

Under the roaring cheers for the Legion that went up from the sidewalks of Fifth Avenue, there was the hopeful silence of 10,000 Negro Legionnaires. They were from North Carolina, South Carolina, Pennsylvania, Maryland, Illinois, Michigan, Missouri, and many other states.

But there was none from Mississippi, the pride of the 1937 Legion. They do not issue Legion charters to Negro veterans in Mississippi. Though these black men were good enough to die for America, the state of Mississippi does not think they are good enough to belong to the Legion.

SAME IN OTHER STATES

Neither [do] Georgia, Texas, and a few other states south of the Mason-Dixon line. Even some of those southern states that issue charters, do so meagerly, hence in most southern states but one or two Negro posts exist.

But just try to get some information on this from the publicity offices of the Legion. You are told very blandly:

"Why, there is no discrimination with respect to race, creed, or color in the American Legion."

Since the officials won't say anything, let's talk to some of the Negro Legionnaires standing up and down Lenox Avenue.

These men are cordial but cagey. They are from the South and they do not want to say anything that can be used against them when they go back home. They have in their own fashion worked out a relationship with the white people of their respective vicinities and they want to keep that relationship unless they know that something better can be done. They are hard-headed and sensible.

And he's courteous; first he'll give you a secret handshake, perhaps, the pass-sign in some fraternal organization. Then he places himself at your service.

"What about hospital facilities for Negro Vets in your state?"

TOUCHY SUBJECT

He looks at you sharply. That's a touchy question. He wants to talk with you and tell you the truth, but he doesn't know who you are.

"They're fine," he says. "They're fine, sir!"

The conversation is changed and he tells you what a fine thing it is to belong to the Legion. With a quiet joy he tells how Negro vets long to place themselves at the service of their country in peace or war.

The conversation again turns to discrimination in the veteran hospitals in the South. You learn that sometimes a sick Negro vet has to be shipped North for treatment, for the one general hospital in the South at Tuskegee, where they are admitted, is not adequate.

LETS LOOSE

He is talking very freely now. "You know what we did in Baltimore? We passed a resolution for the freedom of the Scottsboro boys. . ." [ellipses in original]

But quickly he again changes the subject and talks of other things. That's the psychology of the Negro vet in the South. They resist, but it's done skillfully. They can't lay themselves open to attack. Their protest work must be done under the cloak of loyalty.

"First of all," he explains, "we must be good Legionnaires. Then we make our demands and resolutions and take them to our officers. Of late, they have been acting on them.

SLOW WORK

"In the last few joint meetings we had in the state of Maryland there was no discrimination. Not even in the city hotels. It's slow work, but we're making headway."

In talking with several others you learn that it was only after a stiff fight that Negro vets were allowed to join mixed posts in Rochester and Syracuse, New York. You learn, further, that Negro doctors are not allowed to practice in Northern hospitals for vets.

But, despite all this, the 10,000 black vets are having a good time in Harlem. This traveling from city to city each year to attend the Legion convention is educating them. Many of them have little formal schooling, and their trip across the "pond" in 1917 taught them lots and these trips to conventions are teaching them more.

NO SEGREGATION IN N.Y.

The fact that they can ride around in New York on subways without being segregated is not lost on them. That the Negroes in New York can vote and they can't is a challenge.

They have joined the Legion because it's the most influential organization which an ex-service man can belong to. Yet they know that it does not answer all their problems. When they say, "We're making slow headway" their voices carry a doubt.

These vets are ripe for more forthright action than many realize. The idealistic phrases on their lips are there because that's what they believe the public wants here.

But don't forget that some of these black men seized armories in the South directly after the war to protect themselves. When they see their way clear, when they have before them a well-worked plan of action, they'll act. ■

Daily Worker, AUGUST 30, 1937

Fight Parties in Harlem

HARLEM IS ALL PRIMED for another Joe Louis victory tonight. Up and down the broadwalks of Lenox and Seventh Avenues are pictures of the champion which read: JOE LOUIS, OUR CHAMPION. Due to lack of money, however, betting for the most part is slow; but what is missing in cash is more than made up in enthusiasm.

Among the workers several parties are scheduled at union and unemployed headquarters. The Harlem Bureau of the *Daily Worker* is holding a Joe Louis Radio Party at 415 Lenox Ave. at 9:15 P.M. The moment Joe's hand is lifted in victory, the entire audience will be mobilized to sell the Joe Louis victory issue. The admission is free and refreshments will be served. The YCL is also holding parties.

Many Negroes have journeyed from out of town to see their first heavyweight champion in a quarter of a century defend his crown. And the kids, though they don't have the money to get into the Yankee Stadium, are rehearsing the fight on the sidewalks. Joe Louis' snaky left jab has been imitated a million times by Negro boys in their 'teens.

Harlem for the most part likes the treatment the *Daily Worker* has accorded Joe. They can't forget that when a large part of the press turned thumbs down on Joe because of his defeat at the hands of Schmeling, the *Daily* stood by him. They refer to the *Daily* as "Joe's friend." And they are looking forward to the next time he meets Schmeling. ■

Daily Worker, DECEMBER 6, 1937

Harlem, East Side Honor Hero Who Died in Rescue of Negroes

TWO HOMES—ONE NEGRO AND THE OTHER WHITE; one in Harlem and the other on the East Side—were darkened with anxiety, want, and grief last night as two families took stock of their losses in the fire that gutted a fire-trap tenement in Harlem at 146 W. 121st St. Saturday afternoon.

In the bare front room of Mrs. Mary Campbell's home, 339 E. 45th St., the light of a single candle illuminated a porcelain crucifix over the coffin of her son, William Campbell, the truck driver who gave his life while rescuing two Negro babies.

Campbell's wife and her two children, William, Jr., 3, and Loretta, 4, his grandmother, Mrs. Nana Flynn, 65, and a host of other relatives and friends sat with the body all day yesterday and last night. Their feelings were torn between the loved one they had lost and the problem of his wife's and children's future existence.

HARLEM FAMILY PENNILESS

This morning at 10 A.M. William Campbell's funeral will be held at the St. Agnes Catholic Church, 141 E. 43rd St.

Meanwhile, in Harlem Mrs. Lillian Gills, at 148 W. 121st St., the Negro mother of the two rescued children [two-year-old Mary Jane and one-year-old John], sits in a two-room slum apartment, the air of which is foul with gas leakings and the floors of which are damp from sewage seepings.

About her are her four [older] children, James, 7; Rosetta, 6; Eugene, 4; and Martha, 4.

All they own in the world is what they have upon their backs. This temporary shelter was offered them by kind neighbors and soon, because they have no money and because the place is unfit for human habitation, they must move.

LOSE EVERYTHING

The husband, Eugene Gills, is a plumber and makes $12 a week. "We lost absolutely everything we had in the fire," Mrs. Gillis said. "On what my husband makes we've got to eat, get a new place to stay, new clothes, new everything. And how can we do it?

"My heart is with the wife of that man who was killed saving my children. But I've been so hard pressed for food and shelter all day today and yesterday that I've not had much time really to think of them. That's the way our life is."

Mrs. Gills was away from home when the fire broke out and arrived back just in time to assist in helping to drag her children from the flames.

PLAN BENEFIT

The hearts of Harlem's workers were touched by Campbell's heroism. Last Night the Women's Commission of the Harlem Division of the Communist Party arranged delegations to visit the home of Campbell's mother and offer their sympathy and help. Also plans are on foot to organize a benefit affair for the mother and children. The Commission hopes to involve Harlem churches, clubs, and other organizations in a drive to memorialize Campbell's heroic deed.

The suggestion has come forward that the City Council should be petitioned to pension the Campbell family.

Audley Moore, chairman of the Women's Commission, announced yesterday that floral wreaths will be sent to the Campbell home and to the St. Agnes Church.

AID FOR FAMILY

The *Amsterdam News,* Harlem's Negro newspaper, stated yesterday that they also will throw the weight of their editorial opinion behind an effort to aid the stricken Campbell family.

Sharing honors with Campbell is Curtis Ellison, Negro chauffeur of Dr. Binga H. Dismond [Henry Binga Dismond], who, it was learned belatedly, worked side by side with Campbell in carrying people to safety out of the fire.

It was Curtis Ellison who herded the 30 odd men, women, and children to the roof of the building at 146 W. 121st St. after Campbell had perished in the basement.

On New York's East Side William Campbell's attitude and opinion of the Negro people [were] re-echoed by many who paid tribute to his heroic deed. Campbell's mother told of how her son would bring his fellow Negro workers into her home and give them food and coffee.

Campbell was a member of the International Brotherhood of Teamsters, Local 553, A. F. of L. Because of arrears of dues, however, he is not entitled to death benefits. ■

Daily Worker, December 6, 1937

"He Died By Them"—Hero's Widow Tells of Rescue of Negroes

HE DID NOT PAUSE TO THINK OF THE COLOR OF THEIR SKINS; he saw a building burning and heard cries of distress. He stopped his coal truck, grabbed a hand fire-extinguisher from the cab and rushed into the building. He succeeded in dragging to safety two Negro babies, Mary Jane Gills, age two, and John Gills, age one.

He went into the building again to see who else was in danger; he groped his way through the smoke from one blazing room to the other. He lost his way, and when the fire department put out the blaze, his charred body was found sprawled amid the debris on a sub-basement floor.

That was the end of William Campbell, 204 E. 36th St., age 34, a white worker, a truck driver, a union member, a husband, and the father of two small children.

PLIGHT OF HIS OWN FAMILY

Sunday evening, in the front room of his mother's home at 339 E. 45th St., Mrs. Agnes Campbell and her two children sit about William Campbell's coffin and try to understand. For them the future is a blank wall. William Campbell, like all workers, Negro and white, left no money for food or rent behind. Loretta, age four, and William, Jr., age three, ask their mother every hour:

"What happened to papa?"

"Well," Mrs. Agnes Campbell told her friends, "he drove a coal truck for ten years in Harlem and he liked the Negro people. He died by them."

That's the story of William Campbell's heroism, a heroism which has resulted in a tragic plight for his family.

Mrs. Lillian Gills, who lived in the burned building at 146 W. 121st St., was still too dazed Sunday to tell what she thought of the "white chauffeur who saved my children."

CAN'T TALK OF FIRE

And the other Negro families who live in the block are a little afraid to talk of William Campbell at all. The hordes of Harlem cops and detectives, unable and unwilling to believe that a white worker would give his life to rescue Negroes from a fire, have questioned them to no end about Campbell's presence in the neighborhood.

When pressed for information, they said:

"I can't talk about the fire. You'll have to go to the police station."

An examination of the police records at the West 123rd St. Station revealed that the heroism and the tragedy had been listed officially as "Suspicious."

But James Stevens, William Campbell's friend who lives at 204 E. 36th St., upstairs above the Campbell family, has no difficulty in understanding what happened to his friend.

"He drove a coal truck in Harlem for years. He was always talking about how the Negro people lived," said Stevens. "He was a man forgetful of himself. If he saw someone in danger, he went to them. They could be Negroes, Chinese, anybody. He drew no color line.

"I was shocked to hear about his death, but when I heard how he died I knew that it was he. He was a man who would do just that—die trying to save others."

Stevens told of how he and his friend had planned to celebrate Christmas and New Year's together. But what he is concerned about now most is what will Campbell's wife and children do.

"They are stripped," he said. "They had but little with William. He was driving part time, and not making much. I don't know what they'll do now."

Eye-witness accounts of the rescue and tragedy claim that Campbell was driving along 121st St. around noon Saturday when he saw the building ablaze. Some of the tenants were trying to save themselves by climbing out of windows. The building, a five-story fire-trap, housed in its basement the Pee Wa Wa Democratic Club, in which the fire is said to have originated.

So badly burned was Campbell's body that his employer, Albert Seigler, of the East and West Transportation Co., had to come to Harlem to identify his body. Mrs. Campbell collapsed when informed of the death of her husband.

ANOTHER VICTIM

The fire department was called by Curtis Ellison, a chauffeur employed by Dr. H. Binga Desmond [Dismond], 245 W. 139th St.

Harlem's infamous housing conditions, "the shame of New York," [have] claimed yet another victim, this time a worker who lived in a tenement district on New York's East Side.

Campbell's experience as a truck driver in Harlem had been carried back to his former friends on the East Side for a number of years. And some of the things by which they are remembering him now are his sayings about Harlem: "The Negroes are human beings. They are good people. We ought to treat them equally." ■

Daily Worker, DECEMBER 8, 1937

Harlem Pays Tribute to Truck Driver Who Rescued Negro Children in Fire

PARTIALLY OBSCURED by a veil of this winter's first heavy snow, the pearl-grey coffin of William Campbell was taken yesterday morning from St. Agnes Catholic Church, 141 E. 43rd St., and, escorted by family, friends, and a delegation of Negro workers from Harlem, was driven to a burial ground in Long Island.

This was the end of William Campbell, heroic white truck driver who laid down his life last Saturday to save two Negro babies from burning to death in a Harlem fire.

A few minutes before the funeral procession started, a Catholic priest stood amid a maze of flickering candles and departing from the Latin ritual, declared to the Negro and white mourners:

DELEGATION PLEDGES AID

"This man's death was so exceptional that I feel called upon to say something in English. 'Greater love than this hath no man—that he lays down his life for his friend.'"

The humble Irish-Catholic home of William Campbell's mother, Mrs. Mary Campbell, 339 E. 45th St., was crowded last night as friends, Negro and white, stood by the wife and children through the final hour of their wake.

At 10 P.M. last night a delegation of Harlem workers, headed by Audley Moore, chairman of the Women's Commission of the Communist Party, called upon the family and pledged aid and sympathy. The delegation was received with a veritable demonstration of joy.

"It means a lot to us just to know that the people of Harlem understand," Mrs. Agnes Campbell said.

Not only was the offer of solidarity wholeheartedly accepted, but Mrs. Agnes Campbell insisted that the delegation accompany them to the funeral mass and to the burial ground.

Earlier in the evening the Upper Harlem Section of the Communist Party sent Mrs. Agnes Campbell and her two children the following telegram of condolence:

> Please accept condolences from the Upper Harlem Section of the Communist Party. We recognize in this heroic feat an act that will cement the brotherhood of all working men, a brotherhood which we hold dear and work towards.
>
> The Negro and white workers of Harlem pledge further aid to you and your family.
>
> The Upper Harlem Section of the
> Communist Party Memorial Committee

Meanwhile, the Harlem Branch of the Workers' Alliance is investigating the Negro families who were driven from their homes by the fire last Saturday. Immediate steps are being taken to obtain aid for them through the ERB stations.

Late yesterday afternoon the formation of a William Campbell Memorial Committee was under way headed by Audley Moore.

The Communist Party announced that it would call upon its various Harlem branches to issue collection lists to raise funds for the stricken family.

Section 24 of the Communist Party, 12th A.D., which is situated on the East Side, took steps also to aid the Campbells.

BRANCHES RAISE FUNDS

Florence Cook, administrative secretary, declared in an interview with the *Daily Worker* that:

"We have already sent a delegation of our workers to call upon the family. Also we intend to get them ERB aid. Meanwhile, we are urging our branches to raise funds to tide them over their difficult period."

The Women's Commission of the Communist Party is entertaining several suggestions for possible action to interest various public and civic agencies in the plight of the Campbell family.

The Harlem Tenants' Association announced yesterday that it would conduct a sweeping investigation into mounting violations of the Multiple Dwelling Law. It is known that the burned building at 146 W. 121st St. had no fire escapes of any sort. It was for this reason that the firemen had to take some 30-odd men, women and children from the roofs and windows with the aid of ladders.

It was also learned yesterday that Curtis Ellison, the Negro chauffeur of Dr. Binga [Dismond], 245 W. 139th St., who worked alongside of Campbell in rescuing people from the doomed building Saturday, has behind him a unique record of voluntary fire-fighting. He fought forest fires in Connecticut and left behind him a reputation for conspicuous bravery.

Ellison was complimented by the fire marshalls for the part he played in helping to save children in Saturday's fire. ■

Daily Worker, DECEMBER 18, 1937

Plan Memorial for Heroic Truck Driver

"A HAPPY CHRISTMAS AS A MEMORIAL GIFT to the Campbells!" was the slogan adopted by the Harlem Campbell Memorial Committee, which met yesterday afternoon and drafted plans for a memorial meeting and a Christmas gift for Mrs. Agnes Campbell and her two fatherless children.

Mrs. Campbell is the widow of the heroic truck driver who lost his life in Harlem after rescuing two Negro babies in a tenement house blaze.

The committee met at St. Martin's Episcopal Church, 122nd St. and Lenox Ave., with Miss Audley Moore, chairman of the Women's Commission of the Harlem Division of the Communist Party, acting as chairman.

The memorial meeting was set for Sunday, Jan. 16, at 4 P.M. at the St. Martin Church. Rev. John W. Robinson, pastor, will preside.

SIGNED BY RANDOLPH

A call was issued which was signed by A. Philip Randolph, president of the Brotherhood of Sleeping Car Porters, and read in part:

"A group of broad-minded Negro citizens have come together for the purpose of holding a memorial meeting to raise funds for helping this lonely mother and . . . children whose father died in Harlem in a fire on Dec. 4 saving Negro children. Won't you do your bit to dispel the gloom and sorrow from this home."

Among other organizations cooperating are the Harlem Branch of the International Labor Defense; the Harlem Division of the Workers' Alliance; the Hotel and Restaurant Employees International Union and Bartenders Alliance of America, Local 386; and the Mount Olivet Church.

Miss Moore reported to the committee that Mrs. Agnes Campbell and her two children paid a visit to the one-room home of Mrs. Lillian Gills last Friday.

Mrs. Campbell declared that she wanted her children to know the children her husband died to save. ■

Daily Worker, NOVEMBER 29, 1937

Herndon to Be Honored at Rally Sunday

NEGRO LEADERS YESTERDAY paid warm tribute to Milton Herndon, who was killed in action in Spain, and urged the Negro people to honor the memory of a brave and true fighter of our own.

A. Philip Randolph, president of the Brotherhood of Sleeping Car Porters and president of the National Negro Congress, threw his support behind the Herndon memorial meeting scheduled for Sunday, November 28 at the St. James Presbyterian Church, 141st St. and St. Nicholas Ave. at 3 P.M.

"I think the Negro people should honor Brother Milton Herndon for the role he played in fighting for Spanish democracy, a role which was not only in the interests of Spanish democracy but world democracy."

Audley Moore, chairman of the Women's Commission of the Upper Harlem Section of the Communist Party, declared:

"I can think of no finer tribute to Milton Herndon than build the Communist Party which fights for that democracy for which Milton gave his life in Spain.

"It will be a demonstration for a united struggle for the passage of the Anti-Lynching Bill and for the realization of the demands of the Negro people."

A. W. Berry, organizer of the Upper Harlem Section of the Communist Party declared:

"Sunday's memorial meeting will more than pay homage to Comrade Herndon and the other heroes who gave and are willing to give their lives for Spanish democracy." ■

Daily Worker, JUNE 22, 1938

Why the Eyes of the People Turn to the Ring for the Title Bout at Yankee Stadium Tonight

AT 10 O'CLOCK TONIGHT Joe Louis, America's second Negro World's Heavyweight Champion will climb through the ropes in the Yankee Stadium to the tune of a million dollar gate and 80,000 fight fans and for

15 rounds will try to lay the ghost of Max Schmeling, his challenger, and retain his crown as king of boxers.

Knocked out by the German challenger two years ago in the same ring, Joe Louis says that he will end the fight by a knockout in two rounds. Statements issued by Max Schmeling indicate that he is just as confident of victory.

PRESS SLURS ABILITY

Joe's defeat at the hands of Schmeling two years ago marred one of the most brilliant and dazzling careers in the history of boxing. Perhaps the defeat of no fighter in American history came with such a shock to the public. Due to quarrels among promoters, Louis was given a chance at the title last year, and [he] snatched it from the aging Braddock in Chicago in a bout of thrilling fighting.

Despite the fact that Joe has defeated many men who beat Schmeling, many quarters, and particularly the Nazi press in America and Germany, [have] referred to him as the "so-called champion." Aggressively the Nazi press has sought to symbolize Joe's defeat as a proof of alleged "Negro Inferiority."

After training a solid month at Pompton Lakes in the hills of New Jersey, Joe says he is ready; and Max Schmeling, after training a solid month at Speculator, N.Y. also say he is ready. Both fighters have been examined and certified by doctors as to their physical fitness and the bait to make each man do his brutal best to win is high; for Joe, if he wins $400,000, the retention of the championship, and the right to continue as idol of the American boxing public; for Schmeling, if he wins—$200,000, the championship, and it is rumored that he is to have a place in Hitler's cabinet as a director of physical education of German youth.

EACH A SYMBOL

Joe's from the sun-filled fields of Alabama, the state of the Scottsboro case; Schmeling's from Hitler's Germany. Alabama's tough on Negro and white workers and Joe and his family left there years ago. Germany's tough on all workers. Jews and women, but Schmeling, a good Nazi, likes it and returns there as fast as he can soon after each fight.

In the popular mind the two men have been made to typify and symbolize much more than just two prizefighters. Max Schmeling gave to the newspapers one of the most unsportsmanlike statements ever issued from a fighter's training camp. He claimed that it would be easy for him to whip Joe because (1) Joe's a Negro and Negroes never forget beatings, (2) Joe's afraid of him and (3) he will enter the ring with a "psychological edge" over the Negro.

PUBLICITY MILL AT WORK

On the other hand millions of Americans of all shades of opinion and who otherwise would not be concerned are rooting for Joe to "keep the title from going across the Atlantic to fascist Germany, where Hitler will use it for his own bloody ends." Joe himself has been in a dull rage for two years over the terrific beating he took from Schmeling. He wants to prove in convincing style that: "Last time was just a mistake. This time I'm coming out fighting with all I got." If Louis keeps his work it should be a great fight, for he's "got plenty" in both of his fists. All the things which make such fights a financial success have been done: wild rumors have been peddled to the public; every public figure who would give a statement has picked either Louis or Schmeling; Gov. Frank Murphy of Michigan is among those who have sent their greetings to Joe; the relative merits of each fighter from the size of the pupils of his eyes down to the manner in which he shuffles his feet when he walks have been mulled over in a million conversations; and a daily report of each fighter's process in training has been served up.

NEGROES LOOK TO JOE

The movies will shoot it; the radios will carry it; the newspapers will print pictures and carry columns of print. In every city and village of America millions will gather around their radios or in front of newspaper offices and follow blow-by-blow descriptions of the fight. In each section of the country, among each racial group, there are various reasons for wishing Louis or Schmeling to win.

Throughout America millions of Negroes are looking upon Joe to uphold the honor of his race. Because boxing is simple and the desire to knock out a man is easy to understand, millions are pinning their submerged racial and social hopes upon two men in a ring whaling away at each other.

No great issue, of course, will be settled, no matter who wins; but Joe's winning with a hundred thousand eyes watching and millions of ears listening will be bolstering to many a sagging ideal among 12,000,000 Negroes whose lives have long been misrepresented and vilified in America.

Visits to Joe training camp at Pompton Lakes reveal throngs of curious standing around for hours in a state of deep awe waiting for just one glimpse of the champion. They were good, simple people and when the champion appeared a hush fell upon them and they stared.

They were working people wanting terribly for something to feel deeply about. Something to be loyal to, and a prizefighter such as Joe Louis, young, clean, sportsmanlike, is comprehensible. They can take him into their lives because he is an idol and occupies in the public's mind a place such as they never can.

Many people will deplore the wild elation of millions over a prizefight; but against the background of deadening cynicism, indifference and money-grabbing such wholesome, enthusiasm is bracing. It signifies, if nothing else, that there lies in the simple heart of the masses of people a great capacity for loyalty, devotion and exultation, all of which can be channelized toward meaningful and historic ends.

Under all the excitement it is well to remember that the majority of all prizefighters come from the working class; their capacity to fight stemming from an early life of hard work in steel and iron foundries, coal mines, factories and fields. ■

New Masses, JULY 5, 1938

High Tide in Harlem: Joe Louis as a Symbol of Freedom

THE COLOSSAL BOWL OF SEVENTY THOUSAND hazy faces, an oval-shaped tableau compounded of criss-crossed beams of light and shadow, waited almost in silence for the gong to sound that would start the Louis-Schmeling million-dollar fight. The gaze of the seventy thousand eyes was centered was centered on the "squared circle," a single diadem-like spot of canvas lit to blinding whiteness under the intense glare of overhead floodlights. So dwarfed was the ring by the mammoth stadium that it seemed that each man and woman was straining forward to peer at a colorful puppet show.

The Louis-Schmeling fight for the heavy-weight championship of the world at the Yankee Stadium was one of the greatest dramas of make-believe ever witnessed in America, a drama which manipulated the common symbols and impulses in the minds and bodies of millions of people so effectively as to put to shame our professional play-wrights, our O'Neills, our Lawsons, and our Caldwells. Promoter Mike Jacobs, prompted purely by commercial motives, has accidentally won the rare right, whether he wants to claim it or not, of wearing the purple robes customarily reserved for Euripides and Sophocles.

Each of the seventy thousand who had so eagerly jammed his way into the bowl's steel tiers under the open sky had come already emotionally conditioned as to the values that would triumph if his puppet won. Attached to each puppet, a white puppet and a black puppet, was a configuration of social images whose intensity and clarity had been heightened through weeks of skillful and constant agitation; social images whose emotional appeal could evoke attitudes tantamount to two distant ways of life in the world today.

Whichever puppet went down the Greek route to defeat that night would leave the path clear for the imperious sway of the puppet emerging victorious would be the symbol of a fond wish gratified, would feed the starved faith of men caught in the mesh of circumstances.

Joe Louis, the black puppet who wore black trunks, was the betting favorite; but that was no indication as to how much actual sentiment there was for him among the seventy thousand spectators, for men like to bet on winners. And, too, just how much sentiment there was for Max Schmeling, the white puppet who wore purple trunks, no one, perhaps, will ever know; for now that the violent drama is ended the backers of the loser do not want to parade their disappointment for the scorn of others. But the two puppets were dissimilar enough in "race, creed, and previous condition of servitude" as to make their partisans wax militantly hopeful.

But out beyond the walls of the stadium were twelve million Negroes to whom the black puppet symbolized the living refutation of the hatred spewed forth daily over radios, in newspapers, in movies, and in books about their lives. Day by day, since their alleged emancipation, they have watched a picture of themselves being painted as lazy, stupid, and diseased. In helpless horror they have suffered the attacks and exploitation which followed in the wake of their being branded as "inferiors." True, hundreds of thousands of these Negroes would have preferred that that refutation could have been made in some form other than pugilism; but so effectively and completely have they been isolated and restricted in vocation that they been rarely have had the opportunity to participate in the meaningful processes of America's national life. Jim Crowed in the army and navy, barred from many trades and professions, excluded from commerce and finance, relegated to menial positions in government, segregated residentially, denied the right of franchise for the most part; in short, forced to live a separate and impoverished life, they were glad for even the meager acceptance of their humanity implied in the championship of Joe Louis.

Visits to Joe Louis' training camp revealed throngs of Negroes standing around in a state of a deep awe, waiting for just one glimpse of their champion. They were good, simple hearted people, longing deeply for something of their own to be loyal to.

When Joe appeared, a hush fell upon them and they stared. They took Joe into their hearts because he was a public idol and was respectfully enshrined in the public's imagination in a way they knew they would never be.

But because Joe's a Negro, even though he has to his credit a most enviable list of victories, there have been constant warnings issued by the Bilbos and Ellenders from south of the Mason-Dixon Line as to the wisdom of allowing a Negro to defeat a white man in public. The reactionary argument ran that such spectacles tended to create in Negroes too much pride and made them "intractable."

Naturally, Max Schmeling's victory over Louis two years ago was greeted with elation in reactionary quarters. A close study of Louis' stance, which revealed that he could be hit, together with a foul blow delivered after the bell, enabled the German boxer to win. Louis' defeat came as a shock to the boxing world and provided material for countless conversations and speculations. It was taken for granted that the second-rate Schmeling's defeat of the then reigning champion, the aging Braddock, was but a matter of time. But due to squabbles among promoters, Louis, not Schmeling, fought Braddock for championship and won the title by a knockout in a thrilling bout Chicago. Immediately the Nazi press, in America and in Germany, launched a campaign of slurs against Louis, dubbing him the "so-called champion," and declaring that Schmeling's prior victory over Louis was proof of "Negro Inferiority." Schmeling boasted to the press that it would be easy for him to defeat the Negro again because (1) Negroes never forgot beatings, (2) his mere "white" presence would be enough to throw fear into Louis' heart, and (3) he would enter the ring with a "psychological edge" over the Negro. An open friend of Hitler and an avowed supporter of the Nazis, Schmeling caught the fancy of many reactionary Americans, plus the leaders of Nazi Germany, fascist Italy, Japan, and even certain circles in England.

To bolster the aims of the forces of fascism, Schmeling's victory was interpreted to mean the ability to the "Aryan race to out-think inferior races." The logical implication of such a line of reasoning was that all Negroes, colonial people, and small nations were inherently backward, physically cowardly, a drag upon the rest of civilization, and should be conquered and subjected for the benefit of mankind.

But when faced with this specious proposition, the common people instinctively revolted. They knew that the majority of all prizefighters came from the so-called "backward people," that is, the working class; their capacity to fight stemming from an early life of toil in steel and iron foundries, coal mines, factories, and fields. Consequently, in his fight against Schmeling, Louis carried the good wishes of even the poor whites of the Deep South, something unparalleled in the history of America.

The appearance of the white puppet sent the crowd into frenzy. The black puppet's ovation seemed incidental. The ring was cleared and the fight was on. The entire seventy thousand rose as one man. At the beginning of the fight there was a wild shriek which gradually died as the seconds flew. What was happening was so stunning that even cheering was out of place. The black puppet, contrary to all Nazi racial laws, was punching the white puppet so rapidly that the eye could not follow the blows. It was not really a fight, it was an act of revenge, of dominance, of complete mastery. The black puppet glided from his corner and simply wiped his feet on the white puppet's face. The black puppet was contemptuous, swift; his victory was complete, unquestionable, decisive; his blows must have jarred the marrow not only in the white puppet's but in Hitler's own bones.

In Harlem, that area of a few square blocks in upper Manhattan where a quarter of a million Negroes are forced to live through an elaborate connivance among landlords, merchants, and politicians, a hundred thousand black people surged out of taprooms, flats, restaurants, and filled the streets and sidewalks, like the Mississippi River overflowing in flood time. With their faces to the night sky, they filled their lungs with air and let out a scream of joy that seemed would never end, and a scream that seemed to come from untold reserves of strength. They wanted to make a noise comparable to the happiness bubbling in their hearts, but they were poor and had nothing. So they went to the garbage pails and got tin cans; they went to their kitchens and got tin pots, pans, washboards, wooden boxes, and took possession of the streets. They shouted, sang, laughed, yelled, blew paper horns, clasped hands, and formed weaving snake-lines, whistled, sounded sirens, and honked auto horns. From the windows of the tall, dreary tenements torn scarps of newspaper floated down. With the reiteration that evoked a hypnotic atmosphere, they chanted with eyes half-closed, heads lilting in unison, legs and shoulders moving and touching;

"Ain't you glad?"

Knowing full well the political effect of Louis' victory on the popular mind the world over, thousand yelled:

"Heil Louis!"

It was Harlem's mocking taunt to fascist Hitler's boast of the superiority of "Aryans" over the other races. And they ridiculed the Nazi salute of the outstretched palm by throwing up their own dark ones to show how little they feared and thought of the humbug of fascist ritual.

With no less than a hundred thousand participating, it was the largest and most spontaneous political demonstration ever seen in Harlem and marked the highest tide of popular political enthusiasm ever witnessed among American Negroes.

Negro voices called fraternally to Jewish-looking faces in passing autos;

"I bet all Jews are happy tonight!"

Men, women, and children gathered in thick knots and did the Big Apple, the Lindy Hop, the Truck—Harlem's gesture of defiance to the high cost of food, high rent, and misery. These ghetto-dwellers, under the stress of the joy of one of their own kind having wiped out the stain of defeat and having thrown the lie of " inferiority" into the teeth of the fascist, threw off restraint and fear.

Each time a downtown auto slowed, it became covered with Joe Louis rooters, and the autos looked like clusters of black ripe grapes. A bus stopped and at once became filled with laughing throngs who "forgot" to pay their fares; children clambered up its tall sides and crawled over the hoods and fenders.

It was the celebration of Louis' victory over Carnera, Baer, Pastor, Farr, and Braddock all rolled into one. Ethiopian and American flags fluttered. Effigies of Schmeling chalked with the swastika were dragged through the streets.

Then, nobody knows from where and nobody bothered to ask, there appeared on the surface of the sea of people white placards hurling slogans of defiance at fascist pretensions and calling upon native lovers of democracy to be true to democratic ideals. Oust Hitler's Spies and Agents; Pass the Anti-Lynching Bill; Down with Hitler and Mussolini; Alabama Produced Joe Louis; Free the Scottsboro Boys; Democracies Must Fight Fascism Everywhere.

Carry the dream on for yourself; lift it out of the trifling guise of a prizefight celebration and supply the social and economic details and you have the secret dynamics of proletarian aspiration. The eyes of these people were bold that night. Their fear of property, of the armed police fell away. There was in their chant a hunger deeper than that for bread as they marched along. In their joy they were feeling an impulse which only the oppressed can feel to the full. They wanted to feel that their expanding feelings were not limited; that the earth was theirs as much as anybody else's; that they did not have to live by proscription in one corner of it; that they could go where they wanted to and do what they wanted to, eat and live where they wanted to, like others. They wanted to own things in common and do things in common. They wanted a holiday. ■

Daily Worker, NOVEMBER 27, 1937

Honor Herndon at Harlem Rally Sunday

SOME TWENTY NEGRO LEADERS AND LIBERALS of all races, together with thousands of Harlem workers, will pay tribute to the memory of Milton Herndon, heroic brother of Angelo Herndon, who was killed in Spain on the Saragosa [Zaragoza] Front in October, at a memorial meeting tomorrow at 3:15 P.M. at the St. James Presbyterian Church, 141st St. and St. Nicholas Ave.

Principal among the speakers will be Lieutenant Walter Garland, former commander of the American Training Base in Loyalist Spain, who will make his first public appearance in Harlem since his return from the Spanish front.

During the past week the Herndon Memorial Committee has been the rallying point for several organizations whose representatives will be present at the meeting Sunday, among which are the Workers' Alliance, the Uptown Branch of the City Projects Council, the Young Communist League, the Universal Negro Improvement Association, the Chinese Hand Laundry Alliance, the Italian Workers Club, and the Communist Party.

Outstanding among the individuals who will speak are the Rev. Williams Lloyd Imes, pastor of St. James Presbyterian Church; Capt. A. L. King of the Universal Negro Improvement Association; Lillian Gaskin, executive member of the American Labor Party; the Rev. David M. Corry, of the American Society of Church History; Tito Nunzio, secretary of the Italian Anti-Fascist Committee; Mario Lamar, member of the Spanish Anti-Fascist Committee; J. H. Lin, editor of "China Today"; Gladys Stoner, finance secretary of the National Negro Congress; Joseph Thompson, president of the Harlem International Labor Defense; William Fitzgerald of the Upper Harlem Section of the Communist Party; the Rev. A. C. Powell, Jr., pastor of the Abyssinian Baptist Church; and Dr. James J. Jones, chairman of the Negro People's Medical Committee for Aid to Republican Spain.

Dorothy Height, of the YWCA, and Ethlin Hurd, of the Urban League, are among the sponsors of the meeting. ■

Daily Worker, June 24, 1938

How He Did It, and Oh—Where Were Hitler's Pagan Gods?

Time: when fascist Hitler and his world allies of reaction are trying to conquer all mankind by force of arms and intimidation.

Scene: an oval sea of faces of all races, criss-crossed by powerful floodlights, and centered about a snow-white squared circle.

Place: New York City, where a foul nest of Nazi spies just been routed.

Characters: Joe Louis, Negro Boxing Champion, once defeated by Schmeling, and who is circumscribed because of his color as to where he must eat and live despite his success the ring; and Max Schmeling, friend of Hitler, who believes that his mere "white" presence is enough to throw fear into the heart of a Negro.

Quick as a panther, Joe was out from his corner with the sound of the bell. There was a brief lull during which each fighter looked the other over; it was here that it seemed the entire fight hung in balance. But if there was any doubt which way the battle was going, it was dispelled when Joe shot two straight left jabs to Schmeling's chin and followed them with a blunt, vicious left hook that must have, if only slightly, jarred Hitler's Charlie Chaplin mustache in faraway fascist Germany.

Schmeling must have thought that he was facing one of the Soviet Union's newest army tanks, for he backed away with amazement showing all over his face. But Joe was razor-edged and mad; he followed his challenger. Maybe he was thinking of those countless jibes and taunts let loose upon him for having let a man like this once beat him. He let fly a shower of fistic-destruction, included in which was a nerve-shattering right to Schmeling's chin.

Then Joe leaped back just in time to avoid an over-hand right, which just grazed his jaw. It was the only real blow Schmeling threw during the fight; the Nazi must have thought Joe was afraid of him, because he advanced for the first time in the fight, only to take one of Joe's left chops on his chin.

Again Joe's left bounced twice off Schmeling's face and still another right found the fascist chin. Maybe Hitler's Aryan Gods saved Schmeling from the next whizzing left hook, but all the pagan Gods of Dr. Goebbels could not have saved him from the next left hook, which staggered Schmeling and rocked his very senses.

Hitler's wilted pet looked like a soft piece of molasses candy left out in the sun; he dropped over the ropes, his eyes glassy, his chin nestling in a strand of rope, his widely-heralded powerful right arm hanging ironically useless.

DYING SCREAM

The fight really ended right there. But no one intervened. Joe swept over a right hook to the ribs; but Schmeling's limp body was sagging and caught it in the side; the backbone being crushed with the impact.

Schmeling cried out in agony and the look on his face indicated that he wanted no more of this. Relentlessly Joe plowed forward once again, but the referee pushed him away.

The referee wiped Schmeling's gloves of resin and sent him toward the champion, whose right again clanged against the Nordic chin.

Joe lashed still another right and Schmeling fell like an ox, to all fours. Totally senseless now, the Hitlerite rose at the count of one, had his gloves adjusted and advanced yet again, only to receive one more thunderbolt right to the jaw.

A wet white towel flapped in the glare of the lights, the Nazi sign of "quits," and the fight was over. It was not really a fight; it was a rout. Joe went out and put his feet in Schmeling's face and then turned his back. Schmeling's bluff was as thoroughly called and exposed as was Hitler's during the recent Czechoslovakian crisis. Never in all of his fights has Joe appeared more (according to capitalist standards) deadly and invincible.

It was the shortest and most lopsided heavyweight bout on record, two minutes and four seconds of the first round, and it left no doubt in anybody's mind as to the caliber of the fighter who won. There was a lot of cheering when Joe's hand was hoisted in victory, but there was a lot stunned silence, too; silence stemming not from a lack of respect for Joe, but from inability to grasp the fistic and political significance of what had happened so quickly.

HARLEM RESPONDS

But if the spectators did not respond quickly, Harlem did. The quarter of a million Negroes who live within those narrow confines knew in terms of their daily American life what this fight meant and they gave vent to it in a demonstration, wholly political in character, such as Harlem has never seen.

It was the celebration of Louis' triumph over Baer, Carnera, Pastor, Farr, Braddock all rolled into one plus placards which hurled slogans of defiance at Hitler's pretensions of Aryan superiority and called upon native lovers of democracy to be true to democratic ideals.

> Oust Hitler's Spies and Agents.
> Pass the Anti-Lynching Bill.
> Down with Hitler and Mussolini.
> Alabama Produced Joe Louis; Free the Scottsboro Boys.

With no less than 100,000 persons participating, it was the largest and most spontaneous political demonstration ever seen in Harlem. Joyously, they careened through the streets, on sidewalks and pavement, singing, shouting, yelling, laughing, beating drums, pans, and tubs. Effigies of Schmeling adorned with the swastika were dragged through the swarming crowds.

MOCK NAZI SALUTE

From the windows of high tenements torn scraps of newspaper floated down. The mounted police were literally blotted out in a huge wave of exultant humanity.

From midnight until dawn it seemed that a million horns were ceaselessly blowing. Knowing full well the political effect of Joe's victory upon the popular mind of the world, thousands yelled:

"Heil Louis!"

It was Harlem's mocking taunt to fascist Hitler's boast of the superiority of "Aryans" over other races. And Harlem ridiculed the Nazi salute of the outstretched palm by throwing up their own dark ones to show how little they feared and thought of the humbug of fascist ritual.

What happened in Harlem Wednesday night marks in a certain sense the high[est] tide of popular political enthusiasm ever witnessed among American Negroes. The fascists, even though it was over a mere prizefight, had laid down a dare, and Joe Louis had answered it with his brawny fists. Harlem approved by reiterating a thousand times:

"Say, ain't you glad?"

Can it be said too often that these popular demonstrations, no matter what their specific origin, contain within them seeds of "glad tidings?" The capacity of the people to respond with enthusiasm to what is their ultimate interest has yet to be plumbed to its depths. ■

New Masses, OCTOBER 8, 1935

Joe Louis Uncovers Dynamite

WUN-TUH-THREE-foo-fiiive-seex-seven-eight-niine-thuun!

"Joe Louis—The Winnah!"

On Chicago's South Side Five minutes after these words were yelled and Joe Louis's hand was hoisted as victor in his four-round go with Max Baer, Negroes poured out of beer taverns, pool rooms, barber shops, rooming houses and dingy flats and flooded the streets.

"Louis! Louis! Louis!" they yelled and threw their hats away. They snatched newspapers from the stands of astonished Greeks and tore them up, flinging the bits into the air. They wagged their heads. Lawd, they'd never seen or heard the like of it before. They shook the hands of strangers. They clapped one another on the back. It was like a revival. Really, there was a religious feeling in the air. Well, it wasn't exactly a religious feeling, but it was something, and you could feel it. It was a feeling of unity, of oneness.

Two hours after the fight the area between South Parkway and Prairie Avenue on 47th street was jammed with no less than twenty-five thousand Negroes, joy-mad and moving to they didn't know where. Clasping hands, they formed long writhing snake-lines and wove in and out of traffic. They seeped out of doorways, oozed from alleys, trickled out of tenements, and flowed down the street; a fluid mass of joy. White storekeepers hastily closed their doors against the tidal wave and stood peeping through the plate glass with blanched faces.

Something had happened, all right. And it had happened so confoundingly sudden that the whites in the neighborhood were dumb with fear. They felt—you could see it in their faces—that something had ripped loose, exploded. Something which they had long feared and thought was dead. Or if not dead, at least so safely buried under the pretence of good-will that they no longer had need to fear it. Where in the world did it come from? And what was worst of all, how far would it go? Say, what's got into these Negroes? And the whites and the blacks began to feel themselves. The blacks began to remember all the little slights, and discriminations and insults they had suffered; and their hunger too and their misery. And the whites began to search their souls to see if they had been guilty of something, sometime, somewhere, against which this wave of feeling was rising.

As the celebration wore on, the younger Negroes began to grow bold. They jumped on the running boards of automobiles going east or west on 47th Street and demanded of the occupants:

"Who yuh fer—Baer or Louis?"

In the stress of the moment it seemed that the answer to the question marked out friend and foe.

A hesitating reply brought waves of scornful laughter. Baer, huh? That was funny. Now, hadn't Joe Louis just whipped Max Baer? Didn't think that we had it in us, did you? Thought Joe Louis was scared, didn't you? Scared because Max talked loud and made boasts. We ain't scared either. We'll fight too when the time comes. We'll win, too.

A taxicab driver had his cab wrecked when he tried to put up a show of bravado.

Then they began stopping street cars. Like a cyclone sweeping through a forest, they went through them, shouting, stamping. Conductors gave up and backed away like children. Everybody had to join in this celebration. Some of the people ran out of the cars and stood, pale and trembling, in the crowd. They felt it, too.

In the crush a pocketbook snapped open and money spilled on the street for eager black fingers.

"They stole it from us, anyhow," they said as they picked it up.

When an elderly Negro admonished them, a fist was shaken in his face. Uncle Tomming, huh?

"Whut in hell gotta do wid it" they wanted to know. Something had popped loose, all right. And it had come from deep down. Out of the darkness it had leaped from its coil. And nobody wanted to say. Blacks and whites were afraid. But it was sweet fear, at least for the blacks. It was a mingling of fear and fulfillment. Something dreaded and yet wanted. A something had popped out of a dark hole, something with a hydra-like head, and it was darting forth its tongue.

You stand on the borderline, wondering what's beyond. Then you take one step and you feel a strange, sweet tingling. You take two steps and the feeling becomes keener. You want to feel some more. You break into a run. You know it's dangerous, but you're impelled in spite of yourself.

Four centuries of oppression, of frustrated hopes, of black bitterness, felt even in the bones of the bewildered young, were rising to the surface. Yes, unconsciously they had imputed to the brawny image of Joe Louis all the balked dreams of revenge, all the secretly visualized moments of retaliation, and He Had Won! Good Gawd Almighty! Yes, by Jesus, it could be done! Didn't Joe do it? You see, Joe was the consciously-felt symbol. Joe was the concentrated essence of black triumph over white. And it comes so seldom, so seldom. And what could be sweeter than long-nourished hate vicariously gratified? From the symbol of Joe's strength they took strength, and in that moment all fear, all obstacles were wiped out, drowned. They stepped out of the mire of hesitation and irresolution and were free! Invincible! A merciless victor over a fallen foe! Yes, they had felt all that—for a moment. . . . [ellipses in original]

And then the cops came.

Not the carefully picked white cops who were used to batter the skulls of white workers and intellectuals who came to the South Side to march with the black workers to show their solidarity in the struggle against Mussolini's impending invasion to Ethiopia; oh, no, black cops, but trusted black cops and plenty tough. Cops who knew their business, how to handle delicate situations. They piled out of patrols, swinging clubs.

"Git back! Gawddammit, git back!"

But they were very careful, very careful. They didn't hit anybody. They, too, sensed something. And they didn't want to trifle with it. And there's no doubt but that they had been instructed not to. Better go easy here. No telling what might happen. They swung clubs, but pushed the crowd back with their hands.

Finally, the streetcars moved again. The taxis and automobiles could go through. The whites breathed easier. The blood came back to their cheeks.

The Negroes stood on the sidewalks, talking, wondering, looking, breathing hard. They had felt something, and it had been sweet—that feeling. They wanted some more of it, but they were afraid now. The spell was broken.

And about midnight down the street that feeling ebbed, seeping home—flowing back to the beer tavern, the poolroom, the café, the barbershop, the dingy flat. Like a sullen river it ran back to its muddy channel, carrying a confused and sentimental memory on its surface, like water-soaked driftwood.

Say, Comrade, here's the wild river that's got to be harnessed and directed. Here's a fleeting glimpse of the heart of the Negro, the heart that beats and suffers and hopes—for freedom. Here's that fluid something that's like iron. Here's the real dynamite that Joe Louis uncovered! ■

Daily Worker, November 22, 1937

Memorial for Milton Herndon Next Sunday

A MEMORIAL MEETING for Milton Herndon, brother of the heroic Angelo Herndon, will be held at the St. James Presbyterian Church, Sunday, November 28, at 3:30 PM, it was announced yesterday by the Milton Herndon Memorial Committee.

Praised by his comrades and friends as one of the "staunchest enemies of fascism," young Milton Herndon was killed in action on the [Zaragoza] front in Spain during October. He was widely known among Harlem workers for his militant action on picket lines, in the Scottsboro struggle, in cultural work, and in the struggle for the freedom of his brother, Angelo.

TO DEFEAT TIDE OF FASCISM

William L. Patterson, Negro Communist leader, in issuing a statement for the Milton Herndon Memorial Committee declared:

"We are urging all Harlem to attend this memorial meeting and pay tribute to one of the bravest sons of the Negro people.

"But we believe that the most fitting memorial we can give to Milton is by striving together to defeat the rising tide of fascism!"

The Young Communist League of America, of which Milton was a member, issued the following statement:

"The National Resident Board of the Young Communist League, U.S.A., together with our whole membership, deeply mourn the death of the brother of Milton Herndon, who died in action on the battle fields of Spain. To Angelo and his family we extend our deepest sympathy.

PLEDGE RECRUITING

"At the same time we mourn the loss of young Milton Herndon, we pledge with all our hearts to fill the place left vacant in the ranks of our League by tens of thousands of new members.

"Milton, like Angelo, has shown an example of how to fight for the freedom and equality of the Negro people at home and abroad. We are determined, by the sacrifice made by Milton and all others who have given their lives for democracy, never to stop until fascism is crushed throughout the world. To this end we pledge our lives.

"We call upon all members and friends to join us at the Milton Herndon Memorial Meeting."

The statement was signed by Carl Ross, executive secretary of the Young Communist League of America, and Henry Winston, administrative secretary of the Young Communist League of America.

MANY INVITED

The Milton Herndon Memorial Committee has sent out hundreds of letters to organizations in Harlem, Brooklyn, and the Bronx inviting them to send contingents of their membership to attend the memorial services.

Among those who will officiate are the Rev. William Lloyd Imes of the American League Against War and Fascism; Capt. A. L. King, president of the Universal Negro Improvement Association; Timothy Holmes, assistant editorial director of the New York State Communist Party, and Harry Heywood, former political commander of the Abraham Lincoln Brigade in Spain. ■

Daily Worker, October 12, 1937

Negro Gets Job as City Buyer of All Chemicals

FOR THE FIRST TIME IN HISTORY, a Negro was sworn in as the chief buyer of chemicals and drugs for the City of New York, it was learned this morning.

Maurice Moore, the Negro who was the recipient of this signal honor, is a graduate of Fisk and Columbia Universities. His position pays $4,000 per year.

Moore took the civil service examination for the position, making the highest mark, 86.76. He is the head of his own firm, the Davis and Moore Chemical Manufacturing Laboratory Co., 107 Fulton St., Brooklyn. Moore was born in Texas, and as the chief buyer of chemicals for America's first city, he will supervise the purchase of $5,000,000 worth of drugs annually. ■

SECTION FOUR

A BURST OF FISTS ON A NEW HORIZON

I am black and I have seen black hands
Raised in fists of revolt, side by side with the white
fists of white workers,
And some day—and it is only this which sustains
me—
Some day there shall be millions and millions of
them,
On some red day in a burst of fists on a new
horizon!

RICHARD WRIGHT, "I HAVE SEEN BLACK HANDS"

In his poem "Scottsboro, Too, Is Worth Its Song," Countee Cullen, one of the major poets of the Harlem Renaissance, wondered aloud why more poets and other artists did not speak out against the outrage in Scottsboro:

Here too's a cause divinely spun
For those whose eyes are on the sun,
Here in epitome
Is all disgrace
And epic wrong,
Like wine to brace
The minstrel heart, and flare it into song.[1]

Cullen certainly had reason to bemoan the artistic community's silence on the Scottsboro case. The press, however, was far from silent, especially the leftist press. Foremost among those calling for justice for the Scottsboro defendants was the *Daily Worker*. From the very outset of the case, the newspaper was tireless in its coverage of the story and in its championing of the defendants' cause. For his part, Wright contributed over twenty pieces about the Scottsboro case to the *Daily Worker,* most of them brief but all of them designed to keep the reading public informed about developments in and events related to the case, one of the most controversial in the history of American criminal justice.

The story of the "Scottsboro Boys," as they were called, began in 1931 and ended nineteen years later, when in 1950 the last one of them was released from prison. The nine youths—eight in their teens (two as young as thirteen) and one barely twenty—were accused of one of the most serious crimes that a black man could be charged with in the South or anywhere in America: the rape of a white woman. The nine were accused of raping two women, Ruby Bates and Victoria Price. The rapes were alleged to have occurred in a boxcar on a freight train rolling through Alabama in late March 1931. On March 25, 1931, having been alerted that a group of black youths had beaten up a group of white youths and thrown them off a train, a deputy sheriff and his hastily assembled posse stopped the train at Paint Rock, Alabama. The sheriff and his posse had little trouble finding the nine black youngsters they were supposed to detain, but to their surprise they also found two young white women in the same boxcar with the boys. Before long the women claimed that the boys had raped them aboard the train. The nine youths were promptly arrested and brought to Paint Rock's small jailhouse. To ensure their safety—an unruly mob had formed outside the jail—they were transferred by the Alabama National Guard to a jail in neighboring Scottsboro, the small town with which they would be forever identified. In short order the nine youths were tried, convicted, and sentenced to death in the electric chair. Before the execution date, however, a groundswell of protest not only throughout America but from around the world resulted in a stay of execution pending an appeal. The Communist Party and the National Association for the Advancement of Colored people, though often at odds with each other in the Scottsboro case, were instrumental in securing justice for the defendants. They were the ones who early on drew national and international attention to the case, who provided legal assistance by top-echelon, high-profile criminal defense attorneys such as Samuel Leibowitz, who formed the Scottsboro Defense Committee, and who otherwise labored tirelessly to win the defendants' freedom. The trials, retrials, and appeals spanned two decades, with enough twists and turns to furnish sufficient material for countless essays and books.

Although the Scottsboro case had been ongoing for over six years before Wright arrived in New York in 1937, the story was still receiving continual coverage in newspapers throughout the nation. The trials, verdicts, sentencing, appeals, retrials, reconvictions, and further appeals all garnered heavy attention from the press during the thirties, making the Scottsboro case, as historian Dan Carter has stated, "one of the top news stories of the 1930's."[2] In July 1937, a mere month after Wright began his duties at the *Daily Worker*, four of the nine defendants were found innocent and released from prison.

As historians have noted, the Communist Party played an instrumental role in the Scottsboro defense and ultimate victory. Yet to multitudes of African Americans in the 1930s, in Harlem and throughout America, the Communist Party was an organization whose beliefs and objectives were mysterious and misunderstood. Even Wright, prior to joining the party in 1933, harbored suspicions about its motives and sincerity. "I felt," he relates in his autobiographical *American Hunger,* "that Communists could not possibly have a sincere interest in Negroes. I was cynical. . . . I did not think that there existed many whites who, through intellectual effort, could lift themselves out of the traditions of their times and see the Negro objectively."[3] But by degrees Wright's skepticism melted away and he joined the Communist Party, making, he reveals, "the first total emotional commitment of my life."[4]

As a realist with one foot in Marxism and the other in grassroots black culture, Wright realized that the early skepticism he himself had felt about the party and his own initial ill-formed conception of the Communist agenda were shared by a multitude of African Americans. Typical of many blacks' conception of—and reaction to—Communists was Wright's own mother's. In *American Hunger* he describes his mother's reaction when she comes into his room one morning and notices the stack of Communist magazines he had spent the night reading:

My mother opened the door and stared curiously at the pile of magazines that lay upon my pillow. She hobbled to the bed on her crippled legs and picked up a copy of the *Masses* that carried a lurid May Day cartoon. She adjusted her glasses and peered at it for a long time.

"My God in heaven," she breathed in horror.

"What's the matter, mama?"

"What is this?" she asked, extending the magazine to me, pointing to the cover. "What's wrong with that man?"

With my mother standing at my side, lending me her eyes, I stared at a cartoon drawn by a Communist artist; it was the figure of a worker clad in ragged overalls and holding aloft a red banner. The man's eyes bulged; his mouth gaped as wide as his face; his teeth showed; the muscles of his neck were like ropes. Following him was a horde of nondescript men, women, and children, waving clubs, stones, and pitchforks.

"What are those people going to do?" my mother asked.

"I don't know," I hedged.

"Are these Communist magazines?"

"Yes."

. . .

My mother's face showed disgust and moral loathing. She was a gentle woman. Her ideal was Christ upon the cross. How could I tell her that the Communist party wanted her to march in the streets, chanting, singing?

"What do Communists think people are?" she asked.

. . .

"They don't quite know how to appeal to people yet," I admitted, wondering whom I could convince of this if I could not convince my mother.

"That picture's enough to drive a body crazy," she said, dropping the magazine.[5]

Wright's mother's "disgust and moral loathing," he knew, were by no means atypical of blacks' reaction to Communism. In *Lawd Today!*, the posthumously published novel he wrote during the 1930s, Wright presents another typical response to Communists, this time from one of the lumpenproletariat. Jake Jackson, the novel's black protagonist, is reading the morning newspaper when he spots an article about a Communist riot in New York. "Gawd damn!" he says to his wife. "Wonder how come the police let them guys go on like that?"[6] Jake then launches a verbal assault on "them Reds," as he calls Communists: "Now them guys, them Commoonists and Bolshehicks, is the craziest guys going! They don't know what they want. They done come way over here and wants to tell us how to run *our* country when their *own* country ain't run right. Can you beat that for the nerve of a brass monkey? I'm asking you? Why don't they stay in their own country if they don't like the good old USA? That's what I want to know! And they go around fooling folks, telling 'em they going to divide up everything. And some folks ain't got no better sense than to believe it, neither. Just weak-minded, that's all!"[7]

Later on in the novel, Jake walks into Doc's barbershop for a haircut and finds Doc in a heated discussion with a young black Communist named Duke. Jake joins in, and he and Doc belittle Duke and his "crackbrain" ideas. The scene closes with Jake dismissing Duke as "a fool" and "a nutty bastard" and Communists in general as "chumps."[8]

Jake's disdain for "them Commoonists" and Wright's mother's "moral loathing" are transformed into puzzlement in Wright's magnum opus, *Native Son*. Early in the novel, Bigger Thomas asks one of his friends, "What's a Communist?" Bigger's friend replies, "Damn if I know. It's a race of people who live in Russia, ain't it?"[9]

It was precisely such a distorted image of the Communist Party that Wright was intent on correcting. "Here, then, was something that I could do, reveal, say," he relates in *American Hunger*.[10] That "something" was vivifying what the Communist Party stood for and what it was trying to accomplish. Wright therefore "set [himself] the task of making Negroes know what Communists were."[11] In several of his articles in the *Daily*

Worker, Wright tries to do exactly this. In one of the best, he takes his readers into the very heart of a Communist Party branch meeting. Aptly titled "What Happens at a Communist Party Branch Meeting in the Harlem Section," the article delivers what its title promises: a detailed look at what actually goes on at a party meeting held in Harlem, on Lenox Avenue. Wright must have realized that for many people few things were more boring than reading the minutes of a committee meeting, or of any other kind of organizational gathering. He therefore faced a hefty challenge: how to write an interesting article about a meeting that was, well, just a meeting. Much to his credit, he rose to the occasion. Far from being a boring account of boring people doing boring things, the article he penned turned out to be lively and interesting (and still holds up well over seventy years later). The party members featured in the piece are not dull, wooden figures moving and seconding dry-as-dust motions; nor are they priggish philosophers debating the nature of reality, and they are certainly not crazed Bolsheviks plotting violent destruction. Instead, they come across as affable, down-to-earth people committed to securing justice and equality for those whom Wright has elsewhere termed "the disinherited."[12] Wright nicely captures their humanity. One man, for instance, grouses about being assigned "women's work" and is swiftly reprimanded by, fittingly, a woman. At one point some members even discuss recipes (this in connection with a planned reception for the mother of a Scottsboro defendant). Humanity in the raw.

These seemingly ordinary people, Wright points out, are nonetheless dedicated reformers and activists, and their meeting is far from a coffee klatch. The meeting itself, Wright discloses, centers on some of the most pressing issues of the day: the Scottsboro case, housing conditions in Harlem, Japan's war on China, and the upcoming National Hunger March to Washington (which did indeed take place in December 1937). These issues are not simply discussed, though; the members forge plans how best to assist where needed. Volunteers, for example, are called for to walk a picket line in a strike against a department store (in all probability a store that was still selling Japanese-made goods—a hot issue at this time). A specific plan is adopted to aid in the effort to free the remaining five Scottsboro prisoners. A course of action is mapped out for addressing neighborhood problems.

Throughout the article, Wright never loses sight of his primary reasons for writing the piece: to demystify what the Communist Party is trying to accomplish and to put a human face on those men and women whose image, Wright knew, was so grotesquely distorted in the minds of many. What emerges from the article is a group portrait of "men and women with courage and guts enough to take the world into their hands and mould it," always with the intent of "changing that world into a more human one."[13]

In other articles Wright takes a different approach to his self-imposed task of "making others see what was in the Communist heart."[14] Two especially noteworthy stories that do precisely this are portraits—profiles of two figures, both Communist converts, who have dedicated their lives to the party and its goals: "Born a Slave, She Recruits 5 Members for Communist Party" (August 30, 1937) and "Mrs. Holmes and Daughter Drink from the Fountain of Communism" (September 7, 1937). The members Wright profiles are not male party notables like Ben Davis or James W. Ford but women, both black, both elderly. One of these women is Mrs. Hattie Holmes, a Harlem resident whose twenty-year-old daughter, Artie May, is visiting her from Florida, where the girl attends a Catholic nursing school. Rescued by the party from near starvation and impending eviction, Mrs. Holmes tells her daughter about the wonderful work that the party is doing to bring about justice for the downtrodden, and in the process the mother dispels the distorted image of Communists as "a band of bearded and violent agents of destruction."[15] In their drive for social reform, Mrs. Holmes points out to her daughter, the Communists are as much about extending a helping hand as they are about shaking a balled fist. The *hand,* Wright then explains in his authorial voice, is the appropriate symbol of the Communist Party; it is the emblem of its fight against oppression ("the hard, clenched fist" smashing injustice) as well as the visual representation of its empathy for the suffering masses ("[the] hand of compassion stretched forth to the poor and downtrodden").[16]

The article reverses the traditional association of old age with passivity and youth with radical action. In the dialogue between Mrs. Holmes and Artie May, Wright shows the older woman, who according to the stereotype should be religious and passive, lecturing and converting her daughter, who has been taught by Catholic nuns that Communists are scruffy, bomb-tossing anarchists. In the end the mother wins the daughter over to communism, and in turn the daughter, Wright suggests, will go on to convert others.

If Mrs. Holmes is presented as an inspiring example of a modern-day apostle preaching and practicing the gospel of communism, the other woman Wright profiles emerges as downright heroic. She is seventy-one-year-old Mother Ross, a woman who has survived not only chattel slavery on a southern plantation in the nineteenth century but also the demeaning jobs she was forced to work at in both the South and the modern urban North. Part of the Great Migration, Mother Ross journeyed north at the turn of the century only to endure "the steaming suds of laundries" and grueling domestic work ("the red hot stoves of wealthy people" and "12 and 16 hours of standing on her feet each day at the ironing board").[17] But her spirit remained unbroken, Wright relates, as she searched tirelessly for some organization, some movement that would give her life meaning and purpose. She found such an organization in the Communist Party, becoming one of its most zealous, productive members, successfully recruiting new blood into the Party and laboring to free the Scottsboro prisoners and Angelo Herndon (see below.)

In both articles we see the rudimentary outlines of a project that Wright had envisioned as early as his Chicago days but then abandoned. In *American Hunger* he relates that he planned to compose a series of biographical sketches of black Communists. "I wanted to make the lives of these [people] known," he declares. "I wanted to voice the words in them that they could not say, to be a witness for their living."[18] He abandoned the project after learning that it would surely meet with disfavor from party officials. ("We Communists don't dramatize Negro nationalism," he was told).[19]

Equally noteworthy about the two articles is the heroic role Wright assigns to women. It has long been a staple of Wright criticism that the role women play in his novels and short stories is a subordinate, often demeaning one. They are killed off, like Bessie in *Native Son,* or seduced/raped like Sarah in "Long Black Song," or are mistresses like Gloria and Gladys in *The Long Dream* or are weak, whimpering souls like Lil in *Lawd Today!* Sylvia Keady goes a long way in summing up what many critics contend is, in the words of Margaret Walker, "Wright's negative treatment of women . . . particularly black women" in his fiction.[20] "[Wright's] characterization of women," Keady argues, is "prejudiced and stereotyped." "Most of Wright's female characters," she adds, "are frequently [portrayed] as childlike, whimpering, and stupid . . . [and] are at the bottom of the scale of human intelligence."[21] In the two *Daily Worker* articles, however, the women Wright profiles—Mother Ross and Mrs. Holmes—are a far cry from the women who will later emerge from the pages of his novels and short stories. Mrs. Holmes and Mother Ross are courageous, dynamic people, who, despite their gender and age, are committed to bringing about a better world through adherence to the Communist gospel. They are just as heroic, Wright is suggesting, as any of their male comrades.

In these articles, then, Wright puts human faces on a movement and its ideology, demystifying Communist Party members' beliefs and goals and clarifying what the party offers. As a Communist and a writer and an African American, Wright felt an obligation to do so. He realized that to much of America, communism was a mysterious and misunderstood social system. Further, he realized that one valuable contribution he could make was to lift that veil. Through his pen, he affirmed in *American Hunger,* he could "[make] others see what was in the Communist heart."[22] The *Daily Worker* provided the perfect forum for him to do exactly that. In its pages he elucidated the party's objectives and motivating philosophy and humanized its members in his own inimitable way. While some Wright critics, such as Michel Fabre and Keneth Kinnamon, dismiss Wright's articles on the Communist Party as lifeless propaganda pieces, a close, more attentive reading of those articles belies such a judgment. They are, in truth, as engaging as they are informative.

■

"But I want to tell 'em," shouts Fred Daniels, the protagonist of Wright's quasi-surrealistic tale "The Man Who Lived Underground." Daniels is referring to the amazing metaphysical discoveries he has made during his Dantean sojourn in the sewer beneath the city, discoveries that he is eager to share with society above. In real life, Wright said almost the same thing. Unlike his character Fred Daniels, however, Wright was not referring to metaphysical discoveries. He was talking about the Communist Party and about what he felt was his mission as a black Communist, and, more important, as a black writer, to act as a kind of light bearer to the benighted. Wright knew from personal experience that most Americans, black and white alike, harbored misconceptions about communism and Communists, that to most people the party's principles, objectives, and strategies were alien and mysterious. Communists, so many believed, were bomb-tossing lunatics, and their political philosophy might have been imported from another planet. As someone who had once felt the same confusion and doubts, Wright set himself the task of dispersing the mist draping communism. He resolved to set the record straight and not only clarify communist philosophy and aims but also to humanize its members. And so he did. Using the *Daily Worker* as his platform, Wright in a number of articles successfully demystified the party's basic tenets and aspirations, thus keeping the promise he made to himself to "[make] others see what was in the Communist heart," as he wrote in *American Hunger.*

The Communist Party, Wright also underscores in many of his *Daily Worker* articles, was instrumental in securing justice for the Scottsboro case defendants. Falsely accused of raping two white women in rural Alabama in 1931, the nine black youths collectively known as the Scottsboro Boys were sentenced to death by an all-white jury but were able to win stays of execution and retrials. Their case became a cause célèbre, both nationally and internationally, and has since gone down in history as one of the most flagrant miscarriages of justice in twentieth-century

America. For its part, the *Daily Worker* tirelessly championed the Scottsboro defendants' cause, and Wright contributed more than twenty articles on the case, steadily informing the reading public about developments in the case.

■ ■ ■

Daily Worker, November 24, 1937

2 Scottsboro Boys Leave on National Tour

RICHARD B. MOORE, vice president of the International Labor Defense and secretary of the Harlem Scottsboro Defense Committee, left New York yesterday on a national tour with Roy Wright and Olen Montgomery, two of the freed four Scottsboro boys.

Moore expects to touch more than a dozen cities and will collect thousands of signatures calling for release of the five remaining Scottsboro boys.

His schedule in part includes the following stops: Providence, R.I. on Nov. 24, Pittsburgh, Nov. 26 and 27 [for] the Fourth National Congress of the American League Against War and Racism; Richmond, Va., Nov. 28 and Charleston W. Va., Nov. 29.

ASK ANTI-LYNCH BILL

In a statement issued before he left New York, Moore called upon all ministers, union leaders and Harlem organizations to continue to flood the Senate with resolutions urging the passage of the Anti-Lynching Bill.

When questioned as to his opinion of the effectiveness of the Anti-Lynching Bill, Roy Wright, one if the freed Scottsboro boys declared:

"The passage of the bill will help to free the other five boys and will help to put a stop to other Scottsboro frame-ups."

Among Harlem organizations which sent telegrams protesting the Senate filibuster are the Harlem Swing Club, the Harlem Scottsboro Defense Committee, the Upper and Lower Harlem Nat Turner Clubs, and the Harlem Council of the Workers Alliance. ■

Daily Worker, October 21, 1937

Ask Aid for Scottsboro Defense Drive

STRESSING THE NATIONAL IMPORTANCE of the forthcoming all-Harlem Scottsboro Conference, Richard B. Moore, vice-president of the International Labor Defense, issued an urgent call last night for volunteers and technical workers to assist in handling the initial phases of the campaign.

The conference is scheduled to convene Monday night, October 25, at 8 o'clock at the St. Philips Parish House, 213 W. 133rd St.

"More than fifty individuals and organizations are sponsoring the conference," Moore stated. "We expect a large number of delegates to attend. We have sent out calls to more than 5,000 Harlem people.

"Those lovers of justice and democracy who want to see the five remaining Scottsboro boys can do their part by reporting for volunteer work at the office of the Provisional Scottsboro Defense Committee, 200 W. 135th St., Room 204."

Moore said that all organizations are being requested to arrange for their delegates to make financial contributions to aid in the Scottsboro drive.

It was indicated that the work of the volunteers would consist of visiting churches in Harlem to distribute conference calls. ■

Daily Worker, AUGUST 30, 1937

Born a Slave, She Recruits 5 Members for Communist Party

BORN IN SLAVERY, IN 1865—just a few months before the ratification of Lincoln's Emancipation Proclamation—she has lived for 72 years through wars, strikes, depressions and boom periods to stand finally in the ranks of the Communist Party, the vanguard of the working class.

Mother Ross, as she is called by the workers of Harlem, was born in Petersburg, Va., and at the age of 16 she stopped attending the skimpy school [there] because of the death of her father.

She spent 23 of the best years of her life slaving in a tobacco factory, from the time she was 16 until she was 39. During those years she had eight children, six of whom died in infancy because she did not have time enough to give them the attention they needed. But there is in her no bitterness when she speaks of this; she talks of it calmly, matter-of-factly—she spoke of it like a worker who knows that certain conditions of life are inescapable under capitalism.

In 1904 this black woman and her husband decided to come North to lighten their burden and to seek a better life. Factory work changed to domestic work. Her oldest child, her son, strayed from her; and today she does not know where he is. She speaks of him as being "somewhere in this world."

IN KITCHENS

But she kept her daughter with her and reared her in the kitchens of "white folks."

But she was restless. Surely there was some way out of this. The death of her husband in 1912 intensified her restlessness.

During a period of 18 years Mother Ross joined no less than 20 Negro organizations, "seeking a way out." But none of them answered her desire for a better life. As she puts it:

"All they wanted was money, and more money. . ." [ellipses in original]

Her life alternated between the red-hot stoves of wealthy people and the steaming suds of laundries. Years of raising other people's children so they could rule the earth on which she lived; 12 and 16 hours of standing on her feet each day at the ironing board; living a life bound by Saturday nights when a few cents would be dropped in her roughened hands; all this bent her hopes toward some organization whose voice was sharp enough to enlist her energies in the fight for a better life.

UNEMPLOYED COUNCILS

In 1930 she heard of the Unemployed Councils. She joined because, as she phrases it: "They were lively. They were people like me. And they did things."

It was not long before she joined the Communist Party and became a day to day worker. She plunged into the fight to free the Scottsboro boys, to free Herndon; she helped to organize the locals for the Workers Alliance; and she began to spread the message of Communism among Negro women.

Since the Party announced its recruiting drive, she has brought five Negro workers into the Party. And before the drive ends she hopes to recruit five more.

"I like to move about," said Mother Ross. I will be 72 yeas old on my next birthday and I want to keep up with this 20th Century." Despite her 71 years, Mother Ross is planning to attend the National Negro

Congress in Philadelphia on October 15, 16, and 17. A few days ago she applied for membership in the American Labor Party and she is peeved because the officials of that organization are so slow in sending her her membership card.

SOVIETS IN U.S.

"I would like to see Soviets in these United States," she says. "And I hope to live to see it happen."

When the Young Communist League of Harlem, composed of Negro and white youth, meets this Wednesday it will extend to Mother Ross the honor of becoming an honorary member and the adopted mother of the group.

"I am glad to accept the honor," says Mother Ross modestly. "I like to see Negro and white youth fight together."

This woman has seen the face of her country changed more than once during her 71 years, and she has the strength, the courage and faith to fight and wait for still another change.

"I live in the 20th Century," she said simply, turning away and thumbing through a pile of application cards. ■

Daily Worker, AUGUST 15, 1937

What Happens at a Communist Party Branch Meeting in the Harlem Section?

HOW DOES THE COMMUNIST PARTY WORK? What do Communists do when alone and among themselves? Let's visit a meeting and see.

Leaving the blare and glare of Lenox Avenue, you walk up one flight of stairs and enter an oblong room whose walls are covered with murals depicting the historical struggles of the Negro in America. This is the Nat Turner Branch of the Harlem Division of the Communist Party. It was so named in honor of a black slave who died struggling for freedom.

Before you have time to sit down, your eyes are drawn to a huge black placard.

"IN MEMORY OF OUR BELOVED BROTHER, ALONZO WATSON,
WHO DIED FIGHTING FOR DEMOCRACY IN SPAIN."

GIVE LIVES

So you know, even before the meeting starts, and you hear them talk, that there are people here who will give their lives for what they believe.

The Nat Turner Branch has a membership of about 20; of that 20, 16 were present. The composition according to class and sex was as follows: 9 women and 7 men. Of the 7 men, 2 were white. The Negro men and women were of the working class in manner, accent, and deportment.

There is absolutely no difference between the Negro and white in the Communist Party. They participate on an equal footing in the carrying out of their tasks.

TO THE POINT

As the meeting gets under way you notice that there are no abstractions, no splitting of intellectual hairs. Every word is simple and straight to the point. They are not concerned about whether or not the world exists or what reality is; they know the world exists and they know from their own harsh lives just what kind of world it is. They meet here to devise ways and means of changing that world into a more human one.

The extent of the activities of these seemingly ordinary people is amazing. When Wilhe[l]mina Plummer, a Negro woman organizer of the Nat Turner Branch, rises to read the agenda and announcements, you learn that two delegates from this branch are to attend a conference on Harlem housing conditions; there are announcements urging members to attend classes to learn public speaking; and there is a call and response for two comrades to picket a department where a strike is in progress.

Then a startling discussion arises over the American Labor Party.

There is no desire here to "grab" the A.L.P. Members are urged to join to help build that organization. The whole attitude is more of giving one's self to something more important than a mere petty grasping for control. Suffused through every speaker's words is the burning desire to see the A.L.P. become a popular political party. The women volunteered to join that party and give their services.

THIS IS COMMUNISM!

Education and the process of education is the keynote of everything said and done here by these black men and women. Next, they decide to give a lawn party to raise funds to send a comrade to the Workers' School.

Then comrades are urged to buy and sell tickets to aid the National Hunger March to Washington on August 23. "We must support this," says the organizer. "We in Harlem know what hunger is."

SCOTTSBORO FIGHT

Petitions demanding of Congress and the state of Alabama the freedom of the five remaining innocent Scottsboro Boys are passed around. Comrades are urged to have them filled out as soon as possible. The meeting is going fast now; they want to get through as soon as they can in order to listen to an educational report on the situation in China.

An open-air meeting is planned on neighborhood problems; comrades having difficulties of any kind are invited to attend the next buro meeting of the branch (three or four leading comrades in a branch who formulate policies for endorsement of the membership by whom they are elected constitute a buro).

The weakest spot in the entire meeting is the discussion regarding the *Daily* and *Sunday Workers*. The comrade who had been delegated to obtain the *Daily* and deliver it to the members of the branch had failed. He tried desperately to shunt his responsibilities onto the shoulders of someone else. Hot words flew to and fro. He was finally made to realize that it was his fault and that next time he had to get those papers and deliver them!

RECEPTION

A reception for the mothers of the Scottsboro Boys was planned next. From high political issues they went without a change in the tone of the discussion down to ice cream, fried chicken, how to bake a cake, and how to make a good punch, etc. A committee was elected to arrange this reception. A "man" comrade refused to serve on this committee on the grounds that it was a "woman's affair," and a "woman" comrade bawled him out with strong words.

"What's good for one Communist is good for any Communist!" she said.

Party recruiting came next. One new member was introduced, a Negro woman worker. She was welcomed unanimously and voted in.

Business over, a white comrade, a student, rose to give a talk on the international scene with an emphasis upon China. Before he spoke, many questions were asked, among which were: To what extent are American interests involved in China? What is the role of the Party in relation to Japan's aggression? What is the relationship between China, Spain, and Ethiopia? What of Japan's boast of protecting the "darker races" and then making war on them? What of the Chinese Soviets and the Chinese Red Army? A concrete analysis of how these events and facts were interlinked proceeded. The entire room was dead quiet. There was applause when the speech ended. A comrade rose and demanded that hereafter business meetings should be made shorter so that more and longer educational discussions could be had.

This is the same Party that took power in Russia, that fulfilled the two Five-Year Plans, that built the Red Army, and that is now building Socialism.

These black people who meet here in Harlem are hungry more than in one sense. They love this Communist Party which is the only organization caring enough for them to give them this world-view of things. It is through such meetings as these that Bolsheviks are forged, men and women with guts and courage enough to take the world into their hands and mould it and in moulding it remake themselves.

And it is through such meetings as these that for the first time in American history the Negro is receiving his highest possible pitch of social consciousness. When you listen to them talk, you know that the future is fraught with conflict, but you feel that here are people capable of dealing with that conflict.

Denied university educations, they are receiving an education from the vanguard of the working class, the Communist Party. Farmers, intellectuals, and middle-class people who [are] drifting about in a shoreless sea, wondering what straw they can grasp, should look here, for this is a new pole of strength about which the life of the whole world can regroup itself. These working people may not have polished accents, graceful gestures, etc., but they have what it takes to build a new world—the ability to ACT and a singleness of VISION. ■

Daily Worker, OCTOBER 13, 1937

Harlem Plans Scottsboro Defense Rally

PLANS FOR A SUCCESSFUL Harlem-wide Scottsboro conference for Oct. 25 were virtually assured this morning when it was announced that fifty Harlem leaders and organizations had indicated their willingness to participate.

The conference will be held at the St. Philips Parish House, 213 W. 133rd St.

The call which the Harlem Scottsboro Defense Committee sent to organizations, churches, clubs unions, societies, etc. read in part:

"The Harlem Scottsboro Defense Committee appeals to all justice-loving organizations and persons to take an active part in this vital defense struggle. A powerful, united Scottsboro defense movement in Harlem will inspire like action throughout the country."

Quickening the efforts of the Scottsboro friends in Harlem is the news that the Scottsboro boys are still being terrorized in Alabama.

Mrs. Ada Wright, Scottsboro mother who visited the boys, will speak at the Manhattan Opera House, 8th Ave. and 34th St., Thursday night, Oct. 14. Among the speakers are Roy Wilkins, editor of the CRISIS magazine; Rev. Knight Chalmers, chairman of the Scottsboro Defense Committee; Richard B. Moore of the International Labor Defense, and Ruby Bates, chief defense witness.

The National Scottsboro Defense Committee has urged the speeding of the collection of petitions to help free the five remaining Scottsboro boys. All organizations are urged to secure hundreds of petitions for distribution to their members.

Other meetings and conferences are being organized throughout the United States and plans are on the way for the collection of a million signatures. ■

Daily Worker, JULY 30, 1937

Harlem Spurs Scottsboro Boys Fight

"Carry the fight on to the end!"

THAT TODAY IS THE WAY HARLEM FEELS about the nation-wide fight to free the five remaining Scottsboro boys confined in the torture prisons of Alabama.

Outstanding leaders in the thickly-populated Negro Community almost uniformly considered that "mass action and mass pressure" was the determining factor in the freedom of the four Scottsboro youths freed on July 23. The Negro youths freed are Olen Montgomery, Eugene Williams, Roy Wright, and Willie Robertson.

Among those who commented on the Scottsboro "partial victory" to the *Daily Worker* yesterday: Donelan J. Phillips, president of the Harlem Consolidated Tenants League; Theodore Bassett, educational director of the Harlem Division of the Communist Party; the Rev. William Lloyd Imes, pastor of the St. James Presbyterian Church; and Frank Crosswaith, chairman of the Negro Labor Committee and general organizer of the International Ladies' Garment Workers Union.

CONGRATULATIONS

Several congratulated the Scottsboro Defense Committee, in charge of the boys' defense; Samuel Leibowitz, chief Scottsboro defense counsel; and the International Labor Defense, the first organization to defend the nine Scottsboro boys and which is today one of the eight organizations comprising the Scottsboro Defense Committee.

When the I.L.D. entered the Scottsboro cases in April 1931, all except one of the boys had been condemned to die. Sharply exposing the frame-up as one directed against the Negro people as a whole, the I.L.D. lead a four-year fight which resulted in death convictions being reversed twice in the United States Supreme Court.

D. J. Phillips, president of the Consolidated Tenants' League and Negro leader, stated:

"I think the mass pressure and mass action employed by the Scottsboro Defense Committee, together with the I.L.D. and Mr. Leibowitz have been extremely effective in bringing about the liberation of the four boys. I think it should be continued by all means until the other five are free."

Frank R. Crosswaith, leading Negro Socialist, stated:

"My reaction to this partial victory is implicit in my 20 years of struggle for Socialism. I am opposed to the crucifixion of the Negro on the cross of rape or any other cross. There were times, however, during the course of the struggle when I would have counseled a course other than the one taken. But now that we have come this far, I say that the state of Alabama should be made to free all nine of the boys. If four are innocent, then all nine are innocent."

Alan Dingle, well-known Negro attorney, stated:

"I want to congratulate anybody who has had anything to do with this victory. The manner in which the case has been fought is the only way. I say carry on until all nine are free. Every Negro and white should fight to this end and support the struggle."

MASS EFFORTS

Rev. William Lloyd Imes, pastor of the St. James Presbyterian Church, stated:

"I think the mass efforts used in forcing the state of Alabama to free four of the nine Scottsboro boys have been highly successful. It aroused public opinion as nothing else could have done. The spirit of cooperation which has existed has been wonderful. I hope the Scottsboro Defense Committee, the I.L.D., and Mr. Leibowitz can continue such good work. There is but one thing that matters in this case, and that is—FREE THE BOYS! The people want this fight to go on to the end!"

Theodore Bassett, Educational Director of the Harlem Division of the Communist Party, and chairman of the Grievance Committee of the Permanent Committee for Better Schools and Houses, stated:

"I am elated over this partial victory. The Communist Party was the pioneer in the struggle to free these boys; naturally I am glad now that four are free.

"It represents a tremendous victory for the Negro people, a landmark in the struggle for Negro rights. It is the result of the struggle of our Party and the role it has played in the Scottsboro campaign. We are proud of the struggle of not only our Party, but of all liberals, progressives, and others who have helped. Let's carry the fight on till the five remaining boys are free." ■

Daily Worker, AUGUST 30, 1937

Harlem to Get Scottsboro Defense Group

THE NATIONAL SCOTTSBORO DEFENSE COMMITTEE has issued a call to leading Harlem organizations and individuals to co-operate in forming a Harlem Scottsboro Defense Committee, it was reported yesterday.

Letters have gone out to the Urban League, the National Association for the Advancement for the Colored People, the YWCA and YMCA, and leading individuals, including ministers, civic and trade union leaders.

The organization of the Harlem Scottsboro Committee is in line with the recent move to concentrate upon the struggle for Negro rights and civil liberties in Harlem. A few weeks ago the International Labor Defense opened a branch office in Harlem at 200 W. 135th St. Room 204 with a staff of three in charge. ■

Daily Worker, SEPTEMBER 7, 1937

Mrs. Holmes and Daughters Drink from the Fountain of Communism

TIME: The present, when rents and food are high; when starvation hangs over a quarter of a million Negroes living in Harlem.

PLACE: The front room of a Negro home on West 153rd St.

DAUGHTER: Mother, whose picture is that you've hung on the wall since I've been away to school?

MOTHER: That's Angelo Herndon, darling.

DAUGHTER: Who' he?

MOTHER: A Communist.

DAUGHTER: Oh, he's what the Sisters at the Convent called hell-raisers.

MOTHER: He's a Communist hero, darling.

DAUGHTER: What did he do?

MOTHER: Well, that's a long story.

DAUGHTER: Well, tell me about it, Mother!

MOTHER: Angelo Herndon went to jail in Georgia because he led a demonstration of Negro and white to demand bread to eat. He stood up in a Southern court room and told the landlords of the South that they could not kill the working class. . . . [ellipses in original]

IT WAS IN THIS WAY that a black Communist mother told her daughter who had been educated in a Florida Catholic convent about Communism and extracted from her a pledge to join the Communist Party.

Down South, 20-year-old Artie May Holmes had heard of the Communist Party as being a band of bearded and violent agents of destruction. It had never occurred to her while she had been pursuing her course of nursing at the Catholic school that the Communists—a people she had been taught by [the] sisters and priests to hate—were taking care of her mother, offering her friendship and guidance in one of the most difficult periods of her life.

WITHOUT FOOD

Not only did the mother, Mrs. Hattie Holmes, 268 W. 153rd St., tell her daughter of Angelo Herndon, but also of how she had been alone and out of work in New York. She told her daughter of how she had been without food, about to lose her flat, and of how she had not known where to turn.

"But, Artie May, living above me was a Communist woman with whom I had been friendly. I had never thought that some day she could or would help me. By accident she learned of my condition and told me not to worry."

The mother told the daughter of how she had been taken to the Workers' Alliance.

"She took me to the Workers' Alliance. I went with her because I didn't have any other place to go. But in 24 hours they got me food to eat and made sure that I would not be set outdoors. At first I was afraid. Whenever I went into the ERB station I would try to tell the clerks that I was hungry and I would break down and cry. But they soon got me out of that. They taught me how to stand up and fight.

NEW FRIENDS

"So, you see, daughter, when you were away at school worrying about me, wanting me to come down South, I had found new friends."

The mother told the daughter that Negro and white work together in the Party.

"It made no difference to them that I was a black woman. They helped me anyhow. And I was grateful to them."

Mrs. Holmes told her daughter that when she expressed her gratitude to her Communist friends, they asked her to come to meetings of the Alliance.

"They told me I could express my gratitude that way and I did. Even though I was not well, I served on delegations, stood on picket lines in the snow and rain. I fought side by side with them.

"You see, I wanted to help them to help others as they had helped me. Surely, you understand that, Artie May? The Catholics say they believe in that, too. Well, we do it!"

EXECUTIVE MEMBER

A few months after Mrs. Holmes had joined the Workers' Alliance, she was asked to serve on the executive committee. She accepted and a year later she was honored by being asked to join the Communist Party.

"I was glad to join. I want to see my people free. And I want to see the kind of people who helped me when I was down, take power and rule.

The Party's been wonderful to me. Since I've been out of work here in Harlem it's been all I've had."

She told Artie May of how at one time she lain sick in the hospital. Negro and white had come to help her. They offered to place day and night nurses at her bedside.

ROCK AND SHELTER

"The Party has been a rock and a shelter to me in the time of storm," said the mother.

"Mother," said Artie May, "I was looking about the house the other day and I saw some Communist literature you had hidden. Now that I know you're a Communist, may I read some of it?"

"Yes; I hid it. I didn't know how you would take it, coming from a Catholic school in the South."

Artie May read Angelo Herndon's "Let Me Live" and she wept over it, for in the South she had lived near the conditions it depicted. She gave the book to a friend of hers who, like [her], had lived in Florida and the friend joined the Party.

The summer vacation days for Artie May are over. She has packed her trunk to go back to Florida to resume her school work. But besides her new clothes and other things, she is taking a load of pamphlets, books, and magazines along. And she's resolved to tell her grandmother—her mother's mother—about the Communist Party, the group of black and white comrades who helped her mother while she lay flat on her back, alone and without friends in Harlem.

THEY'LL JOIN

"When people learn the kind of people we have in our Party, they'll join," said Mrs. Holmes. "It's what they're looking for. It was what I was looking for."

But the millions who are out of work in America should not have to wait and stumble accidentally upon the Party that helped Mrs. Holmes. What the Party is and means should be carried to them. Not a dead Communism, but a living Communism; the Communism that Mrs. Holmes told her daughter about and made her change her mind.

PARTY SYMBOL

Paradoxically, the hard, clenched fist is not the only symbol of Communism. There is a fist thrust into the faces of capitalist exploiters, but there is also a hand of compassion stretched forth to the poor and downtrodden.

The clenched fist is not a bluff; it's a fist reaching for power. And the hand of compassion is not sticky with false kindness[—]it is not the kind that gives Hearst Milk Funds; instead it touches the downtrodden to quicken them to new life, to give them courage to struggle for the possession of the earth on which they live. ■

Daily Worker, October 26, 1937

Parley Maps Scottsboro Defense Campaign

THE SUPREME COURT'S REFUSAL to review the case of Heywood [Haywood] Patterson, one of the framed Scottsboro boys, was met in Harlem last night with a pledge to arouse a mass pressure campaign to force freedom for the five boys that are still held.

At a conference of 50 representatives of Harlem organizations and prominent individuals held on the call of the Provisional Scottsboro Defense Committee, at St. Philips Parish Church, 213 W. 133rd St., a plan for a campaign was adopted which includes the following:

A plea will be sent to all churches in the country that they join in observing Scottsboro Sunday; a mass protest meeting will be held in Harlem in the near future; speakers will be sent to all theatres throughout the city to appeal for signatures on Scottsboro defense petitions and funds; a tag day will be held to raise funds; a delegation will go to Washington to see President Franklin Roosevelt and Congress in behalf of the boys; and a resolution condemning the decision of the Supreme Court will go to the President and the Alabama authorities.

TO PUSH FIGHT

Among those who took part in the conference were Scottsboro mothers and the freed boys. Mrs. Ada Wright, mother of Roy, who is free and Andy who is still imprisoned, said:

"I feel that the good people of the country will do all they can to free the five remaining boys despite the unfavorable decision handed down today."

Roy Wright said: "The Supreme Court decision should not stop us. We need help now more than ever. If they freed four of us, then the other five are also innocent." ■

Daily Worker, November 1, 1937

Plan to Push Scottsboro Campaign

THE NEW YORK ORGANIZATION of the National Negro Congress with its 60 awaited bodies will participate in joint action with the Harlem Scottsboro Defense Committee for the freedom of the five remaining Scottsboro boys it was announced yesterday.

To launch the campaign on a Harlem-wide basis a mass meeting sponsored by both organizations is scheduled for Nov. 15 the details of which will be made public soon. Also a joint delegation will go to Congress on Nov. 16 to protest the recent adverse Supreme Court decision denying Haywood Patterson a new trail.

James H. Baker Jr., chairman of the New York Council of the Congress, has issued a call for a meeting of all delegates in the city for Nov. 16 to revamp the present organizational structure of the New York organization.

The purpose of the reorganization is to create conditions under which the 15,000 members in New York can participate more effectively in struggles for Negro rights.

Richard B. Moore, vice president of the International Labor Defense, declared that the joint actions of the Harlem Scottsboro Defense Committee and the National Negro Congress provide a real united front basis for continuing the Scottsboro campaign. He expressed a hope that the momentum of the New York campaign would be reflected throughout the nation. ■

Daily Worker, AUGUST 21, 1937

Scottsboro Boys on Stage Is Opposed

"I AM A LITTLE FEARFUL of the boys spending too much time [on] the stage," said Rev. Thomas S. Harten yesterday in an interview with the Daily Worker.

Rev. Harten is the guardian of the four freed Scottsboro boys, and he was making this statement in reply to an avalanche of criticism directed against the boys appearing at the Apollo Theatre on W. 125th St. near 8th Ave., in Harlem.

"They have been caged up too long and they want to go places," he continued. "They are 21 years old and a long as they keep within the law [and] say or do nothing to jeopardize the five boys who are still in prison, why should they be held up to public vilification as is being done in some newspaper?" the Reverend asked.

NO RIFT

Harten, pastor of the Holy Trinity Baptist Church, Brooklyn, denied that there existed any rift or deep differences of opinion among those now working to free the five remaining boys.

"It is true," Harten stated, "that the boys did release a letter to the public in which they claimed that I was the one who started the fight for their release in 1931. I wish to say that that is a mistake.

"It was the international Labor Defense that began the fight and I am happy to say that I joined it. Meetings were held at my church where Ford, Patterson and others spoke."

CREDIT TO PARTY

Rev. Harten next scouted the rumor that the boys were ungrateful for what "their friends had done for them." And in relation to the notion that the boys were being kept from the Communists, he stated:

"If I had been told that the boys were to be kept from the Communists, I would not have accepted the guardianship. I am not a Communist but I do say that if it were not for the Communists the nine boys would have been dead long ago."

The Reverend expressed concern over the boys' adjustment to their new life after six and one-half years of prison confinement. He felt that the newspapers should give them a chance to live normal lives.

ASSAILS ATTACKS

"Any misrepresentation or attack upon the boys or their decisions might do them an injustice that will be hard for them to overcome; and it further discredits the loyalty and friendship that burns in the hearts of millions of Negro people for these boys."

Meantime under the auspices of the Scottsboro Defense Committee the struggle to free the five remaining boys was getting well under way.

The argument for a new trail for Weems, Norris, and Wright will be held in Decatur, Ala., before Judge "Speed" Callahan on Aug. 27.

RUSH FIGHT

To intensify the struggle among the Negro people a Scottsboro Defense Committee is now being formed in Harlem. Throughout the country more defense committees are forming spurred on by the freedom of the four boys.

The International Labor Defense working in conjunction with the Scottsboro Defense Committee, is making every effort to get hundreds of thousands of the new petitions addressed to Gov. Bibb Graves filled out. ■

Daily Worker, November 17, 1937

Scottsboro Delegation Is Chosen

A DELEGATION OF 15 LEADING HARLEM NEGROES was selected Monday night to go to Washington and urge Congress and the president to act upon the Anti-Lynching Bill. The delegation was organized at a mass meeting held at the Abyssinian Baptist Church, 132 W. 138th St.

The meeting was held under the auspices of the Harlem Scottsboro Defense Committee and the New York Council of the National Negro Congress, with the Rev. A. Clayton Powell, Jr., acting as chairman.

In the capital the delegation will be joined by representatives of defense and church groups from Philadelphia, Baltimore, and Richmond. It will call upon Congress and urge the passage of the Anti-Lynching Bill, and will later call upon the President and urge him to throw his support behind the measure.

The delegation will also urge the President to speak over the radio or otherwise on the constitutional rights of the Negro people and minority groups; the delegation will ask him to connect his talk with Scottsboro and other such cases.

THE COMMITTEE

Among the members of the delegation are Mrs. Ada Wright, mother of two of the Scottsboro boys, Roy and Andy; William Gaulden, organizer of the State, County and Municipal Workers of America; Alonzo D. P. Bellis, representing the American Federation of Musicians, Local 802, AFL; Richard B. Moore, vice-president of the International Labor Defense and secretary of the Harlem Scottsboro Defense Committee; the Rev. D. H. Licriosh [David N. Licorish], chairman of the Church Division of the National Negro Congress; Max Yergan, director of the International Committee on African Affairs and acting secretary of the National Negro Congress; George Blake, organizational secretary of the Harlem Division of the Communist Party; Gladys Stoner, secretary of the New York Council of the National Negro Congress; Mrs. Lillian Gaskin, member of the executive committee of the American Labor Party; James H. Baker, Jr., chairman of the New York Council of the National Negro Congress; and the Rev. A. P. Cheeks, representing the Baptist Ministers Alliance. ■

Daily Worker, October 15, 1937

Scottsboro Drive Backed by Candidate

OSCAR GARCIA RIVERA, United Front candidate for assemblyman in the 17th A.D., announced that he would attend one or more sessions of the National Negro Congress which convenes today in Philadelphia.

Rivera, himself a Puerto Rican, is also supporting the Scottsboro Defense Conference which is scheduled to take place in Harlem on Oct. 25. In his campaign Rivera has constantly emphasized his determination to fight in the common interests of the Puerto Rican and Negro people in his assembly district as well as in the interests of the Negro people throughout the country. In his candidacy Rivera is supported by the American Labor Party, the Republican Party, City Fusion, the Communist Party, and the Puerto Rican Independent Democrats. ■

Daily Worker, November 15, 1937

Scottsboro Drive Backed by State C. P.

THE NEW YORK STATE COMMITTEE of the Communist Party issued a statement yesterday throwing the full weight of its organizational apparatus and membership behind the struggle to free the five remaining Scottsboro boys, and urging the passage of the Anti-Lynch Bill which is slated for consideration in the special session of Congress convening Nov. 15.

The statement, signed by I. Amter, state organizer, and Charles Krumbein, state secretary, called for support at all mass meetings, and stressed particularly the mass meeting to be held in Harlem Monday night, Nov. 15, at the Abyssinian Baptist Church, 132 W. 138th St., from which delegations urging the passage of the Anti-Lynch Bill will be sent to Washington.

C. P. STATEMENT

The statement issued yesterday reads as follows:

"The New York State Committee of the Communist Party urges all members of the Communist Party, members of trade unions, and other members of mass organizations to unite in the mass protest movement against the attempts of the reactionaries in Congress to remove the Anti-Lynch Bill from second place on the calendar.

"The Committee urges Party members and sympathizers to rally to the call of the New York Council of the National Negro Congress and support this united front movement to defeat the reactionaries in Congress and to mobilize nationwide support to free the five innocent Scottsboro boys.

IMMEDIATE PASSAGE

"With the opening of Congress on Nov. 15, every working-class organization and liberty-looking American should rally to the support of the various organizations carrying on the fight for the passage of the Anti-Lynch Bill by adopting resolutions and sending telegrams to the chairman of the Senate and to the President urging its immediate passage.

"Telegrams and resolutions should be addressed to Gov. Bibb Graves of Alabama protesting the constant threats and provocation directed against the boys in Kilby Prison, and urging their immediate transfer to Birmingham and their safe and unconditional release."

CHARLES KRUMBEIN, *State Secretary*
I. Amter, *State Organizer* ■

Daily Worker, OCTOBER 6, 1937

Scottsboro Drive Gains in Harlem

PLANS FOR AN ALL-HARLEM CONFERENCE to spur the work of freeing the five remaining Scottsboro Boys were announced the morning by the Provisional Harlem Scottsboro Committee.

The conference will convene on Oct. 25, at St. Phillip's Episcopal Church 215 W. 133rd St.

Elated over the partial victories so far obtained in the case, many outstanding Harlem leaders signed the call for the conference. Among the names announced by the committee are the Rev. Shelton Hale Bishop, pastor of the St. Phillip's Episcopal Church; the Rev. William L. Imes, pastor of the St. James Presbyterian Church; Max Yergan, director of the International Committee on African Affairs; Dr. P. H. M. Savory, co-editor of the Amsterdam News; Angelo Herndon, nationally-known Negro leader; Frank Crosswaith, chairman of the Negro

Labor Committee; Jack Hardy, secretary of the Retail Grocery Clerks' Union; Richard B. Moore, of the International Labor Defense; Sabina Montenez, of the Laundry Workers' Union, and many others.

Among the organizations, which have pledged aid, are the National Association for the Advancement of Colored People and the Brotherhood of Sleeping Car Porters. ■

Daily Worker, SEPTEMBER 18, 1937

Scottsboro Drive Pushed by Harlem Communist Party

ACTING WITH SWIFTNESS in the campaign to snatch Haywood Patterson from death on an Alabama chain gang and to press for the freedom of the remaining five Scottsboro boys, the Harlem Provisional Defense Committee is staging an open-air street rally tonight at 125th Street and Seventh Avenue.

Al Murphy, Harlem secretary of the International Labor Defense, in issuing the call for the meeting, stated:

"All progressive, justice-loving people, Negro and white, are urged to unite and throw their support behind this drive we are launching to free these boys. We must act quickly for the Alabama lynchers are trying to murder them legally."

Richard B. Moore, who has been active in the Scottsboro case from its early days, will outline to the workers of Harlem the national program of struggle which has been drafted to free the boys. Mrs. Audley Moore, also representing the International Labor Defense, will speak.

Tonight's meeting is the first of a series which will mark the beginning of a broad, vigorous campaign of united public pressure and defense activity. ■

Daily Worker, AUGUST 11, 1937

Scottsboro Fight Pushed at Harlem Rally

A MILITANT STREET MEETING took place at 126th St. and Lenox Ave., in Harlem, Monday night and a telegram was sent to Sen. Robert

Wagner and Congressman Gavagan demanding the freedom of the five remaining Scottsboro boys and passage of the anti-lynching bill now pending in Congress.

The telegram read:

> People of New York urge you to support movement to free five innocent Scottsboro boys by speech in Congress today and support the anti-lynching bill and its relation to halting rape frame-ups similar to Scottsboro Case.
>
> (Signed) *Peoples' Mass Meeting* ■

Daily Worker, DECEMBER 8, 1937

Scottsboro Group Warns on T. S. Harten

THE NATIONAL SCOTTSBORO DEFENSE COMMITTEE issued a statement yesterday warning those hundreds of thousands of individuals who have supported the fight for the Scottsboro boys against the false representations of the Rev. Thomas S. Harten, pastor of the Trinity Baptist Church of Brooklyn.

The Committee declared that Rev. Harten had not been authorized to collect funds for the Scottsboro defense work, and stated that moneys collected by Harten had not been turned over to the Committee.

The Committee further stated that Eugene Williams and Willie Roberson, two of the four freed Scottsboro boys, have been from time to time aided by the Committee, and that it was able to arrange for an authorized tour for them with an official representative of the Committee.

Meanwhile, steps were being taken to organize a Brooklyn Scottsboro Defense Committee to coordinate and centralize the work in that area.

Richard B. Moore, vice-president of the International Labor Defense and secretary of the Harlem Scottsboro Defense Committee, has been organizing local defense committees in all of the cities in which he is speaking while on national tour.

Moore expressed the hope that these numerous committees would be functioning before February 1938. ■

Daily Worker, OCTOBER 14, 1937

Scottsboro Meeting in Brooklyn Friday

THE BROOKLYN COUNCIL of the International Labor Defense issued a call today to its 15 local branches and to the people of Brooklyn to support a Scottsboro protest mass meeting to be held tomorrow night at the Girls Commercial High School, at Classon Ave. and Union St.

The meeting is the second of a series and is being held under the auspices of the Scottsboro Defense Committee.

The main speaker will be Norman Thomas, director of the American Civil Liberties Union. Among the other speakers are: Richard B. Moore, vice-president of the I.L.D.; the Rev. John Paul Jones, pastor of the Union Church of Bay Ridge; Dorothy Kenyon, deputy commissioner of Licenses of New York City; Mrs. Ada Wright, mother of Andy and Roy Wright; and Ruby Bates, chief defense witness.

When interviewed by the *Daily Worker,* in relation to the Scottsboro campaign in Brooklyn, Harold Berg, secretary of the Brooklyn I.L.D., declared:

"We urge all our members and friends to rally to the standards of liberty and justice which the I.L.D. stands for. We must continue our fight for the release of the remaining five victims of Alabama injustice. With the same vigorous campaign of protest which forced the release of four of the boys, we can with united action free the remaining five." ■

Daily Worker, OCTOBER 6, 1937

Scottsboro Mother Sees Son in Jail

IN LINE WITH THE DRIVE TO FORCE the Alabama lynchers to release the five boys, the Scottsboro Defense Committee is taking the case before the people of the Bronx tonight at the Bronx Hungarian Center, 809 Westchester Ave. Among the speakers who will address the mass rally will be many who have figured prominently in the case since its beginning.

Mrs. Ada Wright, just returned from a visit to her son, Andy, in Kilby Prison, has been adding fresh impetus to the campaign by telling audiences of the harsh conditions under which the boys are compelled to live.

Mrs. Ada Wright will also give first hand information concerning her recent trip to Kilby Prison. Richard B. Moore, one of the pioneers of the Scottsboro defense work, will speak in the name of the International Labor Defense. ■

Daily Worker, November 15, 1937

Scottsboro Mother to Lead Delegation

A MASS RALLY TO SEND OFF A DELEGATION to Washington to urge the special session of Congress to pass the Anti-Lynching Bill and to urge the President to speak on the Constitutional rights of minority peoples will be held tonight at the Abyssinian Baptist Church, 132 W. 138th St., at 8 p.m.

The rally is being held under the auspices of the Harlem Scottsboro Defense Committee and the National Negro Congress, with the endorsement of the Baptist Ministers' Alliance and the inter-denominational Ministers' Alliance.

It is expected that a delegation of 50 will be selected, among whom will be Mrs. Ada Wright, mother of two of the Scottsboro boys, Roy and Andy; and two of the freed Scottsboro boys, Roy Wright and Olen Montgomery. The balance of the committee will be composed of liberals, ministers, union and working class representatives, and members of leading Harlem civic and fraternal organizations.

TO VISIT PRESIDENT

In the capital the delegation will be joined by representatives of defense and church organizations from Philadelphia, Baltimore, and Richmond. It will call upon Congress and urge the passage of the Anti-Lynching Bill, and will later call upon the President and urge him to throw his support behind the measure.

The delegation will also urge the President to speak over the radio or otherwise on the constitutional rights of the Negro people and other minority groups; the delegation will also urge the President to connect his talk with the Scottsboro and other such cases, thus showing that the Supreme Court is not the defender of the rights of minority people.

Last week, as a result of a plea made by Mrs. Ada Wright, the National Negro Congress threw the weight of its 2,000 affiliated organizations behind the Scottsboro struggle and is supporting the delegation to Washington.

MEETINGS SCHEDULED

Parallel with the mass meeting to be held in New York, there will be mass meetings in Washington, Philadelphia, and Richmond under the auspices of the National Negro Congress.

Preceding the mass meeting tonight at the Abyssinian Baptist Church, there will be three open-air meetings in Harlem taking place at 7 P.M. The locations are as follows: 113th St. and Fifth Ave.; 126th St. and Lenox Ave.; and 138th St. and Seventh Ave.

Tonight's mass meeting will be addressed by Mrs. Ada Wright, Roy Wright, and Olen Montgomery. Other speakers will be Dr. Max Yergan, director of the International Committee on African Affairs and acting secretary of the National Negro Congress; Richard B. Moore, vice-president of the International Labor Defense and secretary of the Harlem Scottsboro Committee; the Rev. J. N. Lenister, representative of the Baptist Ministers' Alliance; the Rev. Thomas J. B. Harris, representative of the inter-denominational Ministers' Alliance; Col. William Schieffelin, of the Scottsboro Defense Committee; Dr. P. M. H. Savory, of the United Aid for Peoples of African Descent; Frank R. Crosswaith, chairman of the Negro Labor Committee; the Rev. D. N. Licorish, of the New York Council of the National Negro Congress; and attorney Thurgood Marshall, of the National Association for the Advancement of Colored People. ■

Daily Worker, NOVEMBER 8, 1937

Scottsboro Mother to Lead Protest

MRS. ADA WRIGHT, mother of two of the Scottsboro boys, will head a delegation of 50 Harlem leaders who will go to Washington and visit Congress and the President on November 16 or 17 and protest the recent adverse Supreme Court decision denying Haywood Patterson a new trial, it was announced yesterday.

The personnel of the delegation will consist of members of the Harlem Scottsboro Defense Committee, the National Negro Congress, heads of trade union and fraternal organizations, and outstanding ministers in Harlem.

Meanwhile the one-million-signature drive in Harlem is being led by the Workers Alliance. Tomorrow thousands of petitions will be circulated in Harlem churches, among which is St. Martin's Church, pastored by Rev. John H. Johnson, councilmanic candidate endorsed by the American Labor Party.

A further development in the Scottsboro campaign in Harlem will be a meeting early next week between the Baptist Ministers' Alliance and a sub-committee of the Harlem Scottsboro Defense Committee to plan for a series of anti-lynch Sunday services on November 14.

On Monday, Nov. 8, Richard B. Moore, vice president of the International Labor Defense, will appear before the inter-denominational Ministers Alliance and keep their co-operation in the fight to free the five remaining boys. ■

Daily Worker, SEPTEMBER 20, 1937

Scottsboro Mother Talks Monday Night

MRS. ADA WRIGHT, mother of two of the Scottsboro boys, Roy and Andy Wright, will tell a Harlem audience of her experiences on a recent trip South to visit her son, Andy, who is now ill in Kilby Prison.

The Meeting will be held on Monday, Sept. 20, 8:30 P.M. at the St. James Presbyterian Church, 141st St. and St. Nicholas Ave.

In an interview with the Daily Worker Mrs. Wright declared:

"I want the public to know just how they are treating those sick boys. And I want to tell them with my own lips."

Richard B. Moore, representing the International Labor Defense, will also speak.

The meeting is being held under the auspices of the United Aid for Peoples of African Descent. ■

Daily Worker, OCTOBER 25, 1937

Scottsboro Parley in Harlem Tonight

A SCOTTSBORO CONFERENCE, called by the Harlem Provisional Defense Committee, will take place tonight at 213 W. 133rd St., at

8 P.M. The conference is being held in response to the urgent plea of the Scottsboro Defense Committee to facilitate the campaign to free the five Scottsboro boys still in prison.

Four of the boys have already been freed. "The release of these four boys," states the conference call, "is a clear admission by the state of Alabama of the innocence of ALL these boys."

More than fifty of Harlem's leading individuals and organizations will participate in tonight's conference.

Richard B. Moore, vice president of the International Labor Defense, and Al Murphy, organizer of the Harlem branch of the I.L.D., declared in an interview with the *Daily Worker*:

"We hope that this conference will be the first of a series held throughout the nation to compel the victorious ending of the Scottsboro Case."

Signers of the conference call include the Rev. A. Clayton Powell, Frank A. Crosswaith, the Rev. Shelton Hale Bishop, Louise Thompson, and George Murphy.

Also Mrs. Ada Wright, Arnold Johnson, the Rev. William Lloyd Imes, Frank Warner, the Rev. F. A. Cullen, and others. ■

Daily Worker, SEPTEMBER 17, 1937

Scottsboro Rallies to Be Held Tonight

IN PROTEST OVER THE REMOVAL of Heywood [Haywood] Patterson, one of the five still imprisoned Scottsboro boys, from the Kilby Prison to a chain gang at Atmore, Ala., a series of open-air meetings will be held in Harlem tonight and tomorrow.

The Nat Turner and the James W. Ford branches of the Communist Party will conduct the first meeting tonight on the corner of 126th St. and Lenox Ave., at 8 p.m. Among the speakers will be Calvin Krim, member of the Party's speakers bureau, and George Blake, organizational secretary of the Harlem Division.

The Provisional Harlem Scottsboro Defense Committee will conduct the Saturday night meeting at 125th St. and Seventh Ave., at 8 P.M. Richard B. Moore, nationally known Negro defense leader, will outline the national campaign to free the remaining five boys. Mrs. Audley

Moore, Harlem labor leader, will also speak. Al Murphy will act as chairman. ■

Daily Worker, NOVEMBER 13, 1937

Scottsboro Sunday Tomorrow in New York Baptist Churches

PASTORS OF NEGRO BAPTIST CHURCHES throughout Greater New York will preach sermons tomorrow on the Scottsboro case and the Anti-Lynching Bill now pending on the calendar of the special session of Congress, it was announced yesterday by Richard B. Moore, vice-president of the International Labor Defense and secretary of the Harlem Scottsboro Defense Committee.

The Baptist Minister Alliance, with headquarters at the Metropolitan Church, 128th St. and Seventh Ave., voted at its regular meeting last week to endorse Nov. 14 as National Scottsboro-Anti-Lynch Sunday, which will begin what is to be termed Scottsboro anti-lynch week, lasting from Nov. 14 to 21.

On Monday, the opening day of the special session of Congress, there will be a mass rally at the Abyssinian Baptist Church, 132 W. 138th St., to send off the delegation of ministers, liberals, union and working class representatives to Washington. In the Capital the delegation will be joined by representatives of defense and church organizations from Philadelphia, Baltimore, and Washington.

This delegation will call upon Congress and urge the passage of the Anti-Lynch Bill, and will later call upon the President and urge him to throw his support behind the bill.

The delegation will also urge President Roosevelt to speak on the radio or otherwise on the constitutional rights of the Negro people and other minority groups; the delegation will also urge the President to connect his talk with the Scottsboro and other such cases, thus showing that the Supreme Court is not a defender of the rights of minority groups and poor middle-class people.

NEGRO CONGRESS BACKING

Mrs. Ada Wright, mother of two of the Scottsboro boys, Andy and Roy, and also two of the freed boys, Roy Wright and Olen Montgomery, will accompany the delegation to Washington.

Last week, as a result of a plea made by Mrs. Ada Wright, the National Negro Congress threw the weight of its 2,000 affiliated organizations behind the Scottsboro struggle and is supporting the delegation to Washington.

Also four huge mass meetings will be held in Washington, New York, Baltimore, and Richmond on the eve of the opening of Congress under the auspices of the National Negro Congress.

Preceding the mass meeting in Harlem Monday evening, at the Abyssinian Baptist Church, there will be an open-air mass rally at the corner of 126th St. and Lenox Ave. at 7 P.M.

The send-off rally for the delegation at the Abyssinian Baptist Church will be addressed by Ada Wright, Roy Wright, and Olen Montgomery.

Other speakers will be Dr. Max Yergan, acting secretary of the National Negro Congress; Richard B. Moore, vice-president of the International Labor Defense and secretary of the Harlem Scottsboro Defense Committee; the Rev. J. N. Lenister, representative of the Baptist Ministers Alliance; Atty. Thurgood Marshall, of the National Association for the Advancement of Colored People; representatives of the Harlem Labor Committee and the National Scottsboro Committee. ∎

Daily Worker, AUGUST 27, 1937

Statement on Scottsboro Is Made by Group

THE NATIONAL SCOTTSBORO DEFENSE COMMITTEE issued a statement today emphatically disclaiming any responsibility for the appearance of the four freed Scottsboro boys upon the stage of the Apollo Theatre in Harlem.

Advertisements announcing the theatrical appearance of the Scottsboro boys contained a tribute to the "devoted, unerring labors of the International Labor Defense Committee, the National Association for the Advancement of Colored People and other organizations."

The Scottsboro Defense Committee asserted that it appreciated the spirit of the statement, but regretted that it carried implications that the committee directly or indirectly supports or approves the theatrical ventures of the Scottsboro boys.

MAY DO HARM

"The Scottsboro Defense Committee and its constituent organizations have joined with Samuel Leibowitz in urging that these theatrical appearances may do more harm that good to the fight in which we are still engaged." A statement issued by the committee declared.

"On this point the boys have listened to contrary and mistaken advice from other sources. Although badly advised, they still continue their interest in the fate of the other boys still in prison, one under death sentence, the others under terms virtually of life imprisonment."

The appeal [for the] death sentence of Clarence Norris has been filed, and motions for a new trail have been made in the cases of Andy Wright and Charlie Weems. Papers are being prepared for permission to file an appeal in the United States Supreme Court in the case of Haywood Patterson and the Scottsboro Defense Committee is studying every possible legal move which might aid in the case of Ozie Powell who was dismissed on rape charge but sentenced to 20 years for an attack upon a deputy sheriff.

"Petitions for ten million signatures calling upon Governor Bibb Graves of Alabama to release the five boys are being circulated."

"In the meantime the Committee urges that all forces seeking the freedom of the five in jail support all meetings which will be held under the auspices of the Scottsboro Defense Committee." ■

Daily Worker, DECEMBER 6, 1937

YCL Pushes Scottsboro Defense Fight

IN ORDER TO THROW THE FULL WEIGHT of its national influence behind the struggle to free the five remaining Scottsboro boys, the National Board of the Young Communist League announced yesterday a plan to organize a Scottsboro Committee of Five-Hundred with members residing and working in the key cities of the country.

The character of the committee was described in a call which was signed by Vice-President Angelo Herndon and sent to all district offices of the Young Communist League.

It read in part:

> The Scottsboro Committee of Five-Hundred will function on a voluntary basis with each member pledging to carry on the fight to free all of the boys, and to involve large numbers of Negro and white youth organizations in the campaign. The campaign should serve as a stimulating force in arousing intense interest in the case. It is especially necessary to emphasize the historical significance of the Scottsboro case in the fight of the Negro people for liberation.

The call recounted the history of the famous case and appealed to all of its branches to support the National Scottsboro Defense Committee in its legal defense work. In addition, each district office has been urged to assign two of its members to push Scottsboro activity and to aid in having American youth sign hundreds of thousands of pledge cards calling for a fight for Negro rights. ■

SECTION FIVE

ART FOR LIFE'S SAKE

All art is propaganda.

RICHARD WRIGHT

Poverty and racial injustice. Housing conditions and rent strikes. Consumer boycotts and unemployment. War in Spain and in China. Headline-making heroism and unsung heroics. While these were some of the major issues that Wright wrote about in his *Daily Worker* articles, there were other subjects that also commanded his attention. One of these was the arts, particularly literature, music, and drama. As a literary artist, Wright took a keen interest in several art forms other than his own, especially when those art forms addressed social issues. There is perhaps no more telling example of Wright's espousal of issue-driven art than his efforts to rescue and transform the literary journal *Challenge*, a project to which he devoted three months of hard work. His earliest article for the *Daily Worker* centered on the resuscitation of this floundering journal. Indeed, one of the reasons he went to New York was to assist in the resurrection of *Challenge*, which had ceased publication in April 1937. *Challenge* had been the brainchild of author Dorothy West. Modern readers know West primarily for her short stories (chief among which is the frequently anthologized tale "The Typewriter") and her novels *The Living Is Easy* (1948) and *The Wedding* (1995). But in 1937 West was not well known nationally—inside Harlem literary circles, yes, but not far outside.

(Margaret Walker's estimation of West's literary reputation is perhaps an overstatement, though not by much. "Anybody with any literary awareness at all in America," Walker told Wright in a letter in November 1937, "knows that [Dorothy West] is utterly unknown."[1]) It was West's money, though, that had launched *Challenge* in 1934, and hence it was not surprising that she considered it *her* magazine. The story behind *Challenge*'s birth, demise, and short-lived revival explains Wright's involvement with the magazine and why his first article for the *Daily Worker*, written barely a week after his arrival in New York, centered on *Challenge*'s impending resurrection—a resurrection that West would ultimately come to resent.

In 1926 at the tender age of nineteen, West, accompanied by her equally young cousin, poet Helene Johnson, had come to New York at the height of the Harlem Renaissance as one of the winners of *Opportunity* magazine's literary contest. Her short story "The Typewriter" had tied for second place with Zora Neale Hurston's "Muttsy.") West was soon "adopted" by several leading lights of the Renaissance, all older than she. Langston Hughes, Countee Cullen, Wallace Thurman, Zora Neale Hurston, Carl Van Vechten—all took her under their wings while she worked away at perfecting her craft, the short story. When the Harlem Renaissance died with the onslaught of the Great Depression, West mourned its passing. But unlike others who also grieved, she resolved to make an attempt to resurrect the movement. To that end she took her own money and put it where she believed it would best serve the cause of black literature. In a letter to Langston Hughes in 1934, she told him, "Miraculously I got a little money, and a magazine suits my purpose better than a newspaper."[2] It was her fondest dream, she went on to tell Hughes, that this magazine would be "the organ for the young Negro voice. . . . Here is our chance to reach young thinking Negroes."[3] Thus was born *Challenge* magazine.

West's intent in founding the magazine was to resuscitate the creative energy of the Harlem Renaissance, to revive the glory of that magical period in literary history by re-instilling in the reading public an appreciation of what black literary artists still had to offer. In his foreword to the premier issue of *Challenge*, dated March 1934, James Weldon Johnson seemed to share West's dream that the magazine would become "the organ for . . .

young thinking Negroes": "It is a good thing that Dorothy West is doing," he wrote, "in instituting a magazine through which the voices of younger Negro artists may be heard."[4] In her "Dear Reader" section of that first issue, which would be a standard feature in each issue of Challenge, West announced to her readers, "This magazine is primarily an organ for the new voice. It is our plan to bring out the prose and poetry of the modern Negroes."[5]

Challenge's debut issue featured short stories (Langston Hughes and Arna Bontemps each contributed one), articles (one written by West herself under the pseudonym Mary Christopher), and several poems (including two by Countee Cullen and one by Helene Johnson). This issue was followed six months later by another, then by a third in May 1935, two issues in 1936 (one in January and one in June), and a sixth and final issue in April 1937. Although it was generally well received, the magazine simply did not enjoy strong financial backing. Most of its funding came from West's own pocket, and the rest, as she pointed out in the "Dear Reader" section of the final issue, came from "subscriptions and the generosity of [the magazine's] well-wishers."[6] Additionally, far too many of the manuscripts she received were of poor quality, prompting her in the final issue to complain of "no inflow of readable stuff" and "a lack of even fair material" coming in.[7] In "Dear Reader" she lamented, "It has been nearly a year since CHALLENGE last appeared."[8] But she assured her readers that "we are not entirely discouraged, for we have become greatly interested in a young Chicago group. . . . These young Chicagoans hold meetings regularly, where their work is read for open discussion."[9] During these meetings, West revealed, "CHALLENGE has come in for considerable dispraise. . . . And we have retaliated by offering them a special section in a forthcoming issue, that they may show us what we have not done by showing us what they can do."[10] West, in effect, recognizing that her magazine was in trouble and in need of help, agreed to see what this "young Chicago group" could do.

One of the "young Chicagoans" that West referred to was Wright, and it was he who answered her call for help, he who embraced the opportunity to help save her floundering "organ in the East," as she once characterized *Challenge*.[11] In a letter to Sterling Brown dated May 20, 1937, Wright expressed and explained his desire to leave Chicago ("this awful city," he calls it) and move to New York. "One of the many reasons why I want to [go to] New York," he told Brown, "is that Dorothy West is turning Challenge into a leftward organ. . . . I want to work on this very much; it's something I've been wanting to do for three years."[12] In another letter, written about a week later (May 29), this time to Langston Hughes, Wright elaborated on his impending move to New York and what he planned to do once he was there. "Dear Langston," he began, "No doubt by the time you receive this I shall be on my way to New York." For the rest of the letter, Wright talks exclusively about *Challenge* magazine and his intention to "help do something with [it]."[13] "Dorothy West and Marian Minus," he continues, "have decided to turn the thing leftward, which is the only way it should turn if it is to live."[14] Wright goes on to outline plans he has to revitalize the magazine, suggesting such improvements as including a book review section, devoting space to excerpts from novels-in-progress, and holding one-act play contests. He also makes it a point to solicit help from Hughes and other writers who might be in a position to assist. "If you have anything you can spare," he tells Hughes, "ship it along. Especially *prose*."[15] On his end, he pledges to drum up support for the magazine: "I shall do my very best to get the Party to support it; have it placed for sale in the Workers' Bookstores throughout the Nation; and get as much liberal and White support for it as possible."[16] Clearly, then, Wright was deeply committed to transfiguring *Challenge* into *New Challenge.*

One indication that resuscitating *Challenge* was "high on Wright's list of priorities" was that his first article for the *Daily Worker* heralded the coming of *New Challenge*.[17] Headlined "Negro Writers Launch Literary Quarterly," it appeared in the June 8, 1937, edition. In it Wright never mentions *Challenge* magazine directly. Instead, he foregrounds the proposed new quarterly, indicating where its emphasis will be placed. *New Challenge,* he promises, will treat "minority themes" and depict the "conditions of life common to the Negro people." It will present "a picture of the whole of Negro life."[18] While the new quarterly, Wright announces, will welcome submissions from white writers, he is careful to point out that "the contributors will in the main be Negroes," and he proceeds to issue a call to "Negro writers interested" in the "active struggle against war, fascism, and reaction in general."[19] Although Wright mentions the title of the proposed new quarterly only once in the article, readers familiar with West's little "organ in the East" would have recognized that this new magazine was designed to be what many believed *Challenge* never was but should have been: political, progressive, leftist. It was to be a magazine that, like *New Masses,* had "balls," as Wright himself phrased it in his May 29 letter to Hughes.[20] The maiden issue of this ballsy new quarterly, Wright pledged in the article, would be off the press in September.[21] For 1937 readers curious or eager to see what would become of *Challenge* in the hands of the "young Chicagoans" West had spoken of, the article must have been an enticing morsel, a preview of the shape of things to come. For modern-day scholars, on the other hand, the article offers a rare glimpse of the planning for the birth of what would unfortunately become the literary left's one-hit wonder of 1937. For both of these reasons, as well as for the rift it points to between the old world of the Harlem Renaissance and the new world of the radical thirties, it is a piece worth reading as much today as it was in 1937.

Just as Wright had promised, *New Challenge* made its debut in September. By all accounts it was generally well received. Wright's close and ever-supportive friend Margaret Walker was ecstatic over the premier issue. "The Magazine is truly an accomplishment," she wrote Wright on November 4, 1937. "It is not difficult to understand that there is a lot of work in it as well as money. Only with painstaking effort and time [could] such a job [have been] done."[22] In another letter to Wright three weeks later, Walker commended him on the marked and wholesome difference she noticed between *New Challenge* and "the preceding issues," meaning the last issues of *Challenge.*[23]

On the other hand, another of Wright's friends, the often hyper-critical Abe Aaron, found very little to like about the magazine. In a letter to Wright written around the same time Walker wrote hers, Aaron told him: "Glad to get your letter. Newsy. Wish I could say the magazine's as interesting. But I can't. It stinks, Dick, stinks bad. Poems are with one exception definitely bad. Stories smell to high heaven. Without exception. If the mag can get no better material, Dick, better let it die."[24] But it was not Wright's decision to make: West held the purse string of the new magazine, and well before *New Challenge* appeared in print, she had come to mistrust and dislike the direction in which Wright and his fellow Communists seemed to be taking her magazine. West was nobody's fool. She realized that the Communist Party had designs on *Challenge,* that it wanted "to turn the thing leftward," as Wright had told Hughes. Not that West was anti-left. Her fear, rather, was that the Chicagoans, as she called them, would sacrifice art on the altar of propaganda. To West, *Challenge* was first and foremost a literary magazine, and it would always remain such. As she explained to her readers in the April 1937 *Challenge,* the reason that no issues had been published for over a year was "due to the lack of even fair material."[25] A year earlier, in January 1936 in the "Dear Reader section," she had directly addressed the dearth of leftist material in the magazine. "Somebody asked us why CHALLENGE was for the most part so pale pink." In response, she admitted, "We would like to print more articles and stories of protest," but quality writing was simply not coming across her desk. "[T]he few red articles we did receive were not literature," she went on to say. "We care a lot about style. And we think a message is doubly effective when effectively written without bombast or bad spelling."[26] She was convinced that if she sat idly by on the sidelines, the cherished magazine she had launched in 1934 would dissolve into a sociopolitical quarterly devoid of literary merit and filled with what she termed leftist bombast. Accordingly, rather than see her "organ for the young Negro voice" turned into a Marxist soapbox, West pulled the plug on it. "[The Chicagoans] decided they were going to take over the magazine," she related in an interview with Katrine Dalsgard. "But the minute they decided they were gonna take over the magazine, I stopped it, and that was the end of that."[27]

West's decision to euthanize *New Challenge* (which is exactly how she would have termed it) probably came as a disappointment to Wright but not as a surprise. During the time he spent working with her on the magazine, he came to know her and her mind-set well enough to realize that *New Challenge* would not be to her liking. For one thing, it was not at all a resuscitated version of her original magazine—it was a whole new creature. Wright knew very well why West had launched *Challenge* in the first place, how she had hoped it would, in the words of Countee Cullen, "recapture the spirit of '26," the high point of the Harlem Renaissance.[28] He also believed that any journal with such an avowed purpose could be nothing else but reactionary and thus doomed to failure. His reason for this belief was that, as he saw it, the Harlem Renaissance was a movement vitiated by its willingness to cater to whites' desire for black exotica and its desire to please what he called "the jaded appetites of New York Bohemians."[29] Unlike *Challenge, New Challenge* under Wright's direction was not intended to revive the New Negro movement of the previous decade. Wright even throws a not-so-veiled jab at West's original magazine when on *New Challenge*'s editorial page he writes, "We are not attempting to re-stage the 'revolt' and 'renaissance' which grew unsteadily and upon false foundations ten years ago." In the same editorial, he announces that with this new journal there will be "a change in policy" and a "reorganization" of emphasis: "We want to see *New Challenge* as the organ of regional groups composed of writers opposed to fascism, war, and general reactionary policies."[30]

One of the essays in *New Challenge* was Wright's now-famous literary manifesto, "Blueprint for Negro Writing." Like his *Daily Worker* article "Negro Writers Launch Literary Magazine," "Blueprint for Negro Writing" makes explicit Wright's disdain for the Harlem Renaissance, which in the essay he dismisses as "the so-called Harlem school of expression."[31] The literary works of the Harlem Renaissance, Wright charges in the essay, were "the fruits of that foul soil which was the result of a liaison between inferiority-complexed Negro 'geniuses' and burnt out Bohemians with money."[32] Wright's caustic evaluation of the literature of the Harlem Renaissance stemmed from his long-held and deeply rooted belief that African American writers had a moral obligation to use their literary talent to speak out against all forms of social injustice, especially racism. As

Wright saw it, the writers of the Harlem Renaissance had spurned that obligation, turning a blind eye to their duty as "race writers." In "Blueprint," one of the cornerstones that Wright insists must be an integral part of progressive black writing is a particular kind of consciousness. "The Negro writer who seeks to function within his race as a purposeful agent has a serious responsibility," Wright contends. "In order to do justice to his subject matter, in order to depict Negro life in all of its manifold and intricate relationships, a deep, informed, and complex consciousness is necessary."[33] This consciousness, Wright argues, was lacking during the Harlem Renaissance and should be ever present in the literary works of the *new* New Negro. To his credit, Wright practiced what he preached as much as he could in his *Daily Worker* articles and later more freely in his major fiction.

Predictably, "Blueprint for Negro Writing" did not endear Wright to Dorothy West. After all, she was a part of that "so-called Harlem school of expression" that Wright sneered at, and she had been intent on reviving it. Even more important, she was not at all happy with what her "organ in the East" had become in Wright's hands. Given her and Wright's differing artistic temperaments and agendas, it is not surprising that she made sure that *New Challenge*'s first issue was its last. That there were no further issues of *New Challenge* after its debut number remains a loss. Had Wright and West gotten along more amicably, or even if they had reached a compromise agreeable to both of them, then surely literature would have been a bit richer, if only for a little while.

But literature, Wright well knew, was not the only art form that enriched, and it was not the only one that received attention in his *Daily Worker* columns. One such other art form was music—and for Wright, a man who fully exemplified music's power to inspire and motivate was Huddie Ledbetter, best known by his nickname, Lead Belly (sometimes spelled Leadbelly). Ledbetter acquired his nickname while serving prison time in Sugar Land, Texas. Given to him because of his toughness and physical strength, the sobriquet stuck. Ledbetter was proud of it and preferred using it rather than his given name.[34] Wright's feature story on

Lead Belly, "Huddie Ledbetter, Famous Negro Folk Artist, Sings the Songs of Scottsboro and His People," appeared in the *Daily Worker* on August 12, 1937, and was one of the most influential, and hence important, articles he ever wrote for the paper.

Lead Belly was a larger-than-life figure, the stuff of legend. He was a womanizer, a heavy drinker, and a brawler—a violent-tempered man who had served time for murder, been pardoned, then convicted again for attempted homicide. But this bear of a man was also an enormously talented musician, a songwriter-singer who left an indelible imprint on American folk music. "Goodnight, Irene," "Midnight Special," "The Rock Island Line," and "Cotton Fields" are perhaps the most well-known of the five hundred songs he is credited with having written. As his biographers Charles Wolfe and Kip Lornell have remarked, Lead Belly led "a life wrapped up as much in legend as in songs."[35] Born in 1888 on a farm near the small town of Mooringsport, Louisiana, Lead Belly was introduced to the guitar at age twelve by two musically talented uncles, and soon became so skillful a player that by fourteen he was performing weekly at house parties, juke joints, saloons, and dances. He was also getting into trouble: fistfights, knife fights, scrapes over women, all forecasting the direction his life would take for years. Wanderlust drew him away from home at sixteen, and to support himself during his rambles he worked as a cotton picker, truck driver, railroad worker, farmhand, maintenance man, and auto mechanic, all the while perfecting his skill on the guitar and expanding his vast repertoire of songs—and doing what he loved best, performing.

But he could not stay out of trouble: between the ages of sixteen, when he left home, and forty-nine, when Wright met him in New York, Lead Belly twice served time for violent crimes, once in Texas for murder and once in Louisiana, where he served time at the Louisiana State Penitentiary (known as Angola) for assault and attempted murder, although Wright suggests that Lead Belly was not innately violent but rather wisely wired for self-defense. While at Angola, Lead Belly met the man who would play an instrumental role in his life, noted folklorist John Lomax. Lomax had long had a deep, passionate interest in American folk songs and had lectured and written several books on the subject. Supported by a grant from the Carnegie Foundation, Lomax had been traveling throughout the South collecting songs, especially African American songs: work songs, prison songs, folk songs, religious songs. These he would record on celluloid disks using what he described as "a 350-pound recording machine—a cumbersome pile of wire and iron and steel."[36] He would then deposit the recorded songs in the archives of the Music Division of the Library of Congress for historical preservation. He was especially interested in the songs coming out of prisons. "[O]ur best field was the southern penitentiaries," he reveals in his autobiography. "We went to all eleven of them and presented our plan to possibly 25,000 Negro convicts."[37] And with good reason. "We had discovered," he told a reporter for the *New York Herald-Tribune*, "that the southern prisons were treasure troves of . . . ballads, for the convicts were encouraged to sing at their work."[38] One of those convicts who needed little encouragement to sing was Lead Belly, who so deeply impressed Lomax that after Lead Belly's release from prison, Lomax hired him as his driver on his song-collecting trek through the South. Lead Belly also became Lomax's liaison, facilitating his meeting and recording black convicts who otherwise might have been reluctant to cooperate with Lomax. Lomax introduced Lead Belly to New York (and vice versa) in 1935. The two men had a bitter falling out, however, and Lead Belly went back home to Louisiana—only to return to New York a year later in hopes of carving out a career as a singer offering up his own special brand of music. "[Lead Belly] is currently singing and playing on the radio," *Life* magazine reported a few months after his return to New York, and went on to suggest that he "may well be on the brink of a new and prosperous period."[39] It was at this point in Lead Belly's career that Wright's all-important article on him appeared in the *Daily Worker*.

Unlike all the other people Wright interviewed for his *Daily Worker* articles, Lead Belly became his friend and drinking partner. The two met either at a rally or a meeting sometime during Lead Belly's return visit to New York in 1937.[40] Wright's admiration for Lead Belly is evident from the outset of his article. "[T]he entire folk culture of the American Negro," he declares, appears to have "found its embodiment in him." Wright goes on to trumpet the sheer number and the wide variety of the songs in Lead Belly's repertoire: "Blues, spirituals, animal songs, ballads, and work songs pour forth [from him] in . . . profusion." It seems, Wright marvels, that Lead Belly "knows every song his race has ever sung." Lead Belly's music, Wright explains, is inspired by "the day-to-day life of his people" as well as by his own experiences in prison and in the "swamplands [and] sun-baked cotton fields" of the Deep South.[41]

Wright follows up these well-deserved accolades with a brief sketch of Lead Belly's life and career. It is here, particularly in his interpretation of Lead Belly's relationship with John Lomax, that Wright's friendship with Lead Belly clouds matters. With barely concealed indignation, Wright proceeds to paint Lomax as a cultural bandit, characterizing his management of Lead Belly as "one of the most amazing cultural swindles in American history." Wright presents the relationship between the two men as a supreme example of white exploitation of black talent. Lomax, he contends, duped Lead Belly, promising the singer that "he would make him rich" if he assisted him in collecting songs from black prisoners throughout the South.[42] In truth, Lomax never promised Lead Belly that he would make him a rich man; indeed, Lomax was never under the illusion that he himself would ever become rich from his adventures as a ballad hunter (to borrow the title of his autobiography). Becoming rich, or making anyone else rich, was never Lomax's goal. Cultural preservation was. Near the conclusion of his autobiography, Lomax writes, "As I look back on the years of my folk song collecting, I do so with mixed emotions. It has been hard work, at times full of disappointment and discouragement, and at other times richly rewarding."[43] The rich rewards that Lomax speaks of were definitely not monetary. Lomax, then, was not the villain that Wright made him out to be; he did not, contrary to Wright's claims, defraud or exploit Lead Belly. This is not to say that Wright fabricated or knowingly distorted Lomax's dealings with Lead Belly. For his contention that Lomax was a cultural swindler, Wright was drawing on what the singer himself had undoubtedly told him during some of their talks over drinks. Wright's objectivity was thus momentarily clouded.

But such inaccuracies are few, and they are far outweighed by the useful purposes that the article served when it appeared. One was that it counteracted the generally sensationalist and demeaning image of Lead Belly that the white media had been projecting for two and a half years. The newspaper article that ushered in the essentially lurid media portrait of Lead Belly was the same one that introduced him to New York as "the sweet singer of the swamplands." Written by Lincoln Barnett, it appeared *New York Herald-Tribune* on January 3, 1935. Barnett's flattering characterization of Lead Belly at the outset as the "sweet singer of the swamplands" is immediately undercut by sarcasm. Lead Belly, he quips, is in town "to do a few tunes between homicides." Barnett then goes on to describe Lead Belly as a "powerful, knife-toting Negro" whose violent ways have landed him in two state prisons. He does not ignore Lead Belly's talent, however, pointing out his "husky tenor" and guitar playing that "ineluctably charm the ears of those who listen." Barnett quotes Lomax, affirming Lead Belly's talent: "There is no question as to his ability. He's better than any radio character I've ever heard." But those acknowledgements are diluted time and again by the article's portrayal of Lead Belly as by turns menacing and obsequious. The mention of his "dreadful charm," for instance, is framed by suggestions of sex and violence: "[His] voice causes brown-skinned women to swoon and produces a violently inverse effect upon their husbands and lovers." He is also seen as stereotypically loyal, and Barnett refers to him as Lomax's "faithful retainer" who with "undying affection" has "pledge[d] . . . his life and services till death should part them." "Boss," he is quoted as telling Lomax at one point, "if you ever get in trouble and some man tries to shoot you I'll jump in front of the bullet before I let you get hurt."[44] In sum, the *Herald-Tribune* article, appearing only a few days after Lead Belly's arrival in New York, gave him a far from flattering introduction.

Equally unflattering was the story on Lead Belly that appeared in *Time* magazine about two weeks later. Its very first sentence homes in on Lead Belly's criminal past and describes him in animalistic terms: "In Texas a black buck murdered a man." The article goes on to characterize Lead

Belly as a "wild-eyed" hellion whose "knife bulged in his pocket." Though the piece notes Lead Belly's "rich and clear" voice and his talented guitar playing, it points out almost gleefully that Lead Belly was such a "hell-raising minstrel" that shortly before performing for a group of agents and scouts, he "had been out on a wild 24-hour rampage in Harlem." Indeed, even before the article begins, its title—"Murderous Minstrel"—forecasts the perspective from which Lead Belly will be presented.[45]

Another article that cast Lead Belly in a harsh light was one that appeared in *Life* magazine on April 19, 1937, a few months after his return to New York, with the demeaning title "Bad Nigger Makes Good Minstrel." Like the story in *Time*, it acknowledged Lead Belly's "skill on the guitar," referring to him as "a walking anthology of unwritten folk music" and dubbing him "the country's No. 1 Negro minstrel." But like the *Time* piece it dwelled on Lead Belly's criminal past—how "in a row involving a girl," he had "shot another man dead" and went to prison for it, and how later "he got into a stabbing fray with a gang of other Negroes" and had been sent back to prison for attempted murder. One of two photos accompanying the article showed hands playing a guitar, and in bold letters under the photo is the caption, "These Hands Once Killed a Man." The story also brought up details of Lead Belly's early sex life, mentioning that "at 15, he was an illegitimate father." It further painted him as a prodigal of sorts who allowed "money and fame [to go] to his head" and caused him to break with his benefactor, John Lomax.[46]

Then there was the March of Time newsreel that was released in movie theaters across the United States in early 1935. Along with a brief look at Hitler's increasingly menacing rise to power in Europe, the newsreel of March 8 featured a segment on Lead Belly. Although intended as a laudatory look at a "fine songster," as he is described in the newsreel, the featurette is nonetheless shot through with demeaning scenes and images of Lead Belly. For the most part, it depicts him as a twentieth-century version of the docile, faithful slave, a stock figure in mid- and late-nineteenth-century southern literature, especially in the works of Plantationists like Thomas Nelson Page, Armistead C. Gordon, and Irwin

Russell. The short stories, novels, and poems of the Plantationists invariably portray the male slave as so obedient and loyal to his master that he is even willing to lay down his life to save the master's. In the newsreel, Lead Belly seems to have stepped right out of the pages of one of these Plantationists. In one newsreel scene, Lead Belly reenacts his catching up with Lomax after being released from Angola, and he is shown pledging his undying allegiance to the white folklorist. "Please, boss, take me with you," he pleads. "I'll use [my knife] on somebody if they bother you . . . You'll never have to tie your shoe strings any more, if you'll let me, long as you keep me with you." Elsewhere he tells Lomax, "No use to try and run me away, boss. I came here to be your man. I got to work for you the rest of my life." Like the *Herald-Tribune* and *Time* articles that came before it and the *Life* story that was to come after it, the newsreel also highlighted Lead Belly's criminal past. It opens with Lead Belly and a small group of black actors all clothed in then-traditional black-and-white-striped prison uniforms. In a voice-over, a narrator announces the setting: the Louisiana State Penitentiary. Lead Belly is then seen strumming out "Goodnight, Irene" in front of a fire. A little later, when Lead Belly offers to work for Lomax, the folklorist at first says no and reminds Lead Belly, "You're a mean boy. You killed two men." Lomax asks whether he has a pistol, to which Lead Belly says no, but he hands Lomax a knife to examine. Finally Lomax relents, and Lead Belly exults: "You be my big boss and I'll be your man. Thank you, sir, thank you!" All told, as Lead Belly's biographers Wolfe and Lornell accurately observe, the newsreel is "hopelessly stereotyped and full of Uncle Tomism."[47] It must be remembered that the March of Time newsreels, as the Henry Luce media empire boasted, were regular monthly features shown in movie theaters across America. "For many people," media historian Raymond Fielding observes, "especially the illiterate, [the March of Time newsreels were] a principal source of news until the coming of television." The newsreel that showcased Lead Belly, Fielding says, "appeared in 417 movie houses in 168 cities."[48] Since the newsreels were shown repeatedly, and since movie attendance was high despite the Depression, it is a safe bet that nearly one hundred thousand people saw the Lead Belly segment.

Viewed in light of such sensationalist and quasi-racist media coverage of Lead Belly, Wright's article stands as a strong and necessary corrective. In place of an obsequious caricature recalling Stepin Fetchit, Lead Belly becomes, in Wright's hands, a proud, righteously rebellious folk artist, a figure more sinned against than sinning, a man who refuses to suffer fools—especially white fools—gladly. Not that Wright ignores or glosses over Lead Belly's prison record—he simply does not magnify and sensationalize that part of his past the way the mainstream press coverage did. Wright's focus is on Lead Belly as artist, as musical giant, not as knife-wielding hellion.

Wright's article's additional value was in reintroducing Lead Belly to a public that had never truly appreciated what he had to offer. It may have compelled that public to take a second look at this musical legend living among them and to recognize, perhaps for the first time, that Lead Belly was as much a protest singer as he was a folk balladeer. Wright closes his article with excerpts from two of Lead Belly's then-new compositions, "Bourgeois Blues" and "The Scottsboro Boys Got Here." Both can rightly be defined as protest songs. Though Lead Belly did not consider himself a protest singer or his songs protest songs, it was due primarily to these songs of his that he was in such high demand as a performer at rallies and protest meetings held by labor groups and leftist organizations night after night in various parts of New York.[49] Wolf and Lornell write that groups such as the Workers Alliance of America, Workers International Relief, the International Workers Order, the Young Communist League, and various organizations supporting the Loyalist cause in the Spanish Civil War were among the many that Lead Belly performed for, and they point out that he always drew large crowds.[50] While it may be exaggeration to hold Wright's article responsible for the interest and attention that leftist groups showered upon Lead Belly beginning in late 1937 and lasting into the early 1940s, it may have helped guide many into the singer's fold. The *Daily Worker*, it must not be forgotten, had an extensive readership in New York, and it cannot be denied that Lead Belly's popularity among the left soared after Wright's article appeared. Even Mike Gold, the party's journalistic superstar, seemed to have been won over, becoming one of Lead

Belly's most enthusiastic admirers and supporters and writing his own article on Lead Belly. On January 26, 1938, in "Change the World," Gold's regular column in the *Daily Worker,* he lauded the singer as a "true and original fountain of poetry . . . a worker with a guitar telling his feelings in song." Like Wright, he branded John Lomax "an exploiter" and praised Lead Belly as one of "nature's bards," going on to contend that "sophisticated poets can learn [much] from such [an artist]."[51] Gold acknowledges Wright's Lead Belly article (though he refers to Wright not as a journalist or the Harlem bureau chief but as "Dick Wright, the Chicago poet"). Wright's article, then, was as much a beacon as it was an antidotal corrective.

No doubt one of the reasons that Wright was drawn to Lead Belly was that the singer, like Wright himself, did not hesitate to use words as a weapon. Wright recognized early on, even before Lead Belly became so sought after as a performer by leftist groups, that in his hands a song became "a tool for social reform."[52] Wright also recognized that, like music, the theater too could be used as a tool for social reform. That recognition is at the heart of "The Negro Tradition in the Theatre," Wright's article in the October 15, 1937, *Daily Worker.* Well researched and smoothly written, accurate in its observations and sincere in its insistence on the crucial role that the theater can play in black life, the article can even today hold its own as an intelligent investigation of the state and direction of early-twentieth-century black theater. The plays that Wright centers on in the article are those that were staged at the Lafayette Theatre in Harlem by the Negro Theatre Project of the WPA's Federal Theatre Project. Wright laments in the article that plays that honestly and realistically depict black life or treat issues germane to the black experience are routinely ignored by black and white audiences alike in favor of productions that are little more than minstrel shows. As evidence, he contrasts the critical reception given Frank Wilson's *Walk Together, Chillun* and Rudolph Fisher's *The Conjure Man Dies. Walk Together, Chillun,* a drama that explored a number of serious issues, premiered at the Lafayette on February 2, 1936, and ran for twenty-nine performances. Fewer than ten thousand people, Wright reveals, came out to see it. On the other hand, he reports, *The Conjure Man*

Dies, an adaptation of Rudolph Fisher's 1932 novel of the same name, drew over sixty-five thousand viewers during its Lafayette run. Wright's dismay at the relatively low turnout for Wilson's play is evident, as is his frustration that many more preferred to see *The Conjure Man Dies*. He could not have chosen two better examples to illustrate what he identifies in the article as "the problems and efforts of the Negro in the American theatre."[53] To Wright, Wilson's drama exemplified the path that he believed black theater should take. The issues that the play treated—the impact of northern urban life on southern black migrants, intra-racial conflict, the necessity of racial solidarity—were ones Wright deemed important and therefore well worth dramatizing, and, once dramatized, well worth viewing. Yet, as Wright noted, viewer attendance at the play was low.

In contrast, *The Conjure Man Dies* was a hit with audiences—"a Harlem crowd-pleaser," as theater historians Hill and Hatch have characterized it.[54] In the hands of Arna Bontemps and Countee Cullen, who scripted the play from Fisher's popular novel, *The Conjure Man Dies* featured a plot that kept its audience in suspense, quite a few Harlem in-jokes that kept them laughing, and strong performances that kept them thrilled. "The entire cast deserves applause for its work in this production," exclaimed Roi Ottley in the *Amsterdam News* a few days after the play opened.[55] So successful was the play that after its run at the Lafayette ended, it went on tour. The popularity of *The Conjure Man Dies* juxtaposed against the lukewarm reception given to Wilson's *Walk Together, Chillun* signaled to Wright the direction black theater was heading. Clearly that was away from serious, thought-provoking drama toward light-hearted, escapist fare. As further evidence of this drift, Wright points to other Federal Theatre Project productions staged at the Lafayette: *Turpentine*, a drama that depicted the brutal treatment and inhumane working conditions endured by black laborers on a turpentine-tapping camp in the Florida pine woods; *Sweet Land*, which centered on the struggle between black sharecroppers and white farm owners, Klan violence, and black unionizing efforts; and *The Case of Philip Lawrence*, a quasi-naturalistic play about a young black college graduate who, unable to find an honest job, goes to work for a Harlem gangster and ends up accused of a murder he did not commit. All of these dramas, Wright notes, met with the same low attendance as Wilson's play. Harlemites, he sadly observes, "were [so] used to being entertained . . . [that] they shied from serious themes on the stage."[56]

It figured that Harlem's preference for musical and comedic stage productions did not sit well with Wright, a man who believed that art should ever be at the service of social issues. Wright, as far back as his Chicago days, "expected true theatre to antagonize an audience," Rena Fraden correctly pointed out in her *Blueprints for a Black Federal Theatre*. He regarded the vaudeville-like productions that so many black audiences frequented as "cheap and ignorant, amusement for the master, a tradition entirely tainted by white racist expectations and stereotypes."[57] Even though his *Daily Worker* article on black theater is not a tirade or an explicit condemnation of popular taste, it does evince Wright's belief in the value of serious drama and his impatience with the "fluff" that he saw masquerading as entertainment. It shows Wright at his idealistic best, believing (and promulgating the belief) that art is an ideal forum for addressing social issues and an ideal means of effecting social change.

It should be noted that Wright was not the only black intellectual of his day to bemoan Harlem's lack of interest in serious drama and its fondness for escapist fare. The *Amsterdam News*, for example, in an editorial that ran not long after Wright's article appeared, remarked how disappointing it was that "there were so few Negroes in the audience" at the Lafayette for the Federal Theatre Project's production of the compelling historical drama *Haiti*. *Haiti*, the editorial pointed out, "is one of the few plays ever shown in New York that is definitely complimentary to all Negroes. It has probably done much already to break down some of the silly prejudices against the race. Yet, Negroes, the ones who should be most enthusiastic about it and pack the Lafayette every night, ignore it almost completely." They were ignoring it, the writer complained, in favor of "can-can, hi-de-ho vaudeville." Like Wright, the editorialist noted with dismay that far too many "Harlemites of all groups and classes jam-pack every can-can house in Harlem daily and nightly [yet] never darken the door of the Lafayette to see a play like *Haiti*" and consistently "fail to patronize other excellent productions." The editorial concluded by charging that Harlem's preference for mindless comedy and hi-de-ho musical shows while neglecting plays with substance is "an indictment not only against the cultural level of Harlemites but also against their desire to keep Negro actors in jobs during these bad times."[58] (One can almost hear Wright somewhere whispering, "Amen to that!")

The one weakness, however, that Wright's article and the *Amsterdam News* editorial share is that they make no attempt to explain why so many Harlemites chose musical-comedic stage shows over dramatic theatrical productions. There were indeed reasons for that preference. The vast majority of Harlemites, Arthur Paris reminds us, were from "a relatively impoverished and uneducated rural background" and were either unemployed or "locked into menial jobs." As such, they "constitute[d] an audience of direct and unsophisticated tastes with a bent more toward vaudeville and burlesque than 'serious drama' or even melodrama."[59] Fraden likewise points to these direct and unsophisticated tastes as a reason for the "disappointingly small black audiences" attending dramatic productions. Citing one of the many audience surveys taken by the Federal Theatre Project, she remarks that Harlem audiences generally found serious dramas—"problem plays" like *Walk Together, Chillun*—too boring and didactic. "Audiences are not anxious to be preached to," she quotes the survey. "They want diversion, entertainment, not just morbid social problems."[60] Also at work was what Paris calls "the economic imperative": the little money that the average Harlemite did have, so the reasoning seemed to go, would be put to more emotionally profitable use by spending it on "feel-good" entertainment rather than on issue-driven social dramas.[61]

As a transplanted southerner himself and a close observer of Harlem life, Wright could not but have been aware of these factors, yet he chose not to mention them. The reason for this omission perhaps is that the sociocultural crusader in Wright eclipsed the country boy in him. Or maybe Wright believed that it was the province of the sociologist to account for the *why* of the matter: his job was to present the *what*. Or perhaps again where others saw reasons for Harlem's taste in popular entertainment, Wright saw excuses. Whatever his motivation, Wright chose not to spend time probing the why of it all, electing instead to make "the rehabilitation of the Negro in the theatre" his primary concern.[62]

That concern, Wright was surely gratified to know, was shared by almost everybody involved with the Federal Theatre Project, from program administrators, producers, and directors to writers and actors. At the close of his article, Wright points out that one of the goals of the WPA's Negro Theatre Project was to "[make] the children of the Negro people theatre conscious."[63] Wright would have been the first to admit (as his article bears out) that one of his goals too was to make Depression-era Harlemites recognize and appreciate theater as a potent form of artistic expression.

Artistic expression is also the focal point of "Every Child Is a Genius," Wright's article spotlighting the opening of the Harlem Community Art Center, which was established with federal funding as part of the WPA's Federal Art Project. On its face, the subject matter of the article seems mundane and uninteresting, but the center would go on to be important to the cultural life of Harlem, and the article is far from dull. Located at 290 Lenox Avenue, the center opened its doors on the evening of December 20, 1937, with a formal program that included an exhibition of paintings, sculptures, and murals fashioned by artists of the Harlem Artists Guild, as well as many by talented Harlem children. Some of the speakers at the opening ceremony included such well-known figures as A. Philip Randolph, James Weldon Johnson, and sculptor Augusta Savage, the center's newly appointed director. Among those in attendance at the evening ceremony were Charles S. Johnson (one of the deans of the Harlem Renaissance), Arthur Schomburg, Mrs. Aaron Douglas, and literary giant Claude McKay. First Lady Eleanor Roosevelt toured the center the afternoon of the opening. The center occupied the entire second floor of the building, with eight thousand square feet of floor space partitioned into ten separate studios. Under the direction of seventeen WPA teachers and staff workers, students would be taught painting, drawing, sculpture, pottery, weaving, and photography. All classes were free of charge and offered both during the day and at night. The timing of the center's opening was probably not lost on Wright, who no doubt viewed it as a Christmas gift to a Harlem sorely in need of cheer.

Wright was not alone in seeing the CAC as newsworthy. The *Amsterdam News*, devoted considerable space to the center's opening in a piece appearing on Christmas Day. The *New York Post* and the *New York Journal and American* covered the story on December 20, while the Sun and the World-Telegram ran articles on December 21. The *New York Times* ran three pieces on the center, from December 19 to December 22. A common thread running throughout all the coverage was Harlem's enthusiasm for the art center. Even before it officially opened, 400 students had enrolled—children, teens, and adults—a clear indication, to many, of Harlem's desire for training in the arts, a desire that had been recognized years earlier. Over a year and a half before the center's opening, *Opportunity*, the journal of the Urban League and kissing cousin of the NAACP's *Crisis*, featured an article titled "Harlem Goes in for Art." Written by Sophia Steinbach, the article pointed out the "intensive desire for creative activity" that existed in Harlem and revealed how the many free art classes that had been established in Harlem by the Federal Art Project had by then attracted over 1,500 children and adults. Lacking a suitable art center, the article went on to say, the classes were held in schools, churches, Y's, and even garages. Harlem's "enthusiastic response" to art training programs, the article concluded, sent a strong message that "Harlem children . . . are helping to shape America's art future."[64] One of those "children" who got his start at the CAC and from there went on to make a profound contribution to the art world was Jacob Lawrence.

Wright's article on the CAC nicely captures every bit of the enthusiasm and hope generated by the newly opened facility. With interest-grabbing clarity, the piece conveys how greatly the newly opened center will benefit Harlemites, especially young ones. The headline—"Every Child Is a Genius"—encapsulates the center's belief in the untapped artistic talent of Harlem's young people and its commitment to cultivating that talent. Granted, there were surely those who argued that Depression-racked Harlem had more pressing needs than a free art center. Truth be told, they were right. Yet it was also true that many Harlemites hungered for more than just bread and butter. It was to satisfy this other hunger that the CAC was established. Indeed, what Steinbach in *Opportunity* says about the

Federal Art Project in general can be applied with equal validity to the Harlem Community Arts Center: "[It] cannot be considered as a substitute for economic justice and security in Harlem, nor is it expected to take the place of recreational and social opportunities which are sadly needed. But it does provide an opportunity for the people of that crowded area to satisfy their creative yearnings and to experience the thrill of bringing new and hitherto unknown sources of beauty and satisfaction into their lives."[65] Beauty and satisfaction, as Wright's article makes clear, were exactly what the CAC delivered to a Harlem where such commodities were all too scarce.

■

"All art is propaganda," Wright reportedly once railed at James Baldwin in response to Baldwin's criticism of *Native Son* as being too didactic. That art should help effect and promote social justice was one of Wright's most deeply held, long-lasting beliefs. It was also one of his earliest. How early is apparent from several *Daily Worker* articles he penned during his time at the newspaper. The resurrection of *Challenge* magazine as an issue-driven journal (*New Challenge*), the opening of the Harlem Community Arts Center, the importance of the plays staged by the Federal Theatre Project's Negro Theatre Project, the music of Lead Belly—these were important stories to Wright, and they stand as some of his most noteworthy contributions to the *Daily Worker*.

■ ■ ■

Daily Worker, JUNE 8, 1937

Negro Writers Launch Literary Quarterly

THE THOUSANDS OF NEGRO WORKERS, students, and intellectuals whose lives have been touched by recent social and economic changes constitute the new audience which young Negro writers are aiming to mold and direct. In contradistinction to the Harlem School of expression which was complemented by the World War and post-War conditions, and in part exploited by publishers for the jaded appetites of New York Bohemians, the new movement among Negro writers is receiving its stimulus from below rather than from above.

Following in the wake of the National Negro Congress which was held in Chicago about a year ago, a group of young writers, among whom are Margaret Walker, Arna Bontemps, Frank Marshall Davis, Marian Minus, Richard Wright, Edward Bland, Russell Marshall, Robert Davis and others, formed the first group whose aims were to render the life of their race in social and realistic terms. For the first time in Negro history problems such as nationalism in literature, perspective, the relation of the Negro writer to politics and social movements were formulated and discussed.

Last Wednesday night a similar group met in New York to unite and channelize the objectives of these writers. The statement drafted at the meeting called for an active struggle on the part of Negro writers against war, fascism, and reaction in general. Negro writers interested can communicate with *New Challenge* at 43 W. 66th Street, New York City.

Similar organizational activities are being manifested in other cities such as Washington, Memphis and Detroit. To mold these young writers who are still on the wing, an organizational plan, similar in purpose and structure to that of the old John Reed Clubs which influenced so many young white writers during the past seven years, is being launched with a literary quarterly, *New Challenge*, as its organ of expression. The first issue will be off the press in September. The new magazine will be edited by Dorothy West, Marian Minus and Richard Wright.

WELCOME WHITE WRITERS

Though the contributors will in the main be Negroes, white writers dealing definitively with minority themes and depicting conditions of life common to the Negro people will be welcomed.

One of the most hopeful and profound symptoms of the new movement is the deep desire on the part of the Negro writers for unity and at the same time the alliance of that unity with all of that which is progressive in American life. An increasing participation of Negro writers in craft unions, congresses and conferences dealing with economic and political problems indicate[s] the new consciousness.

Realizing the need for a picture of the whole of Negro life, the content of folk-lore, explicit and implicit, is being recognized by these writers as an important source of literature to be studied and used. Representative of this folk background were the 574 delegates who attended the Southern Youth Conference of the National Negro Congress in Richmond, Va., Feb. 1937. This step toward unity was an expression which these writers are utilizing in their effort to deal with the indigenous folk material of the Southern plantation masses. ■

Daily Worker, December 28, 1937

Every Child Is a Genius

THREE FLIGHTS ABOVE THE ROAR of 125th St. and Lenox Ave. is one of the strangest sights to be found in Harlem. Occupying an entire floor of some 8,000 square feet, with ten studios lighted by 19-feet high windows, is Harlem's first art school, the Federal-built Harlem Community Art Center.

Situated in the heart of Harlem, at 290 Lenox Ave., the school was opened a few days ago and has as its task the servicing and instructing of a community of 250,000 people who have long been denied access to modern art training.

The school will conduct day and evening classes for Negro children as well as adults, and offers courses in photography, commercial art, lithography, metal work, weaving, pottery, sculpture, painting, and drawing.

In discussing the reasons for opening this elaborate school in Harlem, Audrey McMahon, regional director of the Federal Art Project, declared:

"Harlem's response to art teaching has been more spontaneous than the response of any other section of New York.

"The first classes under Federal auspices were opened in 1935 in neighborhood schools, settlements, and churches. In that same year the average weekly attendance of these Harlem studios was 2,809.

"Talent of a high order, which has received recognition by professional artists, has been uncovered among Negro children. Exhibitions of their work have been circulated through cities of the West and South.

"I look to Harlem as a community which will undoubtedly play an important role in the development of American graphic and plastic arts."

BACKED BY LEADER

Augusta Savage, Harlem's foremost sculptress, has been placed in charge of the art school as director.

The school has been endorsed by outstanding Harlem leaders, among whom was A. Philip Randolph, president of the Brotherhood of Sleeping Car Porters and president of the National Negro Congress. In commenting upon the possibilities of the school, Randolph stated:

"The Art Project under WPA is not just a device to provide jobs to the proverbial starving artist, but to provide the basis and motivation for the expression of art through socialized arrangements that give wider opportunity to individuals as well as masses for development."

Over a long period of time there have been many attempts on the part of individuals and groups in Harlem to build an art center. As early as 1920 the work of Negro artists was exhibited at the 135th St. Branch of the New York Public Library.

Augusta Savage, sensing the handicaps of the young Negro artist, provided a place of study and work for them in their Harlem workshop.

In 1935 the formation of the Artists' Guild aroused interest in the plight of the struggling Negro artist.

So, after two decades of existence as a distinct Negro community, Harlem has at last come into its own as an art center, with a school and an audience of its own.

The canvasses, water colors, etchings, and drawing hung upon the walls of the Art Center tell of hunger, bad housing, lack of recreational facilities, thus bringing together for the first time in a popular manner the economic and cultural aspects of the world's largest Negro community. ■

Daily Worker, AUGUST 12, 1937

Huddie Ledbetter, Famous Negro Folk Artist, Sings the Songs of Scottsboro and His People

WHEN 50-YEAR-OLD HUDDIE LEDBETTER planks himself in a chair, spreads his feet and starts strumming his 12-stringed guitar and singing that rich, barrel-chested baritone, it seems that the entire folk culture of the American Negro has found its embodiment in him.

Blues, spirituals, animal songs, ballads and work songs pour forth in such profusion that it seems he knows every song his race has ever sung.

Shaped and molded by some of the harshest social forces in American life, Ledbetter admits that he knows 500 folk songs, "and maybe many more I can't count."

He makes his songs out of the day-to-day life of his people. He sings of death, of work, of balked love, of Southern jails no better than hell-holes, of chain gangs, of segregation, and of his hope for a better life.

SANG THROUGH SOUTH

This hard stocky black man sang his way through the Louisiana swamp-lands, the sun-baked cotton fields, and out of two state prisons where he was sent for protecting himself against the aggression of Southern whites.

Down South the white landlords called him a "bad nigger" and they were afraid of his fists, his bitter, biting songs, his 12-stringed guitar, and his inability to take injustice and like it. Because they feared him and respected his hardness, they called him "Lead Belly." And at the first opportunity that came their way they threw him in jail.

This folk singer tells tales of dodging white mobs, of wandering at night to save his life, and of how he would snatch a few hours of companionship with his friends when the whites were not looking. He tells of cutting sugar cane in the rain; of picking a bale of cotton in two days; and of seeing a black man drop dead from the heat of Southern suns in the cotton fields.

WINS PARDON

When Ledbetter won himself a pardon for the second time out of a Southern prison by composing folk songs, the Southern landlords exploited him, robbed him of his self-made culture and then turned him loose on the streets of Northern cities to starve.

John A. Lomax, collector of American folk songs for the Library of Congress, heard of Ledbetter and went to see him in prison.

And here begins one of the most amazing cultural swindles in American history. Lomax found in Ledbetter a mine of lore, songs, tunes, and adages of the South.

He persuaded Ledbetter to make a phonograph record. When finished, it contained two songs: one a love song, "Irene," a haunting and tender melody; the other was called "To O. K. Allen." It was a chanted plea to Governor Allen of Louisiana for a pardon. The plea was sung so successfully that exactly one month later Ledbetter was free.

USES LEDBETTER

Lomax then beguiled the singer with sugary promises, telling him that if he helped him to gather folk songs from other Negro prisoners in various prisons throughout the South, he would make him rich.

Lomax used the influence of his official position with the Library of Congress to get into prisons and get songs. But he knew that a white man would have great difficulty in getting Negro prisoners to confide their folk culture in him; so he used Ledbetter as his guide and entrée.

Ledbetter and Lomax traveled through Texas, Arkansas, Alabama, [and] Louisiana, and gathered folk songs which later were compiled into a book, *American Ballads and Folk Songs*. And the only credit Ledbetter got for that book was the "high honor" of seeing his name in print.

BEGINS ATTACKS

In addition, Lomax, in order to make engagements and more profit, gave out a vicious tirade of publicity to the nation's leading newspapers about the Negro folk singer. Ledbetter was represented in the *New York Herald Tribune, Time Magazine* and over the radio as a half sex-mad, knife-toting, black buck from Texas. *Time Magazine,* March of Time and the newspapers generally featured him in such tones.

In due time Lomax toured the Northern and New England states with Ledbetter, charging $100 per night for each appearance and in addition sometimes took up collections which amounted to over $50.

When Ledbetter insisted upon a straight and legal contract, Lomax told him that he was saving his money for him, and that, "If I gave you your money you'd throw it away in Harlem."

When the tour ended, Ledbetter received but $16 for his appearance in the March of Time; nothing for his extensive travels and work save a sum of $255 paid to him in skimpy installments: $55 in cash and the remaining $200 in checks which were so dated that he could not draw but $50 of it each month.

GOES SOUTH

Ledbetter, who had married in the meantime, took the checks and his wife and went to Shreveport, La. He got what few jobs he could, but the Southern whites would have none of him.

Three years ago he came back to New York, this time alone save for his wife, a laundry worker, who since has become his manager.

Even in New York contracts were hard to get; and for the second time Ledbetter was victimized by a prejudiced white Southerner in a theatre engagement. Finally he joined the Workers' Alliance and applied for relief.

THREATEN SONGS

The relief authorities could not believe that Ledbetter did not have money saved from his extensive appearance on the stage and threatened to withdraw his food ticket. In return the folk singer threatened to write a song about the rotten relief methods and the relief authorities granted his demands.

"The folks in the Workers' Alliance are the finest I've ever known," said Ledbetter. "I feel happy when I am with the boys here in the Workers' Alliance. They are different from those Southern white men."

Two of his latest compositions are on the methods of segregation used in Washington, D.C. and his elation over the recent Scottsboro victory. The words of Bourgeois Blues are as follows:

I was in Washington the other day
And I heard a white man say,
"I am a bourgeois. . ." [ellipses in original here and below]

CHORUS:
Aw, bourgeois! Aw, bourgeois!
I got them bourgeois blues!
And I'm sure gonna spread the news!

When I was in Washington
I couldn't understand
How them white folks treat the colored man. . .
We went all over town
Trying to find a place to stay.
Everywhere we went the white folks
Run us away. . .

Me and my wife was standing on a stair
And we heard a white man say,
"We don't want no niggers up there. . ."

I advise colored folks to listen to me
And stay away from Washington, D.C.
'Cause it's a bourgeois town. . .

Them rich white folks in Washington
They sure know how
To throw you a nickel to see you bow. . .

"THE SCOTTSBORO BOYS GOT HERE"

Scottsboro Boys number nine
6 1/2 years they were confined
The only thing everybody hate
6 1/2 years these boys had to wait

CHORUS:
Scottsboro Boys done got here
Scottsboro Boys 6 1/2 years
Scottsboro Boys done got here
Done got here with a mighty good cheer

Now down South it's a shame
How people can frame
Stick you in jail, and stick you in a cell
Judge tell you to plead guilty in spite of old hell

Some can read, but can't understand
Then some is told and then don't know. . .
But the Attorney General broadcast it
Thursday night over the radio

Huddie Ledbetter will sing this Scottsboro song for the first time on the moonlight sail to be held tomorrow night by the Federal Writers Project. The Steamboat "Mayflower," on which the ride will be given, will leave from Pier 1, North River, West of Battery Park, at 8:30.

The Scottsboro Mothers, Mrs. Wright and Mrs. Montgomery, have been especially invited to hear the song in honor of their sons. ■

Daily Worker, OCTOBER 15, 1937

Negro Tradition in the Theatre

THE DEPRESSION BROUGHT a great many paradoxical things into American life, but none so paradoxical as the culmination of a quarter of a century of Negro theatre effort in the triumphant productions of the subsidized Federal Theatre in Harlem.

What the Negro actor had failed to do because of restrictions in the commercial theatre, he did on the dole. Freed for a while from exploiters, talent long stifled rose to the surface and compelled public attention through such startling exhibitions as *Macbeth, The Conjure Man Dies,* and *Turpentine.*

The long evolution of the Negro actor from the clowning minstrel type to Edna Thomas' lofty portrayal of Lady Macbeth represents a span of years crowded with abortive effort. Until the advent of *They Shall Not Die* and Stevedore, the Negro actor was compelled, whether he liked it or not, to portray Negro life in terms of what some audiences thought it should be.

NEGRO PROBLEMS DRAMATIZED

So used had even Negro audiences become to seeing themselves so depicted that they had all but lost the sense of what their own lives should be upon the stage. Hence the rehabilitation of the Negro in the theatre constituted a special problem. Not only had the Negro actor and the Negro theatre to fight for the right to depict life as it was, but both had to convince and win an audience whose faith had almost died.

Never have the problems and efforts of the Negro in the American theatre been so sharply dramatized as in the Lafayette Theatre in Harlem.

How serious these problems were can be seen from the critical reception, from both Negro and white, which greeted Frank Wilson's *Walk Together Chillun,* the first production of this Federal Negro Theatre, in February of 1936. Though this play dealt with labor and its difficult struggles, less than 10,000 people witnessed its performances.

On the other hand, Rudolph Fisher's *The Conjure Man Dies,* their second play, a melodramatic comedy-mystery, played to an audience totaling some 65,000 people. Frank Wilson's play dealt with Negro unity, a theme which was repugnant to many whites and which left many Negro theatre-goers cold. They were used to being entertained, and they shied away from serious themes on the stage.

So the Negro theatre was faced with two difficult problems: it had to create a Negro theatre literature and at the same time create and organize an audience for itself.

To overcome the first difficulty, the Lafayette Theatre organized and conducted classes in playwriting, which were open to any person who had ambition to write plays. To overcome the second, the theatre found plays depicting conditions of life which were familiar to Negroes whose background was the southern rural community.

OUTSTANDING PRODUCTION

While *Turpentine* was in rehearsal, the Lafayette astonished the nation by bringing forward a Negroid version of Shakespeare's *Macbeth.* In some measures this play represented a compromise with the Negro theatre problem: it afforded Negro actors a wide scope for their talent, and it dealt with a theme which was acceptable to a white theatergoing audience.

With its stunning array of brilliant costumes and enacted against the backdrop of a Haitian jungle, *Macbeth* was an innovation so daring that it attracted more people than all of the Lafayette's preceding plays combined and went on a national tour.

Meanwhile, the management of production at the Lafayette had changed hands. Gus Smith, long associated with the Negro stage both as actor and producer, took charge and endeavored to swing the dramatic productions of the theatre into the very center of the life of the Negro people.

The fourth production of the Lafayette was Gus Smith's and Peter Morrell's *Turpentine,* a drama depicting the exploitation of turpentine workers in Florida. From June to September of 1936, some 23,000 saw the play, a slight increase over *Walk Together Chillun.*

PLIGHT OF SHARECROPPER

Nor was the success of *Sweetland,* a play by Conrad Seller dramatizing the plight of the sharecropper in the South, any better. Peter Morrell's Noah and George Kelly's *Showoff* followed in rapid succession.

On June 8 of this year the Lafayette produced George McIntee's *The Case of Philip Lawrence,* a play of Harlem life built around a Negro college boy trying to get a job. *The Case of Philip Lawrence* was followed by Gus Smith's *Just Ten Days* and a children's play, *Horseplay.*

It can be definitely stated that these two years of activity have created an impression upon the Negro people. It has given them an inkling of what a theatre can mean to their lives.

But just as in the realm of politics the Negro's problem is a special problem, so it is true of the Negro's struggle for culture. Divorced from the theatre, publishing houses, and orchestras, the Negro finds that his first step toward creative expression is the fight for the possession of the mere instrumentalities of culture.

When looked at from this point of view, the recent dismissals of 100 of the Lafayette's actors out of a company of 198 is nothing short of tragic. Instead of the Negro actors being given every possible assistance to overcome their historical handicaps, they were cut more severely than any other group.

The success of the Lafayette so far merely serves to demonstrate the imperative need of even larger subsidies and more theatres for the Negro people. The Lafayette brought forward such names as Perry Watkins, Byron Webb, J. DeWitt Spencer, Thomas Anderson, Edward Perry, and Leonard DePeaur [De Paur]. It can bring forward many more if it's given the chance.

Soon the Lafayette will be facing the third year of its existence in carrying forward its four-fold program: developing a theatre literature for the Negro theatre; organizing and educating an audience; training and developing new talent; and making the children of the Negro people theatre conscious. ■

Daily Worker, November 15, 1937

Negroes Win Back Jobs on WPA Theatre

THE REINSTATEMENT LAST FRIDAY of 11 Negro vaudeville artists of Unit 1-C of the Federal Theatre, who were fired July 15, brought to a victorious conclusion one of the most important battles ever waged against Jim Crow practices on the WPA, it was announced yesterday by the Workers' Alliance.

Last July 11, members of the Vaudeville Unit 1-C were fired by Frank Merlin, managing producer of the Variety Theatre. This unit, the only Negro vaudeville unit in the Federal Theatre, had been active in the May 27 stoppage and was widely known as a militant union local.

Merlin had over a long period constantly aired his anti-Negro and anti-union feeling and had openly boasted that he would fire the entire

Negro group at the first opportunity. On July 15, the Vaudeville Unit 1-C was dismissed in a group.

Charges of discrimination were pressed by the Workers' Alliance. The WPA administration, while admitting the merits of the case as presented by Workers' Alliance, refused a hearing on the basis that the Joint Appeal Board should exercise "original jurisdiction" in all cases of discrimination.

MERLIN RESIGNS

Despite an adverse ruling handed down by the Joint Appeals Board on July 22, the publicity and sensational testimony brought out at the hearing were so strong that Merlin resigned.

After four months of tireless activity on the part of Frank B. Griffin and Arnold Wiley, union members and members of Unit 1-C, the administration reluctantly agreed to hear the case on Nov. 5.

The administration admitted at the hearing that the Negroes had been victims of rank discrimination but protested that they did not have the power to act. ■

CONCLUSION

DEPARTURE

Wright's article on the Harlem Community Art Center was the last one he wrote for the *Daily Worker* as one of its staff writers. As 1937 ended, so did Wright's time at the *Daily Worker.* In late December, he severed his ties to the newspaper. What he did not do, however, was inform anybody at the paper that he was resigning. Instead, he told everyone that he was taking a leave of absence. But Wright knew that his days at the *Daily Worker* were over, that he would never return to work at the newsroom. In a letter he wrote to Margaret Walker in mid-January of 1938, less than a month after he left the paper, he confided to her that he was "on a leave [from the *Daily Worker*] which (please, for political reasons, keep this quiet!) I hope to make a lengthy one."[1] The lengthy leave Wright spoke of was in truth a permanent one.

One major reason for his leaving the *Daily Worker* was some very good news that had come his way. On December 15, Wright received one of the most important letters of his life. The letter was from *Story* magazine, and it informed him that he had won first prize in the magazine's literary competition. Only a few sentences long, the letter, dated the day before, signaled an upward swing in Wright's life and fortunes and deserves to be quoted in full:

Dear Mr. Wright:

It is a great pleasure for STORY Magazine to announce that the judges of the W.P.A. contest have voted the $500 first prize award to you as author of "Uncle Tom's Children," a book of novellas.

While this is to serve as a formal announcement to you we would deeply appreciate it if you would consider this announcement strictly confidential and not to be made public or communicated to any one until later when we can make the official announcement at a time which would be of the most favorable value to you. At the same time we are planning to publish the book of long stories as a STORY PRESS-Harper & Brothers book, the exact contents of which are still to be discussed in view of the fact that it is possible that the new novella you have been working on might be utilized to give the book more variety. Could you discuss this matter with us at 3 o'clock Thursday afternoon, December 16th, at the office of Harper & Brothers, 49 E. 33 Street?

With all our congratulations,
Sincerely yours,
Whit Burnett[2]

Wright's big opportunity had finally arrived—he was going to be a paid, published author. Even though he heeded Whit Burnett's injunction to keep the good news of his winning the literary competition "strictly confidential," Wright's friends back in Chicago seemed to sense that something big was waiting for him just around the corner. A week after he learned that he had won first prize in the competition, his close friend and staunch supporter Margaret Walker wrote him, saying, "Seems as though several [of us] are expecting something mighty fine to break for you soon. I hope to God it does."[3] Wright must have been bursting to tell someone—Walker and Ellison especially—about his good fortune, but he kept the matter a secret. Two months to the date that Wright received Burnett's letter, *Story* magazine finally made the official announcement. Wright no doubt was relieved; at long last the good news was public. Faithful friend that she was, Walker was almost more excited about Wright's winning the competition than he was. "Oh boy!" she exclaimed in a letter a few days after hearing the news. "Isn't it great! . . . You'll probably be riding the crest of a wave of exhilaration."[4] In another letter, written the day that *Story* magazine publicly announced that Wright had won the competition, Walker gave him a characteristically fond pat on the back for his having achieved that "something mighty fine" which she had predicted for him two months earlier. "Things are shaping up just the way you wanted them," she declared. "You wanted to sell some of your stuff . . . and now you've sold a book that is going to sell like nobody's business."[5] With prophet-like accuracy, Walker was on target. *Uncle Tom's Children,* published the following month to highly favorable reviews nationwide, did indeed "sell like nobody's business," reconfirming Wright's commitment to his art and, in his eyes, justifying his "impatien[ce] to give up journalism for creative writing."[6]

But the news of his winning first prize in *Story*'s literary competition, along with the knowledge that the award meant grand-scale publication, was not the only reason Wright decided to leave the *Daily Worker.* After constant requests to WPA headquarters in Washington, D.C., and after months and months of waiting, Wright was notified in late December 1937 that his application for admission into the New York Federal Writers' Project had finally been approved. On Monday morning, January 3, 1938, he began working as a writer with the project.[7] The New York section of the Federal Writers' Project was at that time busily compiling a work to be titled *New York Panorama* and to be published by Random House the following year. The book was to be one of the volumes in the American Guides series and was, among other things, designed to draw attention to the accomplishments that President Roosevelt's New Deal had wrought during the Great Depression (which at that time was still in full force). The book's full title gives a clear indication of its scope: *New York Panorama: A Comprehensive View of the Metropolis, Presented in a Series of Articles Prepared by the Federal Writers' Project of the W.P.A. of New York City.* Wright was assigned the chapter on Harlem, and he tackled the responsibility eagerly, devoting to it all the time, energy, and creativity he could muster. His chapter, "Portrait of Harlem," remains one of the best of the twenty-six chapters in *New York Panorama*. Even though, like all the other writers on the project, Wright was allowed to do other work while researching and writing his chapter, "Portrait of Harlem" would not have been so meticulously researched and so well written had he not left his position at the *Daily Worker.*

Another factor that prompted Wright's decision to leave the *Daily Worker* was his psychological well-being. It was never a secret that Wright and his coworkers at the paper did not get along well. Many in the Communist Party distrusted Wright and at times even viewed him with disdain. What Ralph Ellison points out regarding the Communist rank and file perception of Wright applies equally to Wright's coworkers at the 135th Street office. "[They] sneered at his intellectuality," Ellison recalls, "ridiculed his writings, and dismissed his concern with literature and culture as an affectation."[8] For his part, Ellison continues, "Wright had little sense of humor concerning their undisguised hostility, and this led, as would be expected, to touchy relationships."[9] These touchy relationships took a definite toll on Wright, adding stress to his already pressure-filled life. His leaving the *Daily Worker* thus siphoned off a good bit of that stress. A month after Wright left the newspaper, Margaret Walker remarked in a letter to him that she had noticed a definite change for the better in his attitude, a change attributable, she deduced, to his leaving the *Daily Worker.* "I sort of figured," she told him, "that the newspaper work was not too much to your liking; even I could feel the tension and the rush in your letters, but I knew there was nothing to be done about it and eventually according to the law of averages something better just *had* to come along."[10] The "something better" that did was so much better that even party members and coworkers at the paper who had been antagonistic toward Wright were forced to recognize, no doubt to their chagrin, that he "had . . . become one of the literary stars of the Party," as Michael Favre put it.[11]

To the Communists, Wright's literary stardom meant, among other things, favorable publicity for them. He was still one of them, they reasoned. Those at the *Daily Worker*'s main office in Lower Manhattan's Union Square saw his success in this light and wanted him to return to the paper in some capacity. Years later, in April 1944, at the height of Wright's popularity, the newspaper's managing editor, Louis Budenz, wrote Wright inviting him to return to the paper in some capacity. "We are about to change the format and expand the character of the *Daily Worker*," he told Wright. "We would like very much to have you write regularly for the *Daily Worker*, beginning . . . early in May. We have in mind that you might be able to write for us once a week. . . . Please let us know how this fits in with your plans and work, and then we can discuss . . . in more detail the entire matter."[12] Wright never answered his letter. Wright's close friend Ben Davis also tried to get him to contribute something—anything—to the paper. Shortly after the publication of *Native Son*, Davis wrote Wright, asking, "[W]ould you be interested in sending us articles either regularly or irregularly for publication in the *Daily Worker*[?]" In a tone not so much flattering as complimentary, he went on to tell Wright, "I don't think I have to emphasize the great value which our paper and our readers would place upon anything you had to write. . . . As I pick up the various magazines, namely, the *Atlantic Monthly* and *Saturday Review*, my mouth literally waters to have Richard Wright appearing in the Daily Worker."[13] Wright's reply, if he ever sent one, is lost in the mist of history. What we do know is that after his article on the Louis-Schmeling bout in June 1938, Wright never again contributed to the *Daily Worker*.

It is tempting, and perhaps not altogether inaccurate, to read Wright's reluctance to contribute to the *Daily Worker* as an indication that he did not want to be reminded of his newspaper articles, those stories and features which he had written under the gun and which had siphoned off time and energy that he would have otherwise devoted to his creative writing. If Wright did feel this way, literary studies attest that he was not alone. Many established writers who started out as journalists chose to downplay their early newspaper work. Ernest Hemingway, for example, on his way to becoming enthroned as America's premiere writer, became clearly upset with bibliographer Louis Cohn when Cohn wanted to include some of Hemingway's early newspaper articles in the bibliography he was compiling for publication by Random House. "[The] newspaper stuff I have written," Hemingway told Cohn in a letter, "has nothing to do with [my] other writing which is entirely apart" (his "other writing" being Hemingway's fiction). "The first right that a man writing has," Hemingway continued, "is the choice of what he will publish. If you made your living as a newspaperman, learning your trade, writing against deadlines, writing to make stuff timely rather than permanent, no one has any right to dig this stuff up and use it against the stuff you have written [creatively]."[14]

Wright more than likely would have agreed with Hemingway. Given the fame and success that he went on to achieve after leaving the *Daily Worker*, the likelihood of such agreement is understandable. After all, it might be argued, the man responsible for writing *Native Son*, one of the greatest novels of the twentieth century, and *Black Boy*, one of the most widely read and critically acclaimed autobiographies in modern literature, might well have been loathe to remind the world that he once wrote newspaper articles on, say, the opening of a public housing development or rent strikes by irate tenants or protestors picketing the Italian consulate in New York. On the flip side, Hemingway certainly would have understood and concurred with Wright. Both writers, in short, were not fond of what they had written as newspapermen. But the truth is that Wright, like Hemingway, had absolutely nothing to be ashamed of when it came to his early newspaper work. What Arthur Waldhorn has said of Hemingway's journalism in the twenties—that it is characterized by a "remarkable discipline of observation and language"—applies with equal validity to Wright's journalism in the thirties.[15] Like Hemingway's pieces for the *Kansas City Star* and the *Toronto Daily Star*, Wright's articles for the *Daily Worker*, as well as those occasional ones in New Masses, are noteworthy for their ability to draw the reader in to the world they paint in such vivid strokes.

While Wright himself never viewed his *Daily Worker* articles with the same degree of disdain as Abe Aaron and Herbert Caro did, he nonetheless did not have a high regard for his journalism, considering it an incidental effort, much as James Weldon Johnson and his brother, J. Rosamond, considered their composition of "Lift Ev'ry Voice and Sing" an incidental effort. It will be recalled that when James Weldon and his brother composed "Lift Ev'ry Voice and Sing" in 1900 to commemorate Abraham Lincoln's birthday, they did so with the intention of having the song sung by a chorus of 500 black school children at a ceremony honoring the Great Emancipator. The song was composed, Johnson recalls in *Along This Way*, "under stress and with no intention other than to meet the demands of a particular moment" (156). Later, they were both genuinely surprised that the song proved to be so meaningful and enduring. Wright too would probably be surprised at how meaningful his newspaper articles actually were. Wright's *Daily Worker* articles, of course, cannot be placed on the same level of cultural importance and artistic merit as "Lift Ev'ry Voice and Sing," the Negro national anthem. But in both cases the underlying principle at work is the same: perceived worth and true value. Musing on the popularity and longevity of "Lift Ev'ry Voice," Johnson concludes, "The only comment we can make is that we wrote better than we knew."[16] In his newspaper articles for the *Daily Worker,* Wright, like the brothers Johnson, wrote better than he knew. The proof of that is in the reading.

NOTES

PREFACE

1. Margaret Walker, *Richard Wright, Daemonic Genius: A Portrait of the Man, A Critical Look at his Work* (New York: Warner, 1988), 314.

2. Meyer Weinberg, *A Short History of American Capitalism* (New York: New History Press, 2003), 209.

3. Richard Wright Papers, Yale Collection of American Literature, Beinecke Rare Book and Manuscript Library, Yale University.

4. Ibid.

5. Ibid.

6. Ibid.

INTRODUCTION: ARRIVAL

1. Rudolph Fisher, "City of Refuge," in *The City of Refuge: The Collected Short Stories of Rudolph Fisher,* ed. John McCluskey (Columbia: University of Missouri Press), 4.

2. Arnold Rampersad, introduction, in *The New Negro: Voices of the Harlem Renaissance,* ed. Alain Locke (New York: Simon and Schuster, 1997), ix.

3. James Weldon Johnson, "Harlem: The Culture Capital," in *The New Negro: Voices of the Harlem Renaissance,* ed. Alain Locke 1925 (New York: Simon and Schuster, 1997), 309.

4. Claude McKay, *Harlem: Negro Metropolis* (New York: Dutton, 1940), 16.

5. Arna Bontemps, "The Two Harlems," *American Scholar* 14 (Spring 1945): 167.

6. Cab Calloway and Bryant Rollins, *Minnie the Moocher* (New York: Crowell, 1976), 68.

7. Steven Watson, *The Harlem Renaissance: Hub of African-American Culture* (New York: Pantheon, 1995), 8.

8. Nathan Huggins, *Harlem Renaissance* (New York: Oxford University Press, 1973), 24.

9. Ibid., 14.

10. Jimmy Durante and Jack Kofoed, *Night Clubs* (New York: Knopf, 1931), 113.

11. Dan McCall, *The Example of Richard Wright* (New York: Harcourt, 1969), 193.

12. Edward Robb Ellis, A *Nation in Torment: The Great American Depression, 1929–1939* (New York: Cowart-McCann, 1970), 229.

13. Peter Marcuse, "The Beginnings of Public Housing in New York," *Journal of Urban History* 12 (August 1986): 355.

14. Mark Naison, *Communists in Harlem during the Depression* (Urbana: University of Illinois Press, 1983), 31.

15. Quoted in Cheryl Lynn Greenberg, *"Or Does It Explode?": Black Harlem in the Great Depression* (New York: Oxford University Press, 1997), 43.

16. Jervis Anderson, *This Was Harlem: A Cultural Portrait, 1900–1950* (New York: Farrar Straus Giroux, 1982), 235.

17. Richard Wright, *Black Boy* (1945, repr., New York: Harper, 1993), 285.

18. Ibid., 284.

19. Michel Fabre, *The Unfinished Quest of Richard Wright* (New York: Morrow, 1973), 258.

20. Kelly Rusinak and Chris Lamb, "A Sickening Red Tinge: The Daily Worker's Fight against White Baseball," *Cultural Logic: An Electronic Journal of Marxist Theory and Practice 3* (Fall 1999): 9.

21. *Daily Worker,* September 12, 1936, 6.

22. *Daily Worker,* "Daily Worker Gets Harlem News Bureau," September 23, 1936, 1.

23. *Daily Worker,* "New Paper Makes Big Hit in Harlem: Bureau Hailed," September 29, 1936, 5.

24. Benjamin J. Davis, *Communist Councilman from Harlem: Autobiographical Notes Written in a Federal Penitentiary* (New York: International, 1969), 81.

25. Madison D. Lacy, *Richard Wright: Black Boy,* videocassette (San Francisco: California Newsreel, 1994).

26. Sterling Brown Papers, Moorland-Springarn Research Center, Howard University.

27. Hazel Rowly, *Richard Wright: The Life and Times* (New York: Owl, 2002), 129.

28. Lacy, *Richard Wright: Black Boy.*

29. Rusniak and Lamb, "A Sickening Red Tinge," 9.

30. Michael Fabre, in Richard Wright, *The Richard Wright Reader* (New York: Harper, 1978), xxx.

31. Ralph Thompson, "Books of the Times," *New York Times,* November 18, 1941, 29; Horace R. Cayton, "Black Voices: Wright's New Book More Than a Study of Social Status," *Pittsburgh Courier,* November 15, 1941, 13.

32. Richard Wright, *12 Million Black Voices* (1941; repr., New York: Arno, 1969), 98.

33. Ibid., 93.

SECTION ONE: THE SHAME SPOT OF NEW YORK

1. Greenberg, *Or Does It Explode?,* 43.

2. Ellis, *A Nation in Torment,* 234.

3. Wright, "Negro, with 3-Week Old Baby, Begs Food on Streets," *Daily Worker,* August 4, 1937, 3.

4. Ronald Lawson and Mark Naison, *The Tenant Movement in New York City, 1904–1984* (New Brunswick: Rutgers University Press, 1986),88.

5. Greenberg, *Or Does It Explode?*, 182.

6. Ibid.

7. Lawson and Naison, *The Tenant Movement*, 97.

8. Ibid., 94.

9. Marcuse, "The Beginnings of Public Housing," 375, and Greenberg, *Or Does It Explode?*, 184.

10. Marcuse, "The Beginnings of Public Housing," 375.

11. "P.W.A. Leases Harlem River Houses to City," *New York Herald-Tribune*, June 17, 1937, 23.

12. New York Times, "$4,219,000 Housing Goes to City Today," June 16, 1937, 25A.

13. Langdon W. Post, "Harlem River Houses," *Opportunity* 15 (August 1937): 234.

14. "Pick Tenants for Harlem River Houses: List Filled after Many Are Rejected," *New York Amsterdam News*, June 19, 1937, 4.

15. Henry Lee Moon, "Housing Problem Is Still Acute in Harlem," *New York Times*, June 20, 1937, 10E.

16. "P.W.A. Leases Harlem River Houses to City," *New York Herald-Tribune*, June 17, 1937, 23.

17. Wright, "Opening of Harlem Project Homes Shows How Slums Can Be Wiped Out in New York," *Daily Worker*, October 8, 1937, 5.

18. Ibid.

19. *New York Times*, "$4,219, 000 Housing Goes to City Today," June 16, 1937, 25A.

20. Wright, "Opening of Harlem Project Homes," 5.

21. Ibid.

22. Ibid.

SECTION TWO: THE WINDS OF WAR

1. Naison, *Communists in Harlem*, 196–97.

2. Ibid., 197.

3. Hazel Rowley, *Richard Wright: The Life and Times* (New York: Owl, 2002), 126.

4. Langston Hughes, "Hughes Bombed in Spain: Tells of Terror," *Baltimore Afro-American*, October 23, 1937, 1.

5. Langston Hughes, "Madrid Getting Used to Bombs," *Baltimore Afro-American*, November 20, 1937, 3.

6. Ibid.

7. Wright, "Walter Garland Tells What Spain's Fight against Fascism Means to the Negro People," *Daily Worker*, November 29, 1937, 2.

8. Wright "American Negroes in Key Posts of Spain's Loyalist Forces," *Daily Worker*, September 29, 1937, 2.

9. Wright, "Negroes Form Committee to Aid Spain," *Daily Worker*, November 12, 1937, 4.

10. Wright, "American Negroes in Key Posts," 2.

11. Ibid.

12. Langston Hughes, "Hughes Finds Moors Being Used as Pawns," *Baltimore Afro-American,* October 30, 1937, 1.

13. Francesca Patai, "'La Pasionaria'—Dolores Ibarurri (1895–1989)," *People's Weekly World,* March 15, 1997, 1.

14. Robert Low, *La Pasionaria: The Spanish Firebran*d (New York: Random House, 1992), 61–62.

15. Patai, "'La Pasionaria'—Dolores Ibarurri (1895–1989)," 1.

16. Low, *La Pasionaria,* 107.

17. Ibid., 2.

18. Wright, "Harlem Spanish Women Come Out of the Kitchen," *Daily Worker,* September 20, 1937, 5.

19. Low, *La Pasionaria,* 2.

20. Wright, "Harlem Spanish Women," 5.

21. Ibid.

22. Elmer P. Martin and Joanne M. Martin, "Thyra J. Edwards: Internationalist Social Worker," in *African American Leadership: An Empowerment Tradition in Social Welfare History,* ed. Iris Carlton-Laney (Washington, DC: NASW Press, 2001), 163.

23. Ibid., 171.

24. Ibid., 174.

25. Ibid., 170.

26. Wright, "Negro Social Worker Hails Housing, Education in Spain," *Daily Worker,* November 12, 1937, 2.

27. Ibid.

28. Ibid.

29. Ibid.

30. Ben Ray Redman, "Ralph Bates's Spain," *Saturday Review of Literature,* February 11, 1939, 5.

31. Wright, "Bates Tells of Spain's Fight for Strong Republican Army, *Daily Worker,* October 1, 1937, 2.

32. Wright, "Harlem Group Pushes Aid for China," *Daily Worker,* September 22, 1937, 5.

SECTION THREE: HEROES SUNG AND SILENT

1. David Margolick, *Beyond Glory: Joe Louis vs. Max Schmeling, and a World on the Brink* (New York: Knopf, 2005), 60.

2. Ibid., 66.

3. Gene Smith, "The Champion," *American Legacy* 7, no. 4 (Winter 2002), 30.

4. Chris Mead, *Champion Joe Louis: Black Hero in White America* (New York: Viking, 1986), 198.

5. Gerald Astor, *"And a Credit to His Race": The Hard Life and Times of Joseph Louis Barrow, a.k.a. Joe Louis* (New York: Dutton, 1974), 111.

6. Richard Bak, *Joe Louis: The Great Black Hope* (New York: DeCapo, 1968), 95.

7. James P. Dawson, "Louis Stops Baer in 4th at Stadium as 95,000 Look On," *New York Times,* September 25, 1935, 27.

8. Wright, "Joe Louis Uncovers Dynamite," *New Masses,* October 8, 1935, 18, emphasis mine.

9. Ibid.

10. Ibid., 19.

11. Mead, *Champion Joe Louis,* 142.

12. Bak, *Joe Louis,* 160.

13. Mead, *Champion Joe Louis,* 139.

14. Paulette Douglas, *In This Corner: Boxing's Legendary Heavyweights,* documentary produced by Rick Bernstein, written by Brian Brown, and directed by Paulette Douglas (ESPN, 1992).

15. Mead, *Champion Joe Louis,* 145.

16. Bak, *Joe Louis,* 165.

17. Quoted in Bak, ibid.

18. Douglas, *In This Corner.*

19. Ralph Ellison, *Going to the Territory* (New York: Vintage, 1995), 202.

20. Wright, "Why the Eyes of the People Turn to the Ring for the Title Bout at Yankee Stadium Tonight," *Daily Worker,* June 22, 1938, 1.

21. Wright, "And Oh—Where Were Hitler's Pagan Gods?" *Daily Worker,* June 24, 1938, 1.

22. Ibid.

23. Ibid.

24. Ibid.

25. Ibid.

26. Ibid.

27. Wright, "High Tide in Harlem," *New Masses,* July 5, 1938, 18.

28. Ibid.

29. Ibid.

30. Ibid.

31. Margolick, *Beyond Glory,* 349.

32. James Weldon Johnson, *Along This Way: The Autobiography of James Weldon Johnson* (1933; repr., New York: Penguin, 1990), 341.

33. "Legion Pours in 500,000; Convention Opens Today," *New York Herald-Tribune,* September 20, 1937, 1.

34. "Prankish Visitors Keep City on Edge," *New York Times,* September 20, 1937, 3.

35. "Madcap Visitors Keep up Pranks in Times Square," *New York Times,* September 21, 1937, 20.

36. "Battle of 'Firsts' Is on Again, Just Like Old Times," *New York Herald-Tribune,* September 21, 1937, 1.

37. "Legion's Record 18-Hour Parade Ends at 3 A.M.; 2 1/2 Million Line 53 Blocks, Throng Stays to the End," *New York Herald-Tribune,* September 22, 1937, 1.

38. "Welcome Legionnaires," *New York Age,* September 25, 1937, 6.

39. Wright, "10,000 Negro Vets in New York Silent, but They're Talking Up at Home," *Daily Worker,* September 23, 1937, 4.
40. Ibid.
41. Ibid.
42. W. E. B. DuBois, "Returning Soldiers," *The Crisis* 18 (May 1919): 14.

SECTION FOUR: A BURST OF FISTS ON A NEW HORIZON

1. Countee Cullen, "Scottsboro, Too, Is Worth Its Song," in *On These I Stand: An Anthology of the Best Poems of Countee Cullen* (New York: Harper, 1947), 160.
2. Dan Carter, *Scottsboro: A Tragedy of the American South* (Baton Rouge: Louisiana State University Press, 1979), 399.
3. Richard Wright, *American Hunger* (New York: Harper, 1977), 60–61.
4. Ibid., 82.
5. Ibid., 64–65.
6. Richard Wright, *Lawd Today!* (New York: Avon, 1969), 37.
7. Ibid.
8. Ibid., 65.
9. Richard Wright, *Native Son* (New York: Harper, 1996), 33.
10. Wright, *American Hunger,* 65.
11. Ibid., 67.
12. Wright, *American Hunger,* 34.
13. Wright, "What Happens in a Communist Party Branch Meeting in the Harlem Section," *Daily Worker,* August 16, 1937, 6.
14. Wright, *American Hunger,* 123.
15. Wright, "Mrs. Holmes and Daughter Drink from the Fountain of Communism," *Daily Worker,* September 7, 1937, 5.
16. Ibid.
17. Wright, "Born a Slave, She Recruits 5 Members for Communist Party," *Daily Worker,* August 30, 1937, 2.
18. Wright, *American Hunger,* 85.
19. Ibid., 192.
20. Walker, *Richard Wright, Daemonic Genius,* 117.
21. Sylvia H. Keady, "Richard Wright's Women Characters and Inequality," *Black American Literature Forum* 10 (Winter 1976): 124–28.
22. Wright, *American Hunger,* 65.

SECTION FIVE: ART FOR LIFE'S SAKE

1. Richard Wright Papers.
2. Langston Hughes Papers.
3. Ibid.
4. James Weldon Johnson, "Foreword," *Challenge* 1 (March 1934): 2.
5. Ibid., 39.
6. "Dear Reader," *Challenge* 1 (Spring 1937): 40.
7. Ibid.
8. Ibid.
9. Ibid., 41.
10. Ibid.

11. Langston Hughes Papers.
12. Sterling Brown Papers.
13. Ibid.
14. Ibid.
15. Ibid., emphasis in the original.
16. Ibid.
17. Walker, *Richard Wright, Daemonic Genius,* 110.
18. Wright, "Negro Writers Launch Literary Quarterly," *Daily Worker,* 7.
19. Ibid.
20. Langston Hughes Papers.
21. Wright, "Negro Writers Launch," 7.
22. Richard Wright Papers.
23. Ibid.
24. Ibid.
25. "Dear Reader," 40.
26. Ibid., 38.
27. Katrine Dalsgard, "Alive and Well and Living on the Island of Martha's Vineyard: An Interview with Dorothy West," *The Langston Hughes Review* 12 (Fall 1993): 39.
28. Countee Cullen Papers.
29. Wright, "Negro Writers Launch," 7.
30. Wright, *New Challenge* 2 (Fall 1937), 3.
31. Ibid., 63.
32. Ibid., 53.
33. Ibid., 59.
34. Charles K. Wolfe and Kip Lornell, *The Life and Legend of Leadbelly* (New York: Harper, 1992), 82.
35. Ibid., 4.
36. John Avery Lomax, *Adventures of a Ballad Hunter* (New York: Macmillan, 1947), 111.
37. Ibid., 112–13.
38. Lincoln Barnett, "Lomax Arrives with Lead Belly, Negro Minstrel," *New York Herald-Tribune,* January 3, 1935, 21.
39. "Bad Nigger Makes Good Minstrel," *Life,* April 19, 1937, 39.
40. Wolfe and Lornell, *The Life and Legend,* 200.
41. Wright, "Huddie Ledbetter, Famous Negro Folk Artist, Sings the Songs of Scottsboro and His People," *Daily Worker,* August 12, 1937, 7.
42. Ibid.
43. Lomax, *Ballad Hunter,* 294.
44. Barnett, "Lomax Arrives with Lead Belly," 21.
45. "Murderous Minstrel," *Time,* January 14, 1935, 50.
46. "Bad Nigger Makes Good Minstrel," *Life,* April 19, 1937, 39.
47. Wolfe and Lornell, *The Life and Legend,* 167.
48. Raymond Fielding, *The March of Time, 1935–1951* (New York: Oxford University Press, 1978), 4.
49. Wolfe and Lornell, *The Life and Legend,* 205–6.
50. Ibid., 205.

51. Mike Gold, "Change the World!," *Daily Worker,* January 26, 1938, 7.
52. Wolfe and Lornell, *The Life and Legend,* 202.
53. Wright, "Negro Tradition in the Theatre," *Daily Worker,* October 15, 1937, 5.
54. Errol G. Hill and James V. Hatch, *A History of African American Theatre* (New York: Cambridge University Press, 2003), 317.
55. Roi Ottley, "Audience Likes New 'Conjure Man' Drama," *New York Amsterdam News,* March 14, 1936, 8.
56. Wright, "Negro Tradition," 5.
57. Rena Fraden, *Blueprints for a Black Federal Theatre, 1935–1939* (New York: Cambridge University Press, 1996), 115.
58. *New York Amsterdam News,* "Weekly Topics," May 14, 1938, 12.
59. Arthur Paris, "Cruse and the Crisis in Black Culture," *Journal of Ethnic Studies* 5 (Summer 1977): 63.
60. Fraden, *Blueprints,* 151.
61. Paris, "Cruse and the Crisis," 64.
62. Wright, "Negro Tradition," 5.
63. Ibid.
64. Sophia Steinbach, "Harlem Goes in for Art," *Opportunity* 14 (April 1936): 116.
65. Ibid.

CONCLUSION: DEPARTURE

1. Walker, *Richard Wright, Daemonic Genius,* 116.
2. Richard Wright Papers.
3. Ibid.
4. Ibid.
5. Ibid.
6. Fabre, *The Unfinished Quest,* 162.
7. Wright Documents, National Archives.
8. Ellison, *Going to the Territory,* 202.
9. Ibid.
10. Wright Papers.
11. Fabre, *The Unfinished Quest*, 162.
12. Richard Wright Papers.
13. Ibid.
14. William White, *By-Line: Ernest Hemingway, Selected Articles and Dispatches from Four Decades* (New York: Scribner's, 1967), xi.
15. Arthur Waldhorn, *A Reader's Guide to Ernest Hemingway* (1972; repr., Syracuse: Syracuse University Press, 2002), 78.
16. Johnson, *Along This Way,* 156.

WORKS CITED

ARCHIVAL SOURCES

Countee Cullen Papers. Amistad Research Library, Tulane University.

Langston Hughes Papers. Yale Collection of American Literature, Beinecke Rare Book and Manuscript Library, Yale University.

Richard Wright Documents. National Archives.

Richard Wright Papers. Yale Collection of American Literature. Beinecke Rare Book and Manuscript Library, Yale University.

Sterling Brown Papers. Moorland-Springarn Research Center, Howard University.

PUBLICATIONS AND FILMS

Anderson, Jervis. *This Was Harlem: A Cultural Portrait, 1900–1950.* New York: Farrar Straus Giroux, 1982.

Astor, Gerald. *"And a Credit to His Race": The Hard Life and Times of Joseph Louis Barrow, a.k.a. Joe Louis.* New York: Dutton, 1974.

Bak, Richard. *Joe Louis: The Great Black Hope.* New York: DeCapo, 1968.

Bontemps, Arna. "The Two Harlems." *American Scholar* 14 (Spring 1945): 167–73.

Calloway, Cab, and Bryant Rollins. *Minnie the Moocher.* New York: Crowell, 1976.

Carter, Dan. *Scottsboro: A Tragedy of the American South.* Baton Rouge: Louisiana State University Press, 1979.

Cullen, Countee. "Scottsboro, Too, Is Worth Its Song." *On These I Stand: An Anthology of the Best Poems of Countee Cullen.* New York: Harper, 1947.

Dalsgard, Katrine. "Alive and Well and Living on the Island of Martha's Vineyard: An Interview with Dorothy West." *The Langston Hughes Review* 12 (Fall 1993): 28–44.

Davis, Benjamin J. *Communist Councilman from Harlem: Autobiographical Notes Written in a Federal Penitentiary.* New York: International, 1969.

Douglas, Paulette. *In This Corner: Boxing's Legendary Heavyweights.* Produced by Rick Bernstein, written by Brian Brown, directed by Paulette Douglas. ESPN, 1992.

DuBois, W. E. B. "Returning Soldiers." *The Crisis* 18 (May 1919): 13–14.

Durante, Jimmy, and Jack Kofoed. *Night Clubs.* New York: Knopf, 1931.

Ellis, Edward Robb. *A Nation in Torment: The Great American Depression, 1929–1939.* New York: Coward-McCann, 1970.

Ellison, Ralph. *Going to the Territory.* New York: Vintage, 1995.

Fabre, Michel. *The Unfinished Quest of Richard Wright.* New York: Morrow, 1973.

Fielding, Raymond. *The March of Time, 1935–1951.* New York, Oxford University Press, 1978.

Fisher, Rudolph. "City of Refuge." In *The Collected Stories of Rudolph Fisher,* edited by John McCluskey, 3–16. Columbia: University of Missouri Press, 1991.

Fraden, Rena. *Blueprints for a Black Federal Theatre: 1935–1939.* New York: Cambridge University Press, 1996.

Greenberg, Cheryl Lynn. *"Or Does It Explode?" Black Harlem in the Great Depression.* New York: Oxford University Press, 1997.

Hemingway, Ernest. *By-Line: Ernest Hemingway, Selected Articles and Dispatches from Four Decades.* Edited by William White. New York: Scribner's, 1967.

Hill, Errol G., and James V. Hatch. *A History of the African American Theatre.* New York: Cambridge University Press, 2003.

Huggins, Nathan Irvin. *Harlem Renaissance.* New York: Oxford University Press, 1973.

Johnson, James Weldon. *Along This Way: The Autobiography of James Weldon Johnson.* New York: Penguin, 1990.

———. "Harlem: The Culture Capital." In *The New Negro: Voices of the Harlem Renaissance,* edited by Alain Locke, 301–11. New York: Simon and Schuster, 1997.

Keady, Sylvia H. "Richard Wright's Women Characters and Inequality." *Black American Literature Forum* 10 (Winter 1976): 124–28.

Lacy, Madison D. *Richard Wright: Black Boy.* Videocassette. Written, produced, and directed by Madison D. Lacy. San Francisco: California Newsreel, 1994.

Lawson, Ronald, and Mark Naison. *The Tenant Movement in New York City, 1904–1984.* New Brunswick: Rutgers University Press, 1986.

Lomax, John Avrey. *Adventures of a Ballad Hunter*. New York: Macmillan, 1947.

Low, Robert. *La Pasionaria: The Spanish Firebrand*. New York: Random House, 1992.

Marcuse, Peter. "The Beginnings of Public Housing in New York." *Journal of Urban History* 12 (August 1986): 353–90.

Margolick, David. *Beyond Glory: Joe Louis vs. Max Schmeling, and a World on the Brink*. New York: Knopf, 2005.

Martin, Elmer P., and Joanne M. Martin. "Thyra J. Edwards: Internationalist Social Worker." In *African American Leadership: An Empowerment Tradition in Social Welfare History*, edited by Iris Carlton-Laney, 163–77. Washington, DC: NASW Press, 2001.

McCall, Dan. *The Example of Richard Wright*. New York: Harcourt, 1969.

McKay, Claude. *Harlem: Negro Metropolis*. New York: Dutton, 1940.

Meade, Chris. *Joe Louis: Black Hero in White America*. New York: Viking, 1986.

Naison, Mark. *Communists in Harlem during the Depression*. Urbana: University of Illinois Press, 1983.

Paris, Arthur. "Cruse and the Crisis in Black Culture." *Journal of Ethnic Studies* 5 (Summer 1977): 63–66.

Patai, Francesca. "'La Pasionaria'—Dolores Ibarurri (1895–1989)." *People's Weekly World*, March 15, 1987, 1.

Post, Langdon W. "Harlem River Houses." *Opportunity* 15 (August 1937): 233–35.

Rampersad, Arnold. Introduction. In *The New Negro: Voices of the Harlem Renaissance*, edited by Alain Locke, ix–xxiii. New York: Simon and Schuster, 1997.

Redman, Ben Ray. "Ralph Bates's Spain." Review of Sirocco, by Ralph Bates. *Saturday Review of Literature*. February 11, 1939, 5.

Rowley, Hazel. *Richard Wright: The Life and Times*. New York: Owl, 2002.

Rusinak, Kelly, and Chris Lamb. "A Sickening Red Tinge: The *Daily Worker*'s Fight against White Baseball." *Cultural Logic: An Electronic Journal of Marxist Theory and Practice* 3 (Fall 1999).

Steinbach, Sophia. "Harlem Goes in for Art." *Opportunity* 14 (April 1936): 114–16.

Waldhorn, Arthur. *A Reader's Guide to Ernest Hemingway*. 1972. Syracuse: Syracuse University Press, 2002.

Walker, Margaret. Richard Wright, *Daemonic Genius: A Portrait of the Man, a Critical Look at His Work*. New York: Warner, 1988.

Watson, Steven. *The Harlem Renaissance: Hub of African American Culture*. New York: Pantheon, 1995.

Weinberg, Meyer. *A Short History of American Capitalism*. New York: New History Press, 2003.

Wolfe, Charles K., and Kip Lornell. *The Life and Legend of Leadbelly*. New York: Harper, 1992.

Wright, Richard. *American Hunger*. New York; Harper, 1977.

———. *Black Boy*. 1945. New York: Harper, 1993.

———. *Lawd Today!* 1963. New York: Avon, 1969.

———. *Native Son*. 1940. New York: Harper, 1996.

———. *The Richard Wright Reader*. New York: Harper, 1978.

———. *12 Million Black Voices*. 1940. New York: Arno, 1969.

INDEX

ABOUT THE EDITOR

Earle V. Bryant is professor of English at the University of New Orleans where he teaches American and African American literature. He has written extensively on Richard Wright, Charles Chesnutt, Bernard Malamud, and Dorothy West.